DECONSTRUCTING PRIVILEGE

Although scholarly examinations of privilege have increased in recent decades, an emphasis on privilege studies pedagogy remains lacking within institutions. This edited collection explores best practices for effective teaching and learning about various forms of systemic group privilege such as that based on race, gender, sexuality, religion, and class. Formatted in three easy-to-follow sections, *Deconstructing Privilege* charts the history of privilege studies and provides intersectional approaches to the topic.

Drawing on a wealth of research and real-life accounts, this book gives educators both the theoretical foundations they need to address issues of privilege in the classroom and practical ways to forge new paths for critical dialogues in educational settings. Combining interdisciplinary contributions from leading experts in the field—such as Tim Wise and Abby Ferber—with pedagogical strategies and tips for teaching about privilege, *Deconstructing Privilege* is an essential book for any educator who wants to address what privilege *really* means in the classroom.

Kim A. Case is Associate Professor of Psychology and Women's Studies, Director of the Applied Social Issues graduate sub-plan, and Director of the Teaching-Learning Enhancement Center at the University of Houston-Clear Lake, Houston, Texas, USA.

DECONSTRUCTING PRIVILEGE

Teaching and Learning as Allies in the Classroom

Edited by

Kim A. Case

Routledge
Taylor & Francis Group

NEW YORK AND LONDON

KH

First published 2013
by Routledge
8th Floor, 711 3rd Avenue, New York, NY 10017, USA

Simultaneously published in the UK
by Routledge
2 Park Square, Milton Park, Abingdon, Oxon OX14 4RN

Routledge is an imprint of the Taylor & Francis Group, an informa business

© 2013 Kim A. Case

Library of Congress Cataloging in Publication Data
A catalog record has been requested for this book.

ISBN: 978-0-415-64145-6 (hbk)
ISBN: 978-0-415-64146-3 (pbk)
ISBN: 978-0-203-08187-7 (ebk)

Typeset in Bembo and Stone Sans
by RefineCatch Limited, Bungay, Suffolk, UK

10/6/14

Dedicated to Kent, my partner and eternal support system and ally in all things, and to my mother, for teaching me to always give more than I take.

CONTENTS

FOREWORD

Teaching about Privilege: Transforming Learned Ignorance into Usable Knowledge

Peggy McIntosh

Five years ago, I attended an invitational symposium on Race and Reconciliation in America, hosted in Washington, D.C., by Janet Langhart Cohen and her husband, former Secretary of Defense, William Cohen. The conference was held at the Washington Press Club and featured over 40 presentations from journalists, members of congress, lawyers, foundation executives, biographers, entertainers, religious leaders, educators, historians, filmmakers, and people in medical fields. As the speeches on race and reconciliation progressed, it became clear to me that only people from the academic world were among the very few speakers mentioning white privilege as an aspect of racial reality. A mere handful of us—mostly college teachers—mentioned privilege systems, or had an analysis based on the understanding that privilege is a corollary of discrimination; it is the "upside" of oppression; it is unearned advantage that corresponds to unearned disadvantage in society. It was as though white privilege was either an unknown concept or a third rail, too dangerous to touch for both people of color and for White people. A few speakers did refer loosely to privilege using the term "power and privilege" as though they are the same thing. By the time this conference took place, the concept of privilege had become fairly widespread in the universities, but, during this prestigious gathering, only those from liberal arts institutions spoke about the relationship between racial oppression and white privilege. I was sobered, and the conference gave me intense gratitude toward colleges and universities for making the privilege dimension of social reality visible and taking the risks associated with a kind of teaching that calls into question the myths of meritocracy, monoculture, and the racelessness of White people.

In a few decades, citizens looking back will probably wonder how we in the 21st century could have talked about racism without going into. White people's experience of their own race. How could we have protected Whites' sense of their not being part of the picture of "race"? How could historians have talked about prejudice without going into privilege? In this volume, Kim Case has helped to end the avoidance, the ignorance, and the silence, and to accelerate the understanding of privilege. She has brought together a collection, unlike any other, of essays by authors who testify about their experience of teaching about privilege in a wide range of academic fields. The authors are brave. They describe meeting with resistance, denial, refusal to use the course materials, and attacks on their integrity as scholars, but they also describe ways in which students' consciousness grew, knowledge bases expanded, and systemic awareness developed in people who had previously seen only individual lives as the units of society. In other words, the students came to understand racism and other forms of oppression not as individual acts of meanness, but rather as systems embedded in our society that confer dominance through circumstances beyond the individuals' control.

Kim Case has already distinguished herself by co-editing a special issue of the *Journal of Social Issues* devoted to research on privilege systems. In this book, she goes further to answer the questions of teachers: "Shall I teach about privilege systems?" "If so, how?" The authors in this collection testify to the classroom strategies they developed for conducting conversations in what is understandably difficult psychological territory for most people in a classroom. It was probably a shock for teachers themselves, during their educations, to discover that the vesions of history and society they had been taught were very partial in several senses of the word, and had left out an analysis that includes both oppression, which pushes people or ideas below a hypothetical line of social justice, and privilege, which pushes people or ideas above such a line.

Above the hypothetical line of social justice are the operations of circumstantial privilege, or unearned advantage, through which some people, groups, or conceptualizations are elevated, promoted, given the benefit of the doubt, trusted as responsible or sound, and considered to be extra worthy of the support and respect of the society by virtue of the good qualities associated with or attributed to them, regardless of the actual effects and actions of people or ideas.

It matters to me a great deal to write the foreword to this book because I so welcome the prospect of more teachers inspired to teach about privilege, and I appreciate the contributions of these authors in explaining how they do it. The study of privilege adds a whole new dimension to analysis of social systems and individual experiences. It changes everything. People in the academic world are feeling their way through, both in thinking about and in teaching about privilege. These teachers are offering the academy and its students a whole new angle of vision on social reality and individual positioning. They are, each in their own context, increasing the knowledge base of U.S. education.

The authors within this volume know that it is worthwhile and also very difficult to teach about systemic unearned advantage to U.S. students. The myths of meritocracy and monoculture die hard. Teaching about privilege puts one up against the strongly ingrained beliefs that most people in the world have wide freedom of choice and that circumstances do not really matter. Most of our students have been raised with the assumptions of meritocracy, the idea that the unit of society is the individual, and that whatever a person ends up with must be what that person, as an individual, wanted, worked for, earned, and deserved. Most White university students have also been raised with the myth of monoculture. This monoculture myth holds that the United States is basically one big culture, that we are all experiencing it in more or less the same way, and, if we are not satisfied, then there is something wrong with our vision or our behavior. In addition, most students were raised with subtle, implicit assumptions about the actual superiority of dominant groups, the justice of leaving dominance unnamed and "normal," and the idea that higher powers ordained the hierarchies of U.S. culture, which is the myth of Manifest Destiny in all of its variations. To the teacher, taking on these myths can feel like countercultural work, yet it is actually right in line with the purported missions of universities to search for and promulgate truth. In addition, college mission statements that promise development of the full potential of students are supported by academic work that clarifies social systems and thereby helps students to better understand their own lives. The students usually repay their teachers' efforts. Many teachers are thanked in heartfelt ways for teaching about privilege by students who state, "This course changed my life" or "This assignment changed my life." What was wistful or angry confusion about injustice can give way to empowerment through seeing one's situation and then being able to live one's life more intentionally than before. Many students have felt that there were phenomena at work in U.S. culture that did not have to do with outright discrimination against them but which felt oppressive to them. Privilege studies help to validate their feelings and name some of the many intersecting kinds of privilege they were sensing or seeing.

Some critics of privilege studies will say that the purpose of the university is to develop and pass on accurate bodies of knowledge and that the subject of privilege has nothing to do with this. On the contrary, studies of race that do not include studies of race privilege are simply inaccurate. The time will come when it is seen as ludicrous to study gender without studying male privilege, to study sexuality without studying heterosexual privilege, or to comprehend poverty without seeing class privilege as a major dimension of poverty. It will seem illogical to study the U.S. Constitution, or the founding fathers, or colonization, or gay, lesbian, bisexual, or transgender existence, or psychology, or science, or the experiences of children, or the history of any war without tools of analysis that come from privilege studies, seeing the intricate relationships and intersecting dimensions of differential access to and use of power, including the power to name, to categorize, and to judge.

I remember the time nearly 40 years ago when skeptics asked, "Women's Studies? What is there to study?" The answer turned out to be "just about everything." The same will be asked of privilege studies, and the answer will be the same. People will discover they need the concept of privilege, no matter what they study, in any academic field and in their daily lives. They need it to make sense of their experience, going all the way back to earliest childhood. As I have said, the teachers who are authors of the papers in this collection get much gratitude from students despite the difficulty of their work. Students come to understand that their ideas and experiences, material circumstances and life quandaries are illuminated by understanding the privilege systems that have been working in and around them. I am not sure that all college courses are worth the huge costs of tuition these days, but I am convinced that coming to understand privilege systems is worth the tuition. It is a lifelong gift of greater conceptual, emotional, and even spiritual clarity.

Nevertheless, as young people initially find out that things are not as they had been previously taught, it is natural enough for them to have strong feelings of wanting to deny or remedy the new version of reality they are being shown or to reinstate the previous realities they had relied on. Teachers who contributed to this volume describe their key role in helping students make sense of new dissonant realities, including whatever feelings come up. One important key to supporting student growth and development is the classroom strategy of conducting conversation so that students listen to one another. A fellow feeling can develop when students bring their own experiences to class and are able to testify to them, knowing they will not be interrupted or cross-examined. I find it exciting to read teachers' accounts of tapping into students' previous knowledge and bringing them along in company with other students, all of whom have their stories that never did fit in the older frames. A class on privilege may turn out to be the only course in four years of a college student's life in which his or her own experiences count as a valid contribution to the curriculum.

Learning to be an ally is a complex theme of this book. Teachers in the field need several kinds of skill in allying. They can ally with their students over the difficulty of learning new and disconcerting worldviews. They may draw on their own memories of learning about privilege for the first time. This can help them to ally with their own personal experience of having developed over the years and not being finished with their own learning yet. It can alleviate the impulse to be impatient with students. After all, students should not be blamed for being good students of what they have been taught—that there are no systems in place that would create inequity and that the playing field is level. In addition, some contributors to this volume describe helping students to ally with one another within a classroom setting, listening in a lateral way without trying to argue or doubt what others say about their experience. Such discussions can help students to convert their acculturated punitive feelings into allyship with those in U.S. society or the wider world who for any reason beyond their control have been dealt a less powerful hand. Some modes of teaching encourage explicit action for social justice. I feel that in a sense all of those who teach about privilege are engaging in important action; giving minds new ideas to work with is powerful action. But, in addition, some of these authors have also been developing curricula that explicitly help students to conduct action projects. Ending one's silence and using one's power in practical ways for social change is very powerful day-in and day-out ally work with those unlike oneself. Authors in this volume testify in varying degrees to all of these forms of allyship.

Writing the foreword to this book is also important to me because I want to support people who have found this whole new dimension of social and historical analysis dizzying. I have felt empathy especially for straight White men who have been whirled around time after time, first being told, "You are a man and that affects everything you see and do," and "You are a White person and that affects everything you see and do," and "You are a heterosexual person and that affects everything you see and do." They suffer from what I think of as epistemological nausea. My empathy for them has not diminished. It is not their fault that so many of these dominant group assumptions are embedded in them, which previously allowed them to feel "normal." But new intersectional privilege studies whirl us all around repeatedly. I feel empathy also for those who are whirled around through newer naming and recognition of their class positions, socio-economic status, or other enabling factors, such as able-bodied ease, age-related respect, language-of-origin advantage, religious privilege, and parents' relation to money, formal education, arts, architecture, sports, vacations, recreation, and possessions of all kinds. It can be a temptation for the most privileged and least conscious people to give up on the whole discussion and discredit those who speak of privilege at all. Of course, some can do so, finding many pockets of society to keep them apparently, though temporarily, safe. But the authors in this volume find that supportive teaching about privilege cannot only help, but also transform the lives of the most privileged and unconscious people, for they have suffered too. Everybody has a mix of experiences involving both privilege and oppression, and helping everyone to see this is very humanizing for all. For me, it is one major revelation and reward of privilege studies to learn that none of us got here without grief, and none of us has grief as our only experience of life.

I feel that the recent election outcomes of 2012 have to do in part with students' growing awareness of inequities, and their choice of the political party that appears to have the most concern about these inequities. Young voters threaten and annoy elder statesmen who appear not to have taken in the depth of inequity in the United States. The high turnout of young voters makes me hope that young voters are using their privilege to weaken systems of privilege that they have come to see as deterrents to democracy. The universities have been gradually teaching them to be more aware of what the poet and essayist Adrienne Rich termed the "politics of location," the circumstantial positioning of people that has a strong bearing on what they are able to do with and in their lives. Whether or not privilege studies as a field will affect voting patterns, I feel that it will raise empathetic awareness of the "politics of location" as people in dominant groups realize how much unused power we hold and could use for social change.

The authors of this collection's essays are explorers and cartographers of complex and careful pedagogies for the study of privilege. They are doing very important work. I feel that the course of human oppression may be altered by recognition of the workings of privilege systems. America's problems as well as America's accomplishments all involve the workings of privilege systems. We have not been taught to see privilege systems. In fact, we have been taught not to see them and rewarded for not talking about them. But the myths of meritocracy, monoculture, manifest destiny, dominant group neutrality, and dominant group superiority lack explanatory power in accounting for suffering. They do not help us out of our dilemmas. They simply encourage us to blame the victims of any kind of suffering. Clambering out of that irrationality, we need to study the "colonized mind," as social theorist and psychiatrist Frantz Fanon termed it. But privilege studies allows us to go further and study the colonizers' minds, the emperors' minds, the owners' minds, the gatekeepers' minds, the minds of those who created the whole knowledge system as we know it and who pass on the denials and omissions entailed in the building of that knowledge system.

I trust that gradually the understanding of privilege systems will reach and touch journalists, media producers, sports writers, biographers, historians, government officials, administrators, educators, people in medical fields, and ordinary people trying to make more sense of our experiences than we were encouraged to do by our families, teachers, and society in general. I hope that in the next decades more people will come to see they need privilege as an idea to advance their own thinking, lest we stay in personal and policy murk and fog. The admirable authors of the essays in this fine volume refuse to stand still and wait for the fog to clear. They are teaching in clearer, well-lighted spaces, the classrooms of colleges and universities, privileged spaces in which we have the blessing of time and support for deep new learning about the workings of power in and around us.

Peggy McIntosh, Ph.D.
Founder and Senior Associate
The National SEED Project on Inclusive Curriculum
(Seeking Educational Equity and Diversity)
Wellesley, MA

ACKNOWLEDGMENTS

I owe more than I can articulate in words to Kent Case, my ally in learning and growing together to discover ways to dismantle privilege, chip away at oppression, serve as allies to the marginalized, and hopefully leave the world a little brighter than when we arrived. Through the long studying sessions and dissertation writing of graduate school, then the seven-day workweeks of the tenure track, and now the years that went into this project, he provided a strong foundation of infinite and unconditional love and support for my research and professional life.

My mother, Ann Rivera, deserves special recognition for teaching me that everyone deserves fair treatment. She taught me that this world belongs to all of us. She modeled that truth in so many ways—including sponsoring and cooking dinner for all of my gay high school and college friends that had been banned from their own Thanksgiving family gatherings. She always believed in me and made my education the absolute top priority in my life, beginning in first grade and sustaining that encouragement throughout the years.

My professional and personal worlds are immeasurably enhanced by the presence of Terri Culbert, friend and administrative assistant extraordinaire! Terri's commitment and talent for behind-the-scenes support of others is universally unmatched. Her smile motivated me, her soothing words calmed me, her friendship grounded me, and her candy jar provided the necessary sugar boost for writing and editing.

My journey to where I am today as a scholar of both Psychology and Women's Studies began with two amazing professors, both of whom were graduate students teaching at my undergraduate institution, the University of Tennessee, Knoxville. Kecia McBride introduced me to Women's Studies and what it means to be a feminist academic. Kristine Kelly brought me into the world of Social Psychology and defined my career path with one life-changing course.

Thank you to members of the White Women Against Racism discussion groups that I facilitated during graduate school, where I initially began to reflect on my own privilege and form my identity as an ally in the classroom. My passion for research and teaching about privilege grew from these challenging conversations. I hold exponential appreciation for their honesty, compassion, and willingness to dig into privilege even when it was uncomfortable and even painful.

During my graduate studies, I was also extremely fortunate to encounter two very influential and passionate women who advanced my own thinking about privilege and pedagogy. Mary Brydon-Miller always paved the way for me to pursue my research on privilege, from my dissertation to this book almost a decade later. I am thoroughly convinced my dissertation would never have been completed without her guidance, patience, and mentoring. Patricia Hill Collins introduced me to intersectional theory in her course on Black women's sexuality. That experience challenged and transformed my thinking about not only the complexities of social identity and lived experiences, but also my future teaching approaches.

I am particularly grateful for years of unconditional support, encouragement exactly when I desperately need it, professional mentoring, and advice on this project from Sharon Hall, Lillian Benavente-McEnery, Beth Hentges, Arch Erich, and Elizabeth Cole. In undertaking a major project such as this one, the support of faculty colleagues makes all the difference in persevering. I extend my deepest appreciation to the Psychology and Women's Studies program faculty at the University of Houston-Clear Lake for inspiration and enthusiasm for this project.

This book's focus was shaped by encouragement and advice from the institute organizers and participants at the 2012 Institute for Academic Feminist Psychologists, hosted by the Society for the Psychology of Women (American Psychological Association [APA] Division 35). In particular, many thanks to Abby Stewart, Stephanie Shields, and Joan Chrisler for their generosity as mentors and publishing advisors. I also wish to acknowledge the visionary support of the Society for the Psychological Study of Social Issues (SPSSI, APA Division 9), SPSSI leadership, the *Journal of Social Issues* (*JSI*) editor Sheri Levy, and the *JSI* editorial board for supporting me as guest editor of the 2012 journal issue, "Systems of Privilege: Intersections, Awareness, and Applications." That editing journey motivated me to pursue my idea for this book, and I would never have considered this project without that journal editing learning experience.

I simply must thank Catherine Bernard, my editor at Routledge, for believing in this project and making this volume a reality. Catherine, as well as Allison Bush, provided helpful feedback and suggestions that truly improved the manuscript and always answered my detail-oriented questions with grace. As a rookie to book editing, their guidance and patience meant the world to me. This book would never have existed as a thought in mind if it were not for Peggy McIntosh's 1988 essay reflecting on white, male, and heterosexual privilege. Her work introduced me, like it did for so many others, to the abstract concept and daily reality of privilege. I would especially like to thank Peggy McIntosh for taking the time to write the foreword for this collection and providing inspiration and direction for the future of privilege studies.

Of course, this edited collection resulted from the intellectual work of the chapter authors and their commitment and dedication to this editorial and publishing process. My heartfelt thanks to all of the authors for their collaborative and cooperative spirits, infinite patience with my long list of editorial quirks, and unique contributions that will serve educators searching for the pedagogical innovations they provided here. In addition to authors, many generous individuals gave of their time to provide thoughtful feedback and suggestions that clearly strengthened the final manuscript in a multitude of ways that I could not have accomplished alone. My deepest gratitude goes to the following for helpful comments: Lillian Benavente-McEnery, Amy Buddie, Andrew Christopher, Amanda Clinton, Adrienne Dessel, Mary Sue Green, Justin Hackett, Beth Hentges, Sandra Neumann, Lisa Platt, Desdamona Rios, Abigail Stewart, Stephanie Wildman, Stacey Williams, and Kevin Zabel.

The completion of this manuscript resulted from the dedication of my unbelievably talented students who are already changing the world for the better and will continue to work for social justice. I am indebted to my graduate assistants Cara Gillespie, Rachel Hensley, Morgan Hopkins, and Angela Miller for their work on this collection, and also thank all of my research assistants in the Applied Social Issues sub-plan for their dedicated work in my lab and for being so committed to this research.

1

BEYOND DIVERSITY AND WHITENESS

Developing a Transformative and Intersectional Model of Privilege Studies Pedagogy

Kim A. Case

I relive the spring 2001 semester quite often in my mind, when I taught my very own Women's Studies course for the first time at the University of Cincinnati. In April of that term, a White[1] Cincinnati police officer shot and killed an unarmed African American young man who had misdemeanor warrants. The city-wide civil unrest, riots, and white panic that followed coincided with my Psychology of Women class periods devoted specifically to white privilege and intersections of race and gender. Needless to say, as a naïve and inexperienced White instructor, my bag of pedagogical tools came up empty when a White female student yelled out to the class of 70 students that people of color are "all animals." Despite this pedagogical failure, I continued to incorporate white privilege and critical race theory into my gender-focused courses, earning the label of "racist against Whites" on my student evaluations. Similarly, an intersectional focus on heterosexual privilege in my women's studies courses met student resistance. One White woman made it clear to me that she had to drop my course due to her father's religious concerns about the abundance of "lesbian authors."

Each of these instructional experiences propelled me to search and search for resources to inform and expand my own strategies for facilitating student learning about privilege. However, years of less than fruitful searching made it clear to me that the resource I yearned for was yet to be created. When I first began my privilege studies journey in 1998 as a brand new graduate student, my thesis chair unapologetically advised me to drop this interest because he predicted no one would be interested in privilege as a research focus. Despite this discouragement from a mentor I still deeply admire to this day, and potentially directly due to the discouragement, I designed my first research project to develop a scale assessing white privilege awareness and began including privilege content in my teaching.

To me, I was obligated to present a model of an ally in the classroom, presumably aiding the learning of both privileged and marginalized students. Washington and Evans (1991) define an ally as a dominant group member "who works to end oppression in his or her personal or professional life through support of, and as an advocate with and for, the oppressed population" (p. 195). Neumann (2009) outlines the need for allies in the classroom as part of the professional life aspect of ally actions for social justice. Students encountering faculty allies in the classroom and taking social justice action on campus may feel less isolated, ultimately leading to greater academic success (Neumann, 2009). This book developed from that place of constant exploring for a resource I knew I desperately needed to develop my own identity as an ally in the classroom. Now, 15 years later, my research and teaching led me to take the leap and create the book I wanted to read when I first began developing my own pedagogical philosophy and classroom strategies so many years ago.

Defining Privilege as Distinct from Discrimination

Case, Iuzzini, and Hopkins (2012) describe privilege and discrimination as "divergent outcomes created by . . . institutionalized oppression" and "inseparable as codependent structural forces" (p. 4). Privilege refers to automatic unearned benefits bestowed upon perceived members of dominant groups based on social identity (Case, Iuzzini, et al., 2012; McIntosh, 1988, 2012). As described by McIntosh (1988), privilege functions as "an invisible weightless knapsack of special provisions, assurances, tools, maps, guides, codebooks, passports, visas, clothes, compass, emergency gear, and blank checks" (pp. 1–2). Discussions of privilege and research about privilege often shift to discrimination, disadvantage, and oppression (Case, Iuzzini, et al., 2012; Wise & Case, this volume). In order to raise awareness of unearned social group advantages, the conversation must stay tuned in to privilege itself as a concept and tangible benefits in the daily lives of dominant group members. As McIntosh (2012) argues, there are distinct challenges to the development of a focus on privilege studies:

> Many people who think they are writing about privilege are in fact writing about deficits, barriers, and discrimination, and cannot yet see exemptions, assumptions, and permissions granted by privilege. I am convinced that studies of oppression will not go anywhere toward ending oppression unless they are accompanied by understanding of the systems of privilege that cause systems of oppression.
>
> (p. 204)

Her statement highlights the frequent tendency for conversations about privilege to break down because discrimination seems less abstract and more visible, and, therefore, easier to identify.

Bringing Privilege Studies Pedagogy into Focus

Although the scholarship on privilege increased in recent decades since the original McIntosh (1988) paper on white, male, and heterosexual privilege (McIntosh, 2012), privilege studies pedagogy remains neglected. While courses focusing on prejudice currently receive more programmatic support than in the past, classroom discussions of privilege consistently meet with student resistance and a variety of additional pedagogical challenges (Case & Hemmings, 2005; Lawrence & Bunche, 1996; Tatum, 1994). As instructors struggle to navigate the taboo subject of privilege in high school and college-level courses, helpful pedagogical resources remain scarce and scattered. Currently, there exists a clear and distinct need for a book that focuses on privilege studies pedagogy across a variety of domains recognizing privilege based on sex, religion, race, class, and more.

This book explores best practices for teaching and learning about various forms of systemic group privilege by laying the theoretical foundation for a model of privilege studies pedagogy and provides scholarship and practical applications to aid faculty in becoming effective allies to students in the classroom. The three sections of the volume address:

1. transformation privilege studies pedagogy;
2. intersectional approaches to teaching and learning about privilege; and
3. classroom strategies and applications for teaching about privilege.

This innovative collection emphasizes intersections of identity as an essential aspect of faculty development as pedagogical allies and of student ally identity development. In addition, interdisciplinary contributions from various academic fields such as psychology, sociology, women's studies, ethnic studies, social work, education, family therapy, and law provide multiple perspectives for instructors. The main goals of this collection are to:

- provide a *model of privilege studies pedagogy* for effective teaching and learning about privilege;
- develop an *inclusive privilege studies* that incorporates multiple forms of privilege (rather than only white privilege);
- encourage an *intersectional approach* to teaching and learning about privilege; and
- promote an *interdisciplinary privilege studies* that calls for "privilege studies across the curriculum."

Developing a Model of Privilege Studies Pedagogy

Given that faculty teaching about privilege often search unsuccessfully for scholarship that informs their instructional approaches and classroom strategies, a coherent model for effective privilege studies pedagogy is needed to support faculty allies. Incorporating the following ten aspects of this model of privilege studies pedagogy will maximize student learning and raise awareness of privilege across disciplines. This volume calls for allies in the classroom to engage in a model of privilege studies pedagogy that:

- *analyzes privilege and power* in teaching about privilege, pushing the boundaries of teaching multiculturalism, diversity, or oppression and discrimination. We must extend learning goals to consistently include privileged identities and how privilege operates to maintain oppression;
- *emphasizes the definition of privilege* (unearned group advantage) and how it affects lived experiences and dominant group psychology while also allowing for co-constructed knowledge to expand and improve the definition;
- *focuses on the invisibility of privilege*, the consequences of that invisibility for the privileged and the oppressed, and lifting the veil to make privilege more visible;
- *teaches privilege across a wide variety of oppressions*, including not only white privilege, but also the long list of privileges (e.g., male, heterosexual, able-bodied) that are often neglected in the curriculum;
- frames learning about privilege through an *intersectional theory perspective* for deeper understanding of the matrix of oppression and privilege;
- *involves educator personal reflection on privilege*, biases, assumptions, and the ways in which instructor social identity may impact the learning community;
- encourages critical analysis through *student reflection and writing about their own privileged identities* and careful consideration of how those identities shape their own lives, psychology, perceptions, and behaviors;
- *promotes social action to dismantle privilege* through student learning that extends beyond the classroom walls in the form of service learning, community research projects, public education projects, community engagement assignments, and ally action for social change;
- *values the voices of the marginalized and oppressed* by avoiding claims of equal validity awarded to all perspectives. Pedagogical approaches calling for equal validation of all students' lived experiences may in fact lead to further marginalization of the oppressed in the classroom. If privileged voices and experiences are used to deny the existence of oppression and privilege, then effective privilege studies pedagogy must call for student reflection on the invisibility of privilege. In other words, the lived experiences of the privileged may work to maintain invisibility of privilege and work against learning without critical analysis or reflection; and
- *infuses learning about privilege across the curriculum*, including core liberal arts courses not traditionally associated with diversity content (e.g., biology, introduction to psychology, economics, marketing, and math). Writing and critical thinking "across the curriculum" became common phrases in higher

education over the last two decades. We need a movement to infuse *privilege studies across the curriculum* as a common higher education practice and as a potential innovative initiative to be adopted across universities (e.g., as a quality enhancement program).

Toward an Inclusive Privilege Studies: White Privilege and Beyond

In her influential paper on the interlocking structures of male, white, and heterosexual privilege, Peggy McIntosh (1988) described her realization that she "had been taught about racism as something which puts others at a disadvantage, but had been taught not to see one of its corollary aspects, white privilege" (p. 1) which grants her automatic unearned benefits. During graduate school, this essay was introduced to me in the White Women Against Racism (WWAR) discussion groups that I joined and later facilitated. In the WWAR group, we utilized this list to reflect on our own white privilege and grapple with personal definitions of "ally" as we searched for meaningful ways to take action to dismantle racism (Case, 2012). McIntosh's (1988) analysis provided a lens for complex considerations of privilege that had never occurred to me before. Of course, McIntosh's arguments about white, male, and heterosexual privilege parallel additional forms of privilege bestowed on dominant group members. In other words, individuals perceived to be middle or upper class, gender-conforming, or able-bodied, for example, also encounter benefits directly associated with that group membership (whether they identify with the group or not). However, most existing books, anthologies, and articles about privilege, including those on teaching, focus on white privilege (Aveling, 2002; Case, 2007a, 2012; Case & Hemmings, 2005; Frankenberg, 1993; Lawrence & Bunche, 1996; McIntyre, 1997; Rothenberg, 2008; Stewart, Lanu, Branscombe, Phillips, & Denny, 2012; Tatum, 1994) while neglecting additional forms of privilege. In fact, although McIntosh's famous 1988 paper integrates male, white, and heterosexual privilege, references to the work rarely acknowledge male or heterosexual privilege, emphasizing her points about white privilege while rendering her discussion of two other forms of privilege invisible.

Recently, scholars have begun turning their attention to a broader range of privilege systems to expand the literature within privilege studies beyond its racial focus (Case, 2007b; Case & Stewart, 2010; Kimmel, 2008; Kimmel & Ferber, 2009). A special issue on privilege of the *Journal of Social Issues*, which I guest edited, emphasized an inclusive approach to privilege studies, with articles addressing not only white privilege (Case, 2012; Cole, Avery, Dodson, & Goodman, 2012; Pratto & Stewart, 2012; Stewart et al., 2012; Stoudt, Fox, & Fine, 2012), but also gender-conforming privilege (Case, Kanenberg, Erich, & Tittsworth, 2012), heterosexual privilege (Cole et al., 2012; Montgomery & Stewart, 2012), male privilege (Coston & Kimmel, 2012), socioeconomic privilege (Sanders & Mahalingam, 2012; Stoudt et al., 2012), and Christian privilege

(Blumenfeld & Jaekel, 2012). In that issue, we purposely emphasized multiple forms of privilege to widen the scope beyond the current research focus on white privilege. In addition, we called for an interdisciplinary and intersectional approach to privilege studies (Case, 2012; Cole et al., 2012; Coston & Kimmel, 2012; Ferber, 2012; Stoudt et al., 2012). Without a comprehensive privilege studies literature that spans multiple forms of oppression, educational initiatives to teach students about privilege will be severely limited and ineffective.

Developing an Intersectional Privilege Studies Pedagogy

As a graduate student in an experimental psychology doctoral program, my theoretical approach to academic life was forever changed when I took Patricia Hill Collins's intersectionally focused course about Black women's sexuality. This course, coupled with my efforts to take graduate courses in women's studies, sociology, and educational foundations, provided me with new perspectives that reshaped my thinking about pedagogical effectiveness and what it means to be an ally in the classroom. As a result of that intersectional and interdisciplinary training, I designed this volume to examine ways that educators and learners can address issues of privilege intersectionally in a diverse classroom. Introducing the concept of intersectionality, bell hooks (1984) and Kimberlé Crenshaw (1989) theorized that various social identities combine to place each individual at a particular social location informed by group memberships such as gender, class, sexuality, race, ethnicity, ability, religion, nation, and gender identity. In fact, although often treated as distinct aspects of an individual's experiences, these privileged and marginalized identities interact simultaneously in complicated ways typically overlooked in research and in the classroom. As Dill (2009) suggests, "intersectionality is the intellectual core of diversity work" (p. 229), yet remains marginalized within traditional disciplines. Berger and Guidroz (2009) called for transformation of higher education via an intersectional lens. Recently, scholars have recommended intersectional approaches to social science research (Cole, 2009) as well as institutionalizing intersectionality (Fitts, 2009). The intersectionality among various social identities is rarely introduced in diversity and multicultural courses, which typically address only one aspect of privilege, usually white privilege. Courses designed to raise awareness of multicultural issues often fail to simultaneously integrate multiple oppressions or privileges. Pedagogically, intersectional theory offers both students and instructors the critical tools for exploring identity complexities and making privilege and oppression simultaneously visible (Case & Lewis, 2012; Case, Miller, & Jackson, 2012; Collins, 1990; Dill & Zambrana, 2009). By incorporating an intersectional approach to teaching and learning about privilege, faculty can provide students with a framework to complicate identity, consider a variety of privileged and oppressed identities as contributions to the lived experiences of one person, and avoid over-generalizations and group stereotypes.

Organization of *Deconstructing Privilege*

The collection of original essays contains three main sections designed to emphasize transformational pedagogy, intersectional approaches to privilege, and practical strategies for the classroom. The contributors to *Deconstructing Privilege: Teaching and Learning as Allies in the Classroom* bring cross-disciplinary and interdisciplinary perspectives from sociology, law, psychology, literature, education, family therapy, social work, ethnic studies, and women's studies. These authors provide scholarship, theoretical advancements, and reflections that inform and strengthen a new privilege studies pedagogy model while challenging traditional "diversity" and "multiculturalism" pedagogies. Faculty often struggle with identifying ally behaviors as instructors and mentors to students and providing spaces for students' own ally development. This collection offers a model of innovative strategies for moving beyond a whiteness-focused privilege studies and toward an effective pedagogy enacted by allies in the classroom.

Part I—Transformative Pedagogy: Teaching and Learning about Privilege

In the opening section of this volume, chapters 2 to 5 explore the potential for an innovative privilege studies pedagogy that transforms educational approaches and experiences while broadening instructional perceptions of the possibilities for learning about privilege. Authors emphasize teaching with empathy rather than blaming students, effectively addressing resistance to learning, supporting students as social justice allies, and facilitating deconstruction of colorblindness.

Nationally known speaker and anti-racism activist Tim Wise and Kim Case (chapter 2) highlight the necessity of faculty and all educators to develop skills and resources to teach anti-racism and become allies in educational settings. Not only should anti-racist educators have open and honest communication with students about race, racism, and white privilege, they can also seize the opportunity to make unearned privilege visible and dismantle essentialist beliefs about difference and inequality. However, effective pedagogy for the privileged must include understanding of defensiveness, guilt, shame, blame, entitlement, and hopelessness. Wise and Case argue that, with attention to these obstacles, faculty can transform the curriculum and teach students to question privilege and engage in ally behaviors that challenge injustice.

Student resistance to learning is an expected and often difficult part of teaching about power, privilege, oppression, and identity. Case and Cole's (chapter 3) essay addressing resistance to learning describes student disengagement from the course material that manifests as classroom incivility, refusal to read assigned texts, skipping or dropping a class, etc. Qualitative analysis of interviews with faculty members identified three forms of passive student resistance: (a) worldview protection, (b) target group resistance, and (c) narrative resistance. The authors reflect on resistance as part of a student's learning process and suggest that faculty become aware of student resistance strategies to better aid student learning.

Perrin and colleagues (chapter 4) describe the transtheoretical model of behavior change as a pedagogical framework for teaching and developing privileged students as social justice allies. By working with students to make invisible privilege more visible, educators serve to empower privileged students to work for dismantling oppression. The authors apply this five-stage model to student ally identity development and learning ways to use privilege for social justice goals. Students' "privilege investment" provides an action-oriented outlet in response to learning about privilege and oppression, rather than turning away from learning and toward hopelessness.

Armstrong and Wildman (chapter 5) explore colorblindness as it operates to maintain systems of white privilege and render discrimination invisible. They suggest promotion of "color insight," which acknowledges recognition of race for both White students and people of color. The authors note the specific importance of color insight for educational settings and suggest techniques for increasing students' understandings of race and racism. Their strategies include observation exercises, classroom scenarios, and discussion outside of the classroom about the culture of race in the university context.

Part II—Intersectional Privilege Studies Pedagogy

Chapters 6 to 9 provide intersectional perspectives for teaching and learning about privilege across the curriculum. By offering the theoretical framework of intersectionality as an essential component of the model, the authors guide the future direction of privilege studies pedagogy and challenge higher education to systematically integrate privilege and intersectional studies.

Ferber and Herrera's (chapter 6) review of intersectional theory and privilege literature integrates the two fields of research and outlines the benefits of using an intersectional approach in the study of privilege. They assert that incorporating privilege into the discussion of identity and inequality, using Collins's (1990) matrix of privilege and oppression as a pedagogical framework, allows students to understand their own complex social locations and reduces the tendency to focus only on personal oppressed identities while conveniently ignoring systems of privilege. The authors provide examples of specific activities for instructors to address privilege and oppression in the classroom.

In their essay about the influence of intersections of identity on teaching and learning pedagogy, Banks, Pliner, and Hopkins (chapter 7) use their experiences as professors (Banks and Pliner) and student (Hopkins) whose courses focus on issues of oppression and privilege to address the risks and benefits of teaching with an intersectional approach. They also explore how this approach strengthens students' experiences in the classroom, as it allows them to bring their full selves into the space. Lastly, they argue that encouraging awareness of one's own intersecting oppressed and privileged identities increases student involvement with social justice activism.

Rios and Stewart (chapter 8) explore issues of (in)visibility at certain intersections (e.g., as experienced by feminists of color) using the Global Feminisms Project, an archival collection of interviews with female activists. Specifically, the authors use the online database of interviews to describe teaching strategies that address issues of visibility and invisibility in the classroom. Including discussions of invisibility and marginalization allows more students to identify with the curriculum while highlighting the necessity of making privilege visible. This accessible resource provides faculty allies with an abundance of intersectional examples for use in teaching about privilege.

Dessel, Massé, and Walker's (chapter 9) essay describes the difficulty of teaching about privilege and the benefits of using intergroup dialogue, a method of social justice education. This review of the Program on Intergroup Relations at the University of Michigan provides a model for teaching about privilege that emphasizes peer facilitation, open communication among "ingroups" and "outgroups," and discussions of privilege. Specifically addressing heterosexual, Christian, and Jewish identities, the authors summarize qualitative data from student work to demonstrate the effectiveness of intergroup dialogue as a pedagogical approach for teaching and learning about privilege.

Part III—Privilege in the Classroom: Strategies and Applications

Becoming an ally in the classroom requires not only attention to social location and intersections of identity, but also to pedagogical strategies to promote student engagement through experiential learning and making connections between privilege and students' lived experiences. Chapters 10 to 13 of the collection address these challenges and also discuss ways to promote community learning environments, utilize student resistance to enhance learning, and adjust to broader cultural contexts that impact learning.

Blumer, Green, Thomte, and Green (chapter 10) discuss activities that address three themes regarding heteronormativity in the classroom: (a) acknowledging otherness, (b) recognizing heteronormativity, and (c) unpacking heteronormativity. For example, in a cookie role play activity, students must choose cookies of different colors and sizes to represent significant others in the students' lives and explain their own heterosexuality to another classmate. The role play context sets homosexuality as the cultural norm and heterosexuality as deviant. This allows students who benefit from heterosexual privilege to experience a small sample of the coming out process. Through an analysis of student comments, Blumer and colleagues demonstrate that these classroom activities increase awareness of heteronormativity and may even influence behavior changes.

Experiential learning, such as service learning, can be useful in increasing students' awareness of privilege. Williams and Melchiori (chapter 11) explore ways instructors can utilize service learning to deepen students' understanding and awareness of social class privilege. The service learning described involves community work and allows students to understand the real-world implications of social class inequality, as well as the intersectional impact of social class on other identities. The authors suggest that including a service-learning or community engagement component in courses focused on issues of privilege and identity can enhance transformative learning for both the instructor and the students.

In an examination of a typically ignored form of privilege, Case, McMullen, and Hentges (chapter 12) identify the balancing act of addressing Christian privilege in classrooms with predominantly Christian students in the context of a religiously and politically conservative state. The authors investigate practical ways to address Christian privilege in the classroom, including the creation of academic boundaries and a supportive community learning environment. In addition, the chapter reflects on the role of instructor social identity, including ally and religious identity, in enhancing student learning about privilege.

In her essay, Platt (chapter 13) suggests that making privilege personal and relevant for students as well as managing both students' and instructors' emotional responses to the learning process can ease student resistance and foster awareness of privilege. Teaching privilege at small liberal arts colleges often presents unique challenges due to the makeup of the student population. Students at many of these institutions arrive in the classroom from highly privileged backgrounds (e.g., white and middle class or upper class). In such a context, teaching about issues of power and privilege in the classroom can be met with higher than usual levels of student resistance. Platt offers advice for effectively teaching about privilege when students originate from affluent and homogenous hometowns.

Privilege Studies across the Curriculum

In "Reflections and future directions for privilege studies," Peggy McIntosh (2012) calls for an intersectional privilege studies. As outlined in her original well-known paper, McIntosh's (1988) observations that we must challenge the invisibility of privilege and work toward raising awareness and acknowledgement of privilege among dominant group members remain extremely relevant 25 years later. In addition, her 1988 paper addressing male, white, and heterosexual privilege also urges privilege studies that include analyses of age, ability, ethnicity, religion, and nation. Despite her decades of work toward a complex privilege studies across forms of oppression, both privilege studies scholarship and pedagogy need an intersectional expansion to begin to meet these goals.

This edited volume contributes to these goals by providing an intersectional privilege studies pedagogy model connecting theory and practical tools for transformative teaching and learning. As privilege studies expand into all diversity courses, such as those emphasizing gender, race, class, sexuality, and global studies, as well as into courses not traditionally associated with diversity, the goal of developing privilege studies across the curriculum may be realized. The increasing institutional focus on both writing and critical thinking "across the curriculum" spurred a national trend of quality assessment and enhancement programs at the university level. Privilege studies possess the same potential if faculty, departments, and administrators commit to an infusion of privilege studies pedagogy throughout universities. Perhaps by 2020, institutions of higher education will commonly implement quality enhancement programs focusing on *privilege studies across the curriculum* to enhance learning at all levels and throughout a wide variety of disciplines.

Note

1 When referring to individuals or a group of people, "White" is capitalized in accordance with American Psychological Association (APA) style guidelines. However, references to concepts such as white privilege, guilt, and identity are not capitalized in this collection.

References

Armstrong, M. J., & Wildman, S. M. (this volume). "Colorblindness is the new racism": Raising awareness about privilege using color insight. In K. A. Case (Ed.), *Deconstructing privilege: Teaching and learning as allies in the classroom* (pp. 63–79). New York, NY: Routledge.

Aveling, N. (2002). Student teachers' resistance to exploring racism: Reflections on "doing" border pedagogy. *Asia-Pacific Journal of Teacher Education, 30*, 119–130. doi:10.1080/13598660220135630

Banks, C. A., Pliner, S. M., & Hopkins, M. B. (this volume). Intersectionality and paradigms of privilege: Teaching for social change. In K. A. Case (Ed.), *Deconstructing privilege: Teaching and learning as allies in the classroom* (pp. 102–114). New York, NY: Routledge.

Berger, M. T., & Guidroz, K. (2009). *The intersectional approach: Transforming the academy through race, class, and gender.* Chapel Hill, NC: University of North Carolina Press.

Blumenfeld, W. J., & Jaekel, K. (2012). Exploring levels of Christian privilege awareness among pre-service teachers. *Journal of Social Issues, 68*(1), 128–144. doi:10.1111/j.1540–4560.2011.01740.x

Blumer, M. L. C., Green, M. S., Thomte, N. L., & Green, P. M. (this volume). Are we queer yet? Addressing heterosexual and gender-conforming privilege. In K. A. Case (Ed.), *Deconstructing privilege: Teaching and learning as allies in the classroom* (pp. 151–168). New York, NY: Routledge.

Case, K. A. (2007a). Raising male privilege awareness and reducing sexism: An evaluation of diversity courses. *Psychology of Women Quarterly, 31*, 426–435. doi:10.1111/j.1471–6402.2007.00391.x

Case, K. A. (2007b). Raising white privilege awareness and reducing racial prejudice: Assessing diversity course effectiveness. *Teaching of Psychology, 34*, 231–235. doi:10.1080/00986280701700250

Case, K. A. (2012). Discovering the privilege of whiteness: White women's reflections on anti-racist identity and ally behavior. *Journal of Social Issues, 68*(1), 78–96. doi:10.1111/j.1540–4560.2011.01737.x

Case, K. A., & Cole, E. R. (this volume). Deconstructing privilege when students resist: The journey back into the community of engaged learners. In K. A. Case (Ed.), *Deconstructing privilege: Teaching and learning as allies in the classroom* (pp. 34–48). New York, NY: Routledge.

Case, K. A., & Hemmings, A. (2005). Distancing strategies: White women preservice teachers and anti-racist curriculum. *Urban Education, 40*(6), 606–626. doi:10.1177/0042085905281396

Case, K. A., Iuzzini, J., & Hopkins, M. (2012). Systems of privilege: Intersections, awareness, and applications. *Journal of Social Issues, 68*(1), 1–10. doi:10.1111/j.1540–4560.2011.01732.x

Case, K. A., Kanenberg, H., Erich, S, & Tittsworth, J. (2012). Transgender inclusion in university nondiscrimination statements: Challenging gender-conforming privilege through student activism. *Journal of Social Issues, 68*(1), 145–161. doi:10.1111/j.1540–4560.2011.01741.x

Case, K. A., & Lewis, M. (2012). Teaching intersectional LGBT psychology: Reflections from historically Black and Hispanic serving universities. *Psychology and Sexuality, 3*(3), 1–17. doi:10.1080/19419899.2012.700030

Case, K. A., McMullen, M., & Hentges, B. (this volume). Teaching the taboo: Walking the tightrope of Christian privilege. In K. A. Case (Ed.), *Deconstructing privilege: Teaching and learning as allies in the classroom* (pp. 188–206). New York, NY: Routledge.

Case, K. A., Miller, A., & Jackson, S. B. (2012). "We talk about race too much in this class!" Complicating the essentialized woman through intersectional pedagogy. In S. Pliner & C. Banks (Eds.), *Teaching, learning, and intersecting identities in higher education* (pp. 32–48). New York, NY: Peter Lang.

Case, K. A., & Stewart, B. (2010). Changes in diversity course student prejudice and attitudes toward heterosexual privilege and gay marriage. *Teaching of Psychology, 37*(3), 172–177. doi:10.1080/00986283.2010.488555

Cole, E. R. (2009). Intersectionality and research in psychology. *American Psychologist, 64*(3), 170–180. doi:10.1037/a0014564

Cole, E. R., Avery, L. R., Dodson, C., & Goodman, K. D. (2012). Against nature: How arguments about the naturalness of marriage privilege heterosexuality. *Journal of Social Issues, 68*(1), 46–62. doi:10.1111/j.1540–4560.2012.01735.x

Collins, P. H. (1990). *Black feminist thought: Knowledge, consciousness, and the politics of empowerment.* New York, NY: Routledge.

Coston, B. M., & Kimmel, M. (2012). Seeing privilege where it isn't: Marginalized masculinities and the intersectionality of privilege. *Journal of Social Issues, 68*(1), 97–111. doi:10.1111/j.1540–4560.2011.01738.x

Crenshaw, K. (1989). Demarginalizing the intersection of race and sex: A Black feminist critique of antidiscrimination doctrine, feminist theory, and antiracist politics. *University of Chicago Legal Forum, 1989*, 139–167.

Dessel, A. B., Massé, J. C., & Walker, L. T. (this volume). Intergroup dialogue pedagogy: Teaching about intersectional and under-examined privilege in heterosexual, Christian, and Jewish identities. In K. A. Case (Ed.), *Deconstructing privilege: Teaching and learning as allies in the classroom* (pp. 132–148). New York, NY: Routledge.

Dill, B. T. (2009). Intersections, identities, and inequalities in higher education. In B. T. Dill & R. E. Zambrana (Eds.), *Emerging intersections: Race, class, and gender in theory, policy, and practice* (pp. 229–252). New Brunswick, NJ: Rutgers University Press.

Dill, B.T., & Zambrana, R. E. (2009). Critical thinking about inequality: An emerging lens. In B.T. Dill & R. E. Zambrana (Eds.), *Emerging intersections: Race, class, and gender in theory, policy, and practice* (pp. 1–21). New Brunswick, NJ: Rutgers University Press.

Ferber, A. L. (2012). The culture of privilege: Color-blindness, postfeminism and Christonormativity. *Journal of Social Issues, 68*(1), 63–77. doi:10.1111/j.1540–4560.2011.01736.x

Ferber, A. L., & Herrera, A. O. (this volume). Teaching privilege through an intersectional lens. In K. A. Case (Ed.), *Deconstructing privilege: Teaching and learning as allies in the classroom* (pp. 83–101). New York, NY: Routledge.

Fitts, M. (2009). Institutionalizing intersectionality: Reflections on the structure of women's studies departments and programs. In M.T. Berger & K. Guidroz (Eds.), *The intersectional approach: Transforming the academy through race, class, and gender* (pp. 249–257). Chapel Hill, NC: University of North Carolina Press.

Frankenberg, R. (1993). *The social construction of whiteness: White women, race matters.* Minneapolis, MN: University of Minnesota Press.

hooks, b. (1984). *Feminist theory: From margin to center.* Boston, MA: South End Press.

Kimmel, M. (2008). *Guyland: The perilous world where boys become men.* New York, NY: Harper.

Kimmel, M., & Ferber, A. L. (2010). *Privilege: A reader* (2nd ed.). Boulder, CO: Westview Press.

Lawrence, S. M., & Bunche, T. (1996). Feeling and dealing: Teaching White students about racial privilege. *Teaching and Teacher Education, 12*(5), 531–542. doi:10.1016/0742–051X(95)00054-N

McIntosh, P. (1988). *White privilege and male privilege: A personal account of coming to see correspondences through work in women's studies* (Working Paper No. 189). Wellesley, MA: Wellesley Centers for Women.

McIntosh, P. (2012). Reflections and future directions for privilege studies. *Journal of Social Issues, 68*(1), 194–206. doi:10.1111/j.1540–4560.2011.01744.x

McIntyre, A. (1997). *Making meaning of whiteness: Exploring racial identity with White teachers.* Albany, NY: State University of New York Press.

Montgomery, S. A., & Stewart, A. J. (2012). Privileged allies in lesbian and gay rights activism: Gender, generation, and resistance to heteronormativity. *Journal of Social Issues, 68*(1), 162–177. doi:10.1111/j.1540–4560.2012.01742.x

Neumann, S. L. (2009). The "why's" and "how's" of being a social justice ally. In R. A. R. Gurung & L. R. Prieto (Eds.), *Getting culture: Incorporating diversity across the curriculum* (pp. 65–75). Sterling, VA: Stylus.

Perrin, P. B., Bhattacharyya, S., Snipes, D. J., Hubbard, R. R., Heesacker, M., Calton, J. M., Perez, R. M., & Lee-Barber, J. (this volume). Teaching social justice ally development among privileged students. In K. A. Case (Ed.), *Deconstructing privilege: Teaching and learning as allies in the classroom* (pp. 49–62). New York, NY: Routledge.

Platt, L. F. (this volume). Blazing the trail: Teaching the privileged about privilege. In K. A. Case (Ed.), *Deconstructing privilege: Teaching and learning as allies in the classroom* (pp. 207–222). New York, NY: Routledge.

Pratto, F., & Stewart, A. L. (2012). Group dominance and the half-blindness of privilege. *Journal of Social Issues, 68*(1), 28–45. doi:10.1111/j.1540–4560.2011.01734.x

Rios, D., & Stewart, A. J. (this volume). Recognizing privilege by reducing invisibility: The Global Feminisms Project as a pedagogical tool. In K. A. Case (Ed.), *Deconstructing privilege: Teaching and learning as allies in the classroom* (pp. 115–131). New York, NY: Routledge.

Rothenberg, P. S. (2008). *White privilege: Essential readings on the other side of racism* (2nd ed.), New York, NY: Worth Publishers.

Sanders, M. R., & Mahalingam, R. (2012). Under the radar: The role of invisible discourse in understanding class-based privilege. *Journal of Social Issues, 68*(1), 112–127. doi:10.1111/j.1540–4560.2011.01739.x

Stewart, T. L., Latu, I. M., Branscombe, N. R., Phillips, N. L., & Denney, H. T. (2012). White privilege awareness and efficacy to reduce racial inequality improve White Americans' attitudes toward African Americans. *Journal of Social Issues, 68*(1), 11–27. doi:10.1111/j.1540–4560.2012.01733.x

Stoudt, B. G., Fox, M., & Fine, M. (2012). Contesting privilege with critical participatory action research. *Journal of Social Issues, 68*(1), 178–193. doi:10.1111/j.1540–4560.2011.01743.x

Tatum, B. D. (1994). Teaching White students about racism: The search for White allies and the restoration of hope. *Teachers College Record, 95*(4), 462–476.

Washington, R. L., & Evans, N. J. (1991). Becoming an ally. In N. J. Evans & V. A. Wall (Eds.), *Beyond tolerance: Gays, lesbians, and bisexuals on campus* (pp. 195–204). Alexandria, VA: American College Personnel Association.

Williams, W. R., & Melchiori, K. J. (this volume). Class action: Using experiential learning to raise awareness of social class privilege. In K. A. Case (Ed.), *Deconstructing privilege: Teaching and learning as allies in the classroom* (pp. 169–187). New York, NY: Routledge.

Wise, T., & Case, K. A. (this volume). Pedagogy for the privileged: Addressing inequality and injustice without shame or blame. In K. A. Case (Ed.), *Deconstructing privilege: Teaching and learning as allies in the classroom* (pp. 17–33). New York, NY: Routledge.

PART I

Transformative Pedagogy: Teaching and Learning about Privilege

2

PEDAGOGY FOR THE PRIVILEGED

Addressing Inequality and Injustice without Shame or Blame

Tim Wise and Kim A. Case

In my (Tim's) more than 20 years as an anti-racism educator, speaking about and organizing against racism and institutional white supremacy, there are two questions that other educators have asked me far more often than any others: "How can we get Whites to agree that they have unearned privileges, given their day-to-day struggles, which lead most to believe otherwise?" and "If we do convince Whites of their unearned advantages, why would they be willing to give those up in the service of a more equitable society?" The same questions arise with regard to getting men to critically explore patriarchy, upper-middle class and affluent persons to examine the class system from which they benefit, and heterosexual and gender-normative people to interrogate their privilege.

These questions present interesting challenges for K–12 and college educators attempting to act as allies and motivate privileged students to think about unearned advantages they receive via systems of inequality. As a graduate student teaching my (Kim's) own class for the first time, questions of how to address privilege, inequality, and to be an ally to students swirled around in my mind with each lecture preparation. These challenges prove especially daunting given the prominent forces of meritocracy and competitive advantage in American culture. Michael Lewis (1978) described meritocracy as the "individual-as-central" sensibility, the idea that success and material possessions resulted from hard work and initiative within a largely fair and just society (McNamee & Miller, 2009; Miller & Lapham, 2012; Ryan, 1981; Williams & Melchiori, this volume). With the belief in meritocracy comes the desire to maintain one's advantages in a competitive culture. Those advantages provide access to better education, housing, health care, employment, and security compared with oppressed groups. Culturally accepted and politically normalized in the United States (Green, 1981; Lewis, 1978; Ryan, 1981), inequality appears justified and the economically and racially advantaged typically attribute privilege to their own hard work (Feagin, 2010; Steinberg, 1989, 1995). This creates barriers to successfully engaging those with privilege in honest examination of their own advantages, as well as problematizing and seeking eradication of those unearned benefits (Case, Iuzzini, & Hopkins, 2012).

Despite the challenges that make discussions of privilege difficult, in our experience, certain approaches by faculty allies increase the likelihood of success when it comes to critically engaging members of privileged groups with this subject matter. Far from a silver bullet, these methods nonetheless de-escalate the defensiveness that so often surrounds discussions of these topics. In fact, these approaches may even result in the kinds of breakthroughs that allow some among the privileged group to commit to the destruction of unearned advantage and creation of more equitable institutional structures.

Understanding the Obstacles to Learning about Privilege

Before an educator can successfully teach students about their own unearned advantages or aid student development of an ally identity, he or she must recognize the obstacles that may prevent students from absorbing the information being presented. The first step in successfully teaching about privilege and inequity requires fundamental understanding of the forces that present barriers to learning. In the course of my work as an anti-racism educator and activist, I (Tim) identified six principal barriers to effective conversations about racism and white privilege. However, these obstacles to learning may also manifest when discussing other types of privilege. Although my discussion focuses on race, educators might relate each to other identity categories.

Defensiveness and Feelings of Personal Judgment

Racism, typically viewed as an individual character flaw and often conflated with overt bigotry (Brown et al., 2003; Kendall, 2006; Kivel, 2002), includes institutional forces most often invisible to the privileged. Therefore, discussions of racism and white privilege readily provoke feelings of defensiveness among Whites, many of whom experience the discussion as an attack that labels them as personally racist or bigoted (Case & Hemmings, 2005). In my (Kim's) courses and workshops, White students quite often jump to a defense of "I'm not racist" when no one in the room has accused or labeled them, but merely brought up the concept of privilege. The individualistic and interpersonal frame typically brought to the subject of racism leads many White students, when discussing white privilege, to feel that they are being judged as deliberately seeking to harm others, or at least passively accepting advantages over others. Therefore, educator allies hoping to teach effectively about white privilege will need to consider possible ways this obstacle prevents productive learning.

Not long ago, White Americans openly expressed racial prejudices towards people of color with very little misgiving. In fact, most Whites possessed no awareness of their relative advantages and defended their elevated position as a natural result of their own inherent superiority. Although racism remains far too common, Whites now outwardly condemn racism and adhere to social norms labeling racist beliefs unreasonable and unacceptable. Current conceptions of racist beliefs vary and biased views about people of color get defined as something other than racism by those who believe them. Many White Americans redefine their prejudices as something other than racism (Case & Hemmings, 2005; Feagin & Vera, 1995) and insist that they "haven't a racist bone in their bodies." Shifting social norms resulted in exaggeration of racial progress among White Americans. Although institutionalized white advantage over people of color continues as a dominant and normalized social force, most Whites feel compelled to proclaim the nation one of equal opportunity void of racial disparities. While this shifting of social norms is welcomed, it portends a desire on the part of most Americans to embrace an anti-racist or at least non-racist norm. It also complicates discussions about racial subjects, as the desire to see oneself as unbiased often makes grappling with notions of institutional inequity especially difficult.

Guilt or Shame: Feeling Blamed for the Suffering of Others

The fact that open expressions of racism are generally considered unacceptable today represents some progress in race inequality. However, progress brings unintended consequences that complicate honest discussions about racism and privilege. Given the social taboo that prohibits acknowledging one's racism or unearned advantage, discussions of privilege often cause feelings of guilt or shame among Whites. These guilt and shame responses may result from the conflict between (a) the belief in personal "goodness" and (b) being implicated in the suffering of others. To avoid these feelings of guilt and shame, White students often avoid addressing the concept of privilege by resisting understanding and derailing their own learning process in the classroom.

The Myth of Meritocracy

The belief in meritocracy, where individual effort and talent determine one's success or failure, is a deeply held cultural value in the United States. Growing up in a culture that endorses the belief in meritocracy, students face challenges to accept the notion that there are systemic injustices that interfere with the merit system (Case & Cole, this volume). Belief in meritocracy ties into not only national pride, but also psychological necessity for the privileged. After all, to believe that one is the master of one's own destiny allows the perception of control and hope for a better future. To let go of such a faith can be difficult, especially for White Americans confronted with evidence of unearned advantages. To admit the failings of meritocracy and acknowledge the ways in which racism and white privilege elevated them unjustly, Whites must accept personal implication in the suffering of others. This presents a unique challenge for educators seeking to engage their students around the subjects of racism and privilege as allies in the classroom.

The Tendency to Refocus on Marginalized Identities

In an effort to deflect attention away from privilege, and thereby avoid honestly appraising them, Whites often change the subject of discussion to a personal marginalized identity (Case, this volume; Case & Hemmings, 2005). By refocusing the conversation on personal injustice (perhaps as women or on the basis of economic status, sexual orientation, or Jewish identity), the racially privileged avoid facing the reality of systemic unearned benefits. Through discussion of subordination on the basis of other identities, Whites play the metaphorical "get out of jail free" card to avoid critical reflection on unearned advantage. Preparing in advance to navigate this common response is critical for ally educators hoping to engage students in transformative learning. Deconstruction of sexism, classism, heterosexism, gender-normative supremacy, anti-Semitism, and other forms of identity-based subordination requires the development and implementation of critical pedagogical strategies.

Entitlement and the Fear of Loss

Most White Americans seem unwilling to acknowledge race-based advantages and regularly claim racial equality when asked about income, housing, education and health care access (Brown et al., 2003; Wise 2010, 2012). It also seems that Whites fear the loss of social and economic status while publicly minimizing the importance of that status. For instance, Whites often express concern that undocumented immigrants "take our jobs." This formulation signifies a mentality of entitlement. Whites perceive the jobs as belonging to them, even though Whites did not occupy those positions. The claim also suggests Whites recognize they possess status and opportunities not afforded to others, and those others seek to "take" from Whites (Chomsky, 2007). Whites often express fears that affirmative action results in reverse discrimination (Pincus, 2003; Wise, 2005). They perceive this supposed discrimination against the dominant group as costing Whites jobs or college admission slots that rightfully belong to Whites. In addition, Whites fear ongoing demographic changes in the United States will result in the loss of national identity and cultural hegemony (Buchanan, 2011).

Regardless of personal denials that racism and privilege continue to provide Whites with unearned advantages, a belief persists that those privileges and entitlements are threatened by social, economic, and political changes. In my (Kim's) courses focusing on race, gender, sexuality, and intersections of identity, students from dominant groups often express their disdain for affirmative action programs and other social policies that lead to a more level playing field. Their firm and entrenched beliefs in the existence of meritocracy prevents them from recognizing that the privileged may in fact be granted promotions, admission to college, and other entitlements due to their own group membership. Although they label affirmative action as special treatment of women and people of color, they fail to see the institutionalized system of whiteness, white privilege, patriarchy, and male privilege as affirmative action for Whites and men. To engage students with issues of racism and privilege, teachers must negotiate the contours of this white anxiety very carefully.

Hopelessness in the Face of Injustice

Even if an educator manages to effectively teach lessons about privilege to students, unintended consequences may arise. Once students recognize such un-earned advantages exist, many become defeatist and even fatalistic about prospects for social change. This fatalism mitigates against the likelihood that students truly internalized the lesson at anything beyond a surface level and may diminish the prospects that they might become engaged in personal or collective struggle for social justice. If students acknowledge the reality of privilege and injustice, only to withdraw from the larger and more important conversation about social change, pedagogical interventions must be implemented. As such, ally educators will need to explore pedagogical approaches that empower students with a sense of agency in the face of widespread inequity and injustice.

Strategies for Discussing White Privilege with White Students

Given these common obstacles to constructive conversations about white racial privilege and racism, as well as social awareness and potential societal transformation, how might educators address the subject matter forthrightly and effectively? The strategies described below represent the most successful of our approaches to raising awareness of privilege. Although these examples primarily focus on strategies for advancing a conversation about white privilege and racism, they may also be utilized to address other forms of identity-based privilege with students.

Focus on Daily Privilege Rather than Economic Advantage

In my (Tim's) experience, Whites resist understanding the issue of unearned privileges because the word "privilege" leads to assumptions that the conversation revolves around wealth. Told that they possess "privilege," many Whites reject this assertion because they grew up in lower-income or working-class families. My initial rejection of the claim of my personal privilege illustrated this common reaction (Wise, 2011). I remember feeling defensive many years ago when first exposed to the notion that, as a White person, I was ipso facto privileged. Even though I knew I had grown up with certain advantages relative to my friends of color, the use of the word "privilege" to describe those advantages initially struck me as inaccurate.

Once I began to explore some of the literature on white privilege and discuss the matter with people of color, I became aware that the conversation was not primarily money or material advantage per se. Although the discussions sometimes explored the ways in which Whites (even the non-wealthy) experience material advantages over people of color, this was not the actual core of the privilege argument. Much more complex, privilege translated into psychological advantages of whiteness, the ways in which being White allowed me go about my days with "one less thing to sweat," so to speak. I never worried about the ways my racial identity might mark me negatively in the eyes of others. In fact, I safely assumed my racial identity would mark me positively in most instances as capable, intelligent, and hardworking. Scholars seeking to discuss not only white privilege, but also heterosexual privilege, male privilege, and other privilege systems, made similar points (Johnson, 2001).

The idea that I walk through life without worrying about racial stereotypes was one of the principal strengths of Peggy McIntosh's (1988) influential piece, widely regarded as one of the first pieces on white privilege ever authored by a White person. Although McIntosh's essay also noted the very real material advantages enjoyed by Whites (and men and heterosexuals) due to systemic privilege, the work struck me as important and helpful precisely because it dealt principally with the day-to-day, emotional, psychological, and affective aspects of white privilege, rather than focusing on economic positionality. In so doing, she minimized the kind of push-back that focuses on one's modest economic beginnings as somehow disproving white privilege.

The psychological aspects of white privilege were even more poignantly described for me in McIntosh's (2006) lesser-known follow-up to her original piece, an essay addressing white privilege in the justice system (McIntosh, 2006). McIntosh discussed the myriad ways in which White Americans receive fair treatment from law enforcement officials and benefit from being overlooked by law enforcement despite occasional illegal activity. Given my own engagement in illegal activities as a young man (drinking under age, making fake IDs for friends, or using illegal narcotics) and my lack of concern for the potential legal consequences of such actions, McIntosh's (2006) piece focusing on criminal justice stood out as an especially strong pedagogical tool for discussing these matters with students.

In speaking to hundreds of thousands of students over the years about white privilege, I realized students became visibly more receptive to the "lesson" when I switched from a mostly material conception of privilege (which focused on the higher incomes of Whites relative to Blacks, or greater net worth) to a psychological conception. Although I certainly discuss the ways in which Whites enjoy greater economic opportunities than most people of color, beginning these conversations with the ways privilege becomes normalized through the "privilege of obliviousness" dramatically affected audience receptivity. The privilege of obliviousness represents the luxury of not having to think much about race, racism, or one's racial identity in most settings and walking through daily life unconcerned about being targeted for mistreatment because of race.

Draw Privilege Parallels and Introduce Intersectionality

To promote learning about privilege, educators may draw parallels between white privilege and other privilege systems, acknowledging that virtually everyone possesses some kind of privilege based on social identity. Each individual carries privilege in some areas versus subordinate status in others. Intersectional theory scholars point out that many privileged and oppressed social identities interact simultaneously within each individual (Collins, 1990; Crenshaw, 1989; Dill & Zambrana, 2009). Using this theoretical approach helps the conversation move forward for a couple of reasons: (a) it provides students an avenue for conceptualizing privilege outside racism and whiteness, allowing critical examination of privilege within a potentially less threatening context; and (b) it actually pre-empts the common tendency for Whites in these discussions to change the subject to some other identity area in which they are not dominant, but, rather, a member of a subordinate group.

As part of my (Kim's) own approach as an ally in the classroom, I teach my "diversity courses" from an intersectional perspective. In my role as an educator, I view myself as a potential ally that can serve to promote dialogues across rigid ingroup and outgroup boundaries in the classroom. My ally identity informs my pedagogical approaches from the time I design the syllabus and reading list, to the carefully worded discussion questions I pose to the class, to the creation of assignments that involve both intersectional analysis and social action. For example, graduate students in my Psychology of Gender, Race, and Sexuality course spend the entire semester grappling with intersectionality in each week's readings, their reflective papers, class exercises and discussions, and in their major projects (Case & Lewis, 2012; Case, Miller, & Jackson, 2012). By strategically incorporating intersectional theory into student learning and critical analysis throughout the entire course, transformations occurred that fed into their public education projects for social action at the end of the term. As social justice allies, students created projects designed to teach others about the concept of intersectionality or a particular intersectional identity, such as the impact of both race and class on access/no access to quality public education. For example, one student worked with a domestic worker advocacy group in New York City to create flyers that would alert workers to their legal rights in their own languages. By the end of the course, over 1,000 domestic workers had received his pamphlet. Another student designed a packet on intersectional theory and its applications that is now used by women's studies and other faculty teaching courses across the United States.

If educators acknowledge, from the start, other forms of privilege and subordination on the basis of gender, class, sexuality, religion, or disability (and other categories as well) and that everyone possesses both dominant and marginalized identities, students feel validated in their experiences. At the same time, acknowledging complex identities cannot take priority in a manner that prevents discussion of white privilege. This approach allows the instructor to draw parallels across forms of privilege and communicate the importance of all aspects of identity to students. In turn, examples of marginalization based on gender, class, sexuality, religion, and more can be harnessed as illustrative examples of privilege and subordination to facilitate their understanding of white privilege as a phenomenon. In hearing from people of color who read *White Like Me* (Wise, 2011) for a class, they noted that the personal stories of white privilege resonated with them, not only as people deprived of that privilege, but as men with male privilege, upper-income persons with class privilege, or as heterosexual and gender-normative persons with privilege. In other words, students made these parallels across forms of privilege and successfully recognized their own dominant group status.

In my (Tim's) experience, asking students to reflect on the extent to which they paid attention to the way they entered the classroom or the auditorium for my speech illustrates one quick and easy way to get them to think about privilege. In that case, I am asking them to consider their able-bodied privilege. Since most audience members are able-bodied, they rarely pay much attention to the logistics of entering or exiting a building, the time needed to do so, the presence or absence of steps, ramps, or elevators, or the construction and positioning of seats or the classroom space. Considering able-bodied privilege primes them to understand the notion of everyday obliviousness. I ask them to reflect on the luxury of mobility and their advantage or privilege relative to those who face obstacles daily. The disability analogy also primes White students to think more critically about all the ways in which they "miss" evidence of everyday racism in society. Their able-bodied obliviousness (most students) prevented them from noticing the obstacles to mobility. Similarly, they are not required to be keenly aware of race-based obstacles facing people of color.

Several years ago, while participating in a day-long youth conference on diversity and racial equity in Washington, D.C., which brought together public and private school students as well as teachers, staff, and administrators, I (Tim) witnessed the value of this strategy up close. During a workshop session facilitated by others, I received a handout produced by Randolph Carter, the Director of the Eastern Educational Resource Collaborative, which helped develop equity initiatives for years for use in school settings. A simple rubric, it contained several categories of potential privilege, from the obvious, such as race, gender, sexuality, and class, to perhaps less obvious types, such as level of education, religious affiliation, and body type or physical attractiveness.

Participants completed the form, using what at first I considered to be a rather simplistic and not altogether useful scoring system, ranking ourselves in each category as possessing "high level," "medium level," or "low level" privilege in each realm. I was unsure of the pedagogical usefulness of such terminology or exercise and worried it might allow Whites in the room to avoid confronting white privilege by steering discussion to another category in order to claim "low" privilege and focus on personal marginality rather than dominance in the arena of race. Nonetheless, because I knew Randolph and trusted his instincts, I filled out the form and waited patiently to see what would come next.

On the one hand, there were no surprises in terms of how people completed their individual schematics. As one would imagine, almost everyone ended up with a mix of rankings marking at least one category as "high privilege" and at least one category as "low privilege." But, interestingly, the exercise process seemed to open up discussion in a way that allowed White participants to be honest and engage their white privilege, even though they had been handed a golden opportunity to shift discussion elsewhere. It was almost as if by being allowed to "mark their pain," so to speak, and to be honored in the doing of it, rather than being shut down as if to say that white privilege trumps all other systems of oppression at all times, they had been able to relax, open up, and acknowledge the power of whiteness in their lives without shame or guilt. Because they knew that persons of color in the session would have to also acknowledge their high-privilege categories (even if only to themselves at first, since they would not have known as they filled out their rubrics that everyone would ultimately be asked to publicly own a high-status category), Whites in the room could rest assured they were not being singled out and marked as the only privileged persons. This allowed them a certain protection from the stigma that might otherwise have tripped them up in the session.

The experience taught me that by universalizing the notion of privilege for an audience and acknowledging that indeed all have some form of it, Whites being asked to honestly assess and critique whiteness are freed to do so without guilt or the same degree of misgiving that might normally characterize these interactions.

Acknowledge Exceptions

When faced with students that deny privilege, instructors may find it beneficial to carefully contextualize the conversation and validate the perspectives of those students blocking conversational progress. For example, by acknowledging that some people of color also benefit from advantages and privilege based on non-racial aspects of identity, student defensiveness may be reduced. Likewise, some Whites experience disadvantages on the bases of non-racial categories that might render their white privilege virtually meaningless in certain specific situations. Although a case could be made that all Whites enjoy some level of white privilege (Oliver & Shapiro, 1995) and that all people of color are subjected to racism (Feagin & Sikes, 1994), instructors might do well to present this argument after clearly acknowledging that exceptions do exist, thereby bringing the reluctant learner into the critical conversation. For example, I (Kim) regularly encounter students who point out successful Black individuals, such as Oprah Winfrey, Condoleezza Rice, and especially two-term President Barack Obama, as evidence that the idea of white privilege carries no weight. If students perceive an instructor as teaching dogma, they may resist learning new information. Therefore, an instructor's insistence that "all Whites are privileged," "all Blacks are oppressed," "all Whites are racist," or "only Whites can be racist" may prevent learning. From a pedagogical perspective, bringing learners into the conversation must be the top priority. By admitting to the possibility of exceptions, instructors support critical thinking about exceptions while keeping them interested in learning more. This allows the instructor to maintain focus on the larger and more important point that privilege and inequality are about general social truths and systems.

For example, I (Tim) often point to examples that illustrate such exceptions to highlight white privilege as a measurable social phenomenon even though poor White people exist. The link between smoking and cancer offers one such example. Virtually all Americans now accept the idea that smoking can and often does cause cancer. At the same time, many people smoke for decades without developing so much as a cough. Regardless of existence of many cancer-free smokers, few people reject the knowledge that smoking increases the likelihood of cancer. The metaphor of smoking and cancer may help promote understanding of social identity privilege. Whiteness is highly correlated with advantage relative to people of color. Being a man is highly correlated with advantage relative to women. These privileges persist despite the existence of many Whites and men who experience marginalization via other identity categories. Through discussion of individual exceptions to a social rule, instructors foster students' deepened understanding of the rule itself. For example, wealthy individuals with disabilities exist, but this wealth does not lead to claims that their financial security eradicates disadvantage when it comes to the barriers of ableism and able-bodied privilege. Financial means might make their disability easier to manage, but wealth still fails to promote them able-bodied status.

Contextualization

Contextualization is helpful in discussing privilege with students because it helps to narrowly focus on ways privilege relates to the particular students in the classroom. Based on feedback from teachers I (Tim) received over the years, students often approach McIntosh's (1988) original knapsack piece searching for one or two examples of white privilege that do not apply to them personally. Ignoring the rest of the list, students then focus on those examples to torpedo the larger point about privilege being made within the piece. Students critique the example of "flesh-colored bandages," citing recent development of different shades of bandages and clear bandages since the essay was written. To address this tendency to hone in on a specific example to pick apart, I approach my audience with a selected few examples from the McIntosh (1988) list. I purposely limit the examples to those most likely to be applicable to the audience or students in the room. When I use this strategy of targeted daily white privilege examples, student receptivity seems to be quite a bit greater in comparison to using the entire list. In other words, quality trumps quantity when it comes to the white privilege list.

Modeling Self-Reflection on Privilege

Educators serving as ally role models and hoping to effectively engage students around issues of privilege will fare far better in the process by modeling self-reflection around privilege. For example, the *White Like Me* memoir (Wise, 2011) serves as a great tool for modeling self-reflection. In an undergraduate course on race and gender, I (Kim) modeled ally behavior and shared my reflection on my own white privilege with students by reading my "white affirmative action list" to them. This list includes every single individual that ever hired me, promoted me, admitted me to an academic program, or taught the courses that were required to earn my degrees. Every single one of the names belongs to a White person that served as gate-keeper, but opened the gate for me. By personalizing privilege and beginning with themselves, teachers drop the veil of objectivity and model self-reflection for students. Providing a space for students to "own" their privilege without acknowledging one's own privilege presents a pedagogical challenge. Students may fear that by admitting their own privileges, and their direct implication in systems of injustice, they will be judged by instructors who determine their academic grades and by classmates. If the teacher breaks the ice by pointing to examples of privilege in his or her own life, the student will likely be more comfortable opening up about their own experiences and advantages. For White instructors, this means openly discussing their own racialized privilege as Whites. For faculty of color, it means acknowledging privileges associated with their identity (gender, sexuality, economic status, etc.). This modeling can substantially reduce the defensiveness so often manifested by students during discussions of privilege. Additionally, expressing self-reflection on privilege as the instructor serves to open students up to discussing privilege because it signals to them that they will not be judged for admitting their own unearned advantages. This practice contributes to establishing a "safe space" for the acknowledgement of privilege.

Highlight Institutional Privilege

As instructors personalize the face of privilege by sharing their own stories with students, they simultaneously demonstrate the ways white privilege and racism exist as institutional and structural forces. By discussing the way that privilege flows to dominant group members as a matter of institutional course, regardless of an individual's good intentions, educators minimize defensiveness on the part of students, as well as blunt feelings of guilt or shame among those with privilege.

Discussing the role of "old boys' networks" for jobs provides an effective way to highlight the institutional nature of privilege. Most students know that some people benefit from better connections than others and that Whites tend to have the best connections. Such examples help students visualize the unfairness of institutional systems, even without overt individual-level bigotry operating to produce unequal outcomes. For example, students recognize that even without racial bias among individual employers, members of racial groups outside the traditional networks will continue to be overlooked because of systemic exclusion. Most students successfully identify moments when they fell outside of a network that would provide a better opportunity. Reflecting on a personal experience of limited access to opportunities helps them empathize with others facing similar forms of marginalization. Some of the ways I (Tim) highlight the institutional forces that maintain privilege include:

1. the use of standardized tests on profoundly unstandardized students who attended fundamentally unequal schools;
2. the use of property tax revenues as the principal form of K–12 school funding (which favors affluent and Whiter communities, where property values are higher); and
3. tax codes that tax capital gain and investment gains (upper class and wealthy) at lower rates compared to income earned from labor (poor/working class/ middle class).

Talking about institutional forces and the ways they operate regardless of individual intent serves to minimize feelings of guilt and defensiveness, as well as challenge the notion of meritocracy. Highlighting institutional privilege allows teachers to help their students visualize the benefits of whiteness (or maleness, etc.) much like Tatum's (1993) metaphorical "moving walkway," which continues to progress in the same direction regardless of whether those standing upon it actively do anything at all. Unless the privileged actively push against the flow of the walkway (institutional privilege) will the system fail to produce the results for which it was designed (Tatum, 1993).

Explore the Costs of Privilege

Once students begin to acknowledge their unearned advantages, why would they choose to give them up by advocating for a more just and equitable society? After all, U.S. culture promotes actively capitalizing on one's advantages. If educators take special care to explore the ways privilege damages and harms the dominant group, students may begin to weigh the costs associated with unearned advantages. Discussing the downside of privilege became a more common theme among anti-racist activists and educators in attempts to create anti-racist consciousness within the White community (Barndt, 2007; Harvey, Case, & Gorsline, 2004; Kendall, 2006; Wise, 2011, 2012). Although thinking about privilege in terms of costs seems in conflict with the definition, invisible benefits come with a number of costs. Educators might encourage students to explore personal, familial, psychological, cultural, emotional, economic, and health-related costs within their analyses of privilege.

The importance of discussing the downside of privilege became especially clear to me (Tim) after the publication of my memoir, *White Like Me* (Wise, 2011). Although many of the stories concern privilege in my life, the chapter about loss included various costs paid for the receipt of privilege such as: (a) the loss of connection to one's actual cultural heritage, since whiteness comes to serve as a substitute for the rich traditions of one's particular European ancestors; (b) the internalization of racial biases and prejudices despite one's best intentions; (c) the loss of connection to community and the isolation that is bred by profound inequities; (d) the development of an unhealthy mentality of expectation and entitlement that can result in failure when faced with unexpected obstacles; and (e) the perpetuation of an economic order that disempowers the vast majority of people, including most Whites.

With regard to teaching about the harms of racial privilege, I introduce students to the development of whiteness as a concept and the way white privilege was deployed specifically to convince working-class European immigrants they had more in common with other Whites than with people of color who shared their economic status (Thandeka, 2000). This approach, focusing on the downside of privilege and what Marx might have called "false consciousness," helps diminish feelings of guilt, defensiveness, and the sense of being personally judged. Understanding the systemic nature of whiteness and its costs removes personal blame from the students' shoulders and allows them to claim a type of shared victim identity with people of color. At the same time, these costs pale in comparison to the oppression experienced by people of color under a system of white supremacy, and educators must be careful to distinguish the costs to Whites from the primary damage it does to people of color. By creating the sense that Whites and people of color share a common source of injury (although not at the same level), teachers promote empathy and enhance solidarity amongst and between White students and students of color.

Using Levine's (2006) examination of the "price of privilege" among affluent, mostly White youth in her upscale Northern California community, instructors may develop an effective starting place for student learning. As a psychotherapist, Levine observed the emotional costs of having too much and the expectations and sense of entitlement that often result. Because so many of her examples resonate with young people, either in their own lives or the lives of people in their social circle, asking students to explore privilege as an inadvertent psychological stressor and damaging weight leads to recognition that even advantages come at a cost.

Students in my audiences also prove open to an examination of the nation's current economic condition and its relationship to privilege. If simply asked to examine the matter, they recognize the recent housing meltdown and unemployment crisis as connected to inequality and privilege. They acknowledge that the indifference of most national leaders and the media to sub-prime and predatory lending, which began in the mid-1990s in communities of color, ultimately laid the groundwork for the spread of such practices into more neighborhoods. If race and class privilege did not insulate millions from thinking about such matters, perhaps leaders would have implemented regulations to prevent the housing collapse. However, privilege and obliviousness allowed the situation to worsen until it contributed to the collapse of the economy. Likewise, if leaders considered double-digit and long-term unemployment a national emergency when it affected people of color, perhaps action would have been taken at the national level to address it. The privilege of whiteness allowed leaders to ignore the problem, to blame the out of work for their plight, to slash the safety net programs upon which desperate people relied, and avoid facing the consequences of indifference. Instead, millions of Whites experienced the costs of privilege, obliviousness, and disconnection from the larger community they share with people of color (Wise, 2012).

Student Empowerment: Developing Change Agents

In order to develop pedagogical approaches as allies in the classroom, educators must help students discover a sense of their own power by making sure to address the hopelessness, defeatism, and even fatalism that sometimes set in when people become more aware of the depths of social injustice. As the Case (this volume) pedagogical model points out, effective privilege studies education requires students' ally identity development and exploration of social change actions. When confronted with previously invisible matters of racism, discrimination, inequity, and their own privilege, individuals face difficulty in terms of digesting the new awareness. At this stage, students perceive themselves as implicated in systems of unfairness, question their understanding of the society, and recognize deep and interwoven systems of oppression. Unless educators facilitate hopefulness and a sense of possibility, awareness of injustice may lead to student disempowerment.

Peggy McIntosh (2012) makes a strong case for working with privileged persons to challenge injustice and approaching this work to empower rather than deflate students. She discusses the need to view privilege as not only an invisible knapsack, but also a bank account, given to her at birth, from which she makes unconscious and conscious withdrawals every day. In other words, if those with privilege begin to perceive their advantages as tools that can either do great harm or great good, they can develop a sense of ownership and efficacy that would allow them to imagine deploying privilege for the sake of equity. Just as a hammer can be used to build a home or commit a violent assault, privilege can be used for constructive or destructive purposes.

Of course, the privileged must be cautious about deploying privilege, taking special care to empower the marginalized and elevate their voices. Examining the possibilities and encouraging those with privilege to think about ways they may use their advantages to interrupt instances of discrimination, challenge institutional arrangements, and confront overt manifestations of racism can lead to lifelong learning that extends beyond the classroom.

Educating for Social Justice: A Call to Action

Teaching students with privilege to critically examine those privileges and commit to changing the society that bestows them requires effective strategies. In our experiences, the approaches mentioned here and the framing of the issues in the way we have suggested minimize the obstacles and barriers so often erected by resistant students. Without allies in the classroom willing to address privilege in the classroom, model self-reflection, and facilitate student empowerment to take action for social justice, privilege systems will remain intact at the individual and institutional levels. Educators in K–12 settings, higher education, and community organizations have a responsibility to provide spaces for deconstruction of privilege by creating learning environments where students will critically analyze their own privilege, biases, and possible avenues for creating change.

References

Barndt, J. (2007). *Understanding and Dismantling Racism*. Minneapolis, MN: Fortress Press.

Brown, M. K., Carnoy, M., Currie, E., Duster, T., Oppenheimer, D. B., Shultz, M. M., & Wellman, D. (Eds.). (2003). *Whitewashing race: The myth of a color-blind society*. Berkeley, CA: University of California Press.

Buchanan, P. J. (2011). *Suicide of a superpower: Will America survive to 2025?* New York, NY: Thomas Dunne Books.

Case, K. A. (this volume). Beyond diversity and whiteness: Developing a transformative and intersectional model of privilege studies pedagogy. In K. A. Case (Ed.), *Deconstructing privilege: Teaching and learning as allies in the classroom* (pp. 1–14). New York, NY: Routledge.

Case, K. A., & Cole, E. R. (this volume). Deconstructing privilege when students resist: The journey back into the community of engaged learners. In K. A. Case (Ed.), *Deconstructing privilege: Teaching and learning as allies in the classroom* (pp. 34–48). New York, NY: Routledge.

Case, K. A., & Hemmings, A. (2005). Distancing strategies: White women preservice teachers and anti-racist curriculum. *Urban Education, 40*(6), 606–626. doi:10.1177/0042085905281396

Case, K. A., Iuzzini, J., & Hopkins, M. (2012). Systems of privilege: Intersections, awareness, and applications. *Journal of Social Issues, 68*(1), 1–10. doi:10.1111/j.1540–4560.2011.01732.x

Case, K. A., & Lewis, M. (2012). Teaching intersectional LGBT psychology: Reflections from historically Black and Hispanic serving universities. *Psychology and Sexuality, 3*(3), 1–17. doi:10.1080/19419899.2012.700030

Case, K. A., Miller, A., & Jackson, S. B. (2012). "We talk about race too much in this class!" Complicating the essentialized woman through intersectional pedagogy. In S. Pliner & C. Banks (Eds.), *Teaching, learning, and intersecting identities in higher education* (pp. 32–48). New York, NY: Peter Lang.

Chomsky, A. (2007). *"They take our jobs!" And 20 other myths about immigration.* Boston, MA: Beacon.

Collins, P. H. (1990). *Black feminist thought: Knowledge, consciousness, and the politics of empowerment.* New York, NY: Routledge.

Crenshaw, K. (1989). Demarginalizing the intersection of race and sex: A Black feminist critique of antidiscrimination doctrine, feminist theory, and antiracist politics. *University of Chicago Legal Forum, 1989*, 139–167.

Dill, B. T., & Zambrana, R. E. (2009). Critical thinking about inequality: An emerging lens. In B. T. Dill & R. E. Zambrana (Eds.), *Emerging intersections: Race, class, and gender in theory, policy, and practice* (pp. 1–21). New Brunswick, NJ: Rutgers University Press.

Feagin, J. (2010). *The white racial frame: Centuries of racial framing and counter-framing.* New York, NY: Routledge.

Feagin, J., & Vera, H. (1995). *White racism.* New York, NY: Routledge.

Feagin, J., & Sikes, M. P. (1994). *Living with racism: The Black middle-class experience.* Boston, MA: Beacon Press.

Green, P. (1981). *The pursuit of inequality.* New York, NY: Pantheon.

Harvey, J., Case, K., & Gorsline, R. H. (Eds.) (2004). *Disrupting white supremacy from within: White people on what we need to do.* Cleveland, OH: Pilgrim Press.

Johnson, A. G. (2001). *Privilege, power, and difference.* Mountain View, CA: Mayfield Publishing.

Kendall, F. E. (2006). *Understanding white privilege: Creating pathways to authentic relationships across race.* New York, NY: Routledge.

Kivel, P. (2002). *Uprooting racism: How white people can work for racial justice* (Rev. ed.). British Columbia, Canada: New Society Publishers.

Levine, M. (2006). *The price of privilege: How parental pressure and material advantage are creating a generation of disconnected and unhappy kids.* New York, NY: Harper Collins.

Lewis, M. (1978). *The culture of inequality.* New York, NY: Meridian.

McIntosh, P. (1988). *White privilege and male privilege: A personal account of coming to see correspondences through work in women's studies* (Working Paper No. 189). Wellesley, MA: Wellesley Centers for Women.

McIntosh, P. (2006). White privilege, color, and crime: A personal account. In C. R. Mann, M. S. Zatz, & N. Rodriguez (Eds.), *Images of color, images of crime: Readings* (3rd. ed., pp. 52–60). Los Angeles, CA: Roxbury Publishing.

McIntosh, P. (2012). Reflections and future directions for privilege studies. *Journal of Social Issues, 68*(1), 194–206. doi:10.1111/j.1540–4560.2011.01744.x

McNamee, S. J., & Miller, R. K. (2009). *The meritocracy myth.* Lanham, MD: Rowman & Littlefield.

Miller, B., & Lapham, M. (2012). *The self-made myth: And the truth about how government helps individuals and businesses succeed.* San Francisco, CA: Berrett-Koehler.

Oliver, M., & Shapiro, T. (1995). *Black wealth, white wealth: A new perspective on racial inequality.* New York, NY: Routledge.

Pincus, F. (2003). *Reverse discrimination: Dismantling the myth.* Boulder, CO: Lynne Rienner Publishers.

Ryan, W. (1981). *Equality.* New York, NY: Pantheon.

Steinberg, S. (1989). *The ethnic myth: Race, ethnicity, and class in America.* Boston, MA: Beacon.

Steinberg, S. (1995). *Turning back: The retreat from racial justice in American thought and policy.* Boston, MA: Beacon.

Tatum, B. D. (1993). *"Why are all the Black kids sitting together in the cafeteria?" And other conversations about race.* New York, NY: Basic Books.

Thandeka. (2000). *Learning to be White: Money, race, and God in America.* New York, NY: Continuum.

Williams, W. R., & Melchiori, K. J. (this volume). Class action: Using experiential learning to raise awareness of social class privilege. In K. A. Case (Ed.), *Deconstructing privilege: Teaching and learning as allies in the classroom* (pp. 169–187). New York, NY: Routledge.

Wise, T. (2005). *Affirmative action: Racial preference in black and white.* New York, NY: Routledge.

Wise, T. (2010). *Colorblind: The rise of post-racial politics and the retreat from racial equity.* San Francisco, CA: City Lights Books.

Wise, T. (2011). *White like me: Reflections on race from a privileged son* (2nd ed.). Berkeley, CA: Soft Skull/Counterpoint.

Wise, T. (2012). *Dear White America: Letter to a new minority.* San Francisco, CA: City Lights Books.

3

DECONSTRUCTING PRIVILEGE WHEN STUDENTS RESIST

The Journey Back into the Community of Engaged Learners

Kim A. Case and Elizabeth R. Cole

Although college faculty sometimes write about their experiences with students' resistance to material in courses that focus on privileges linked to social identity, this literature most often presents a single instructor's perspective (e.g., Atwood, 2010; Chan & Treacy, 1996; Higginbotham, 1996). The following exploration considers themes of resistance across disciplines and multiple instructors' experiences in diversity-themed courses. Drawing on interviews with teachers of such courses aimed at first-year students, as well as on our own teaching experiences, we identify three forms of resistance. In addition, we reflect on alternative ways to understand student resistance and offer strategies for addressing resistant behaviors to bring students back into the broader community of engaged learners. For faculty aiming to teach from an ally perspective, such strategies for working with and through student resistance may aid the goal of creating inclusive classrooms that minimize marginalization of groups and promotes productive dialogues.

We use the term "resistance" to describe the behavior of students who fail to engage with the course content, whether actively or passively. We do not define thoughtful or critical analysis of readings or theoretical perspectives as resistance to learning. Instead, we apply the term to behaviors that dismiss or fail to acknowledge new and disconfirming information or perspectives. In our view, resistance to learning shuts down the conversation rather than encouraging and opening up the broader discussion. Active student resistance often takes the form of arguing by assertion or insisting on the unassailability of personal opinion (i.e., "that's just what I believe") rather than by providing an explicit and reasoned rationale or academic support. In these situations, students often fall back on labels, generalizations, and catch phrases from popular culture to support their views (i.e., describing new information or perspectives as "politically correct"; citing Bible passages as incontrovertible truths; or invoking the views of radio and television pundits as authorities).When students resist learning, they are unwilling to consider alternative perspectives, especially those different from their own.

Research on resistance often involves a taxonomical approach, identifying types of behaviors, personality predispositions, and classroom dynamics. For example, Chan and Treacy (1996) distinguished between active resistance, in which students assertively criticize and disagree with material presented in class, and the more common passive resistance, which may include marginal cooperation, late or incomplete assignments, tardiness to class, or decreased involvement with material. Similarly, Higginbotham (1996) classified resistance into three forms (vocal, silent, and absent) and noted that members of less privileged groups commonly deploy passive types of resistance. Faculty often face difficulty determining whether student behavior resulted from disengagement with the material or some unknown and possibly unrelated reason. As allies in the classroom, instructors must identify ways to effectively address such barriers to learning and promote critical reflection. Most of these typologies describe resistance without insight into the reasons for the resistance or its dynamics.

Jackson (1999) classified resistance based on the psychological source of the barrier, using the phrase "resistance to content" to describe when students feel trapped and respond with anger, resentment, and silence resulting from demands for examination of their own privileges in required courses. Case and Hemmings (2005) also examined resistance to content in response to anti-racist curriculum in a social inequalities course for pre-service teachers. They found that White women in the course used strategies to distance themselves from the topic of racism by remaining silent when class conversations turned to race or when confronted with racism in their personal lives.

In contrast to resistance to content, "character resistance" (Jackson, 1999) refers to a defensive personal coping style (e.g., denial, projection, reaction formation). Case and Hemmings (2005) noted that the White women in their study separated themselves from learning about racism by focusing on the progress made for civil rights, blaming the racist culture or racist people in the past, blaming affirmative action and reverse discrimination in the present, or blaming the marginalized group for the perpetuation of racism.White women also disassociated themselves from racism by proclaiming colorblindness and denying the label of "racist" (Armstrong & Wildman, this volume; Case & Hemmings, 2005; Tatum, 1992;Wise & Case, this volume). These forms of denial and projection illustrate Jackson's (1999) conceptualization of character resistance. Similarly, LaDuke (2009) found that students verbally protested the defining of a relationship between institutional racism and dominant group power for Whites."Transference resistance" describes students' reactions to instructors, both positive and negative, which interfere with communication and learning (Jackson, 1999). When students' negative emotions lead to shutting down and avoiding dialogue through silence, instructors face the pedagogical challenge of finding ways to bring them back into the community of engaged learners.

Alternatively, Tatum (1992) characterized resistance as a developmental process. Mapping White student resistance to taboo content such as race and racism onto Helms' (1990) racial identity model, Tatum suggested pedagogical attention must be paid to the development of resistance as part of the learning process. She described positive student development as resulting from creating safe classroom spaces, including identity development models in the curriculum, providing opportunities for students to contribute to knowledge creation, and empowering student as agents of social change. By addressing resistance as a developmental process, faculty can better identify effective strategies for maximizing learning.

Yet another strand in the student learning literature focuses on attitude change over the course of a term (Case, 2007a, 2007b; Case & Stewart, 2010; Cole, Case, Rios, & Curtin, 2011; Dessel, Massé, & Walker, this volume; Markowitz, 2005). By comparing students' attitudes at the start and conclusion of the course, these studies explore whether such courses lead students to be more tolerant, democratic, feminist, or likely to engage in activism. Markowitz (2005) found that taking a gender-focused course taught from a feminist pedagogical perspective reduced students' use of dichotomous analysis at the end of the term. Cole et al. (2011) identified student characteristics associated with learning among students taking required race and ethnicity courses in their first year of college. Students exhibited increased understanding of blatant racism, white privilege, and intersectionality, and White students showed decreased endorsement of the Protestant work ethic by the end of the term. However, these general trends cannot address the experiences of individual students who may struggle with and resist content in such courses over the time span of a course.

Exploring Faculty Experiences with Resistance

Given that most of the literature cited above derives from authors' individual experiences as teachers, empirical data are needed to further develop pedagogical theory with regard to student resistance. This study aims to theorize students' resistant behaviors in courses addressing privilege linked to social identities by looking at a sample of instructors' experiences to identify emerging patterns. Any individual's teaching experience is necessarily limited by her or his goals, hopes, fears, and personal qualities. In our own experience, we noted distinct similarities within colleagues' descriptions of frustration with student resistance, and we hoped that in-depth interviews might reveal new insights into the obstacles instructors face in such classes. What type of materials are students resisting? Are there more fine-grained distinctions we can make among these types of resistance? We aim to identify some dynamic, rather than descriptive, ways of thinking about resistance. In doing so, we hope to generate a diagnostic approach to help teachers ask, "What is going on here?" and identify some strategies to address the problems. Through interviews, we draw on college teachers' own practice to generate this analysis.

I (Elizabeth) interviewed 7 faculty members at the University of Michigan teaching first year seminars with a focus on privilege, oppression, and diversity. These seminars are small (20 students) courses offered by many departments focused on specialized topics and provide students opportunities to personally engage with a faculty member. Specific topics included, but were not limited to, race and racism, gender and sexism, heterosexism and homophobia, and other aspects of social power and privilege. The sample was small, heterogeneous, and included: 4 women; 3 men; 2 African Americans; and 5 European Americans (2 were Jewish). Two had been teaching full time for 3 or fewer years, one for 6 years, and four for 20 years or more. The interviewees represented diverse disciplines within the humanities and social sciences, as well as the interdisciplinary areas of women's studies and Afro-American studies. In the analyses that follow, we also include insights from our own teaching. Elizabeth, who has been teaching nearly 20 years, is of biracial background and identifies as African American. Kim has been teaching for 13 years and identifies as White. Both of us are heterosexual.

Semi-structured in-depth interviews lasted an average of one hour and were audiotaped and transcribed. Questions asked respondents to describe their background and interest in privilege and diversity, summarize the course content and goals of their first year seminar, talk about examples and types of student resistance they had encountered and their responses, and to reflect on how student resistance affected them both professionally and personally. Using HyperText software for qualitative analysis, interview transcripts were coded for episodes of resistance, characterizations of types of resistance, and content material eliciting resistance. We focus here specifically on passages in which faculty explain different types of resistance. Close reading, categorizing, and thematic analysis of those passages revealed patterns within the categories. The resulting observations are intended to help understand the types of interactions between students and faculty hidden beneath these umbrella statements by faculty about student resistance.

Emergent Themes

Our analysis of resistance as described by faculty members revealed three main themes, although not mutually exclusive categories:

1. worldview protection;
2. target group resistance; and
3. narrative resistance.

Examples from faculty interviews supplemented with reflections based on our personal classroom experiences below illustrate the three emergent forms of passive resistance.

Worldview Protection

Chan and Treacy (1996) argued that courses on multiculturalism may challenge students' core convictions such as belief in meritocracy, expectation of social justice for all, and emphasis on individuals as separate from society. First year students may resist information they suspect will separate them from homes and families intellectually and emotionally. Information in such courses may be particularly challenging for those whose identities are based on essentialist notions, or the belief that group members share innate characteristics. For instance, a student in a heterosexual marriage based on traditional gender roles may be reluctant to consider new ways of thinking about these roles as socially constructed and inequitable. Some faculty interviewed described students whose failure to engage seemed to be rooted in a desire to protect their existing worldview, as though they aimed to lock certain beliefs in a vault where they could not be questioned or examined. We labeled this form of passive resistance "worldview protection."

For example, one faculty member described an African American man who engaged early in the course, but later refused to consider issues concerning the rights of sexual minorities due to his religious beliefs. This particular student "came from nothing," in the instructor's words, and moved into the upper middle class due to his father's career. He was "very active in the class . . . and very involved in talking." The faculty member went on to say:

> He very much knows the class issues of working-class folks and he's a Black man so really was engaged in race and ethnicity issues. But then when it came to sexual orientation, he was shut down. Religion was very . . . you know, is very strong in his life. And that was his kind of defense. Well, you know, "my religion tells me that's wrong and that's it." And he didn't say anything for the class sessions that we were talking about sexual orientation.

Given that we cannot fully know whether his silence manifested from resistance, this student's uncharacteristic silence may potentially indicate lack of familiarity with this form of oppression or possible emotional reactions to learning about a form of oppression he had not yet considered. However, the instructor characterized the student's silence as defensive, allowing him to disengage from content that challenged his religious background. This behavior was all the more striking given his high level of engagement at other points in the course.

Another instructor described students who were reluctant to consider ways that Malcolm X's life presents problematic gender themes. He reflected:

> They do see that there is some misogyny in this narrative, although there is some resistance there too. Some people, it's probably more men than women, say they want to "give him a pass," so to speak . . . They see it as pulling out one particular component of him, of his like, of his overall

experience and critiquing him for that without seeing the context of all that he's experienced, and so forth. So that is an element, I think, of resistance.

The difficulty that students have with seeing contradictions in one person can lead to resistance. Students appeared to reject any critique of Malcolm X as if that critique would then negate all of his work for racial justice advocacy. Interestingly, the instructor felt students believed that understanding Malcolm's life in context would excuse any sexist behavior, rather than assuming a full and nuanced assessment would require acknowledgement of his complexity.

I (Kim) witnessed a conservative Christian student, typically engaged and enthusiastic during class, retreat during a discussion that included a transgender male-to-female guest speaker. Although fully engaged in all previous class sessions, on this particular day she wore a baseball cap, pulled it down over her face, sat back in her chair with arms crossed, and refused to look up or participate in any way for the full three hours of class. This signaled clearly to me that the topic presented a threat to her own worldview; more specifically, to her endorsement of traditional gender roles and the gender binary. As an instructor striving to serve as an ally through my pedagogical approaches, this particular instance of resistant behavior left me uncertain of any path to bring the student back into the community of engaged learners. Given my own gender-conforming, non-transgender, and heterosexual identity, I felt responsible as an ally for creating a learning environment where all students could remain open to new frames of reference and critiquing systems of gender. In these situations, instructors identifying as allies may feel ineffective due to one specific student's behavior.

Interestingly, these examples illustrate the complexity of learning at the site of intersecting identities (Banks, Pliner, & Hopkins, this volume; Ferber & Herrera, this volume) and suggest that protecting one's worldview as a privileged group member is not confined to the left or right politically. Where privileged identities are concerned, students may passively resist along a political continuum depending on their interpretation of whether the content threatens their previous worldviews.

Target Group Resistance

The second theme we identified in instructors' narratives characterized students' resistance on behalf of collective, marginalized identities, which we describe as "target group resistance." Typically this occurred among students living in social locations that reflect less privilege than many of their classmates. Target group resistance may manifest when a particular class topic makes students' oppressed identities salient due to behaviors and comments by faculty or classmates. For example, a gay male student may refuse to participate in a class discussion of same-sex marriage when privileged students present arguments against marriage equality. Latina/o students may skip class on the day when discussions of immigration are scheduled, for fear that they will be assumed by their classmates to be undocumented immigrants or that the faculty member will ask them to speak for their ethnic group.

Examples of target group resistance highlight the way that behaviors adopted by students as ways to survive marginalization on campuses and cope with prejudice can inadvertently become barriers to their learning. A previous student of mine (Kim) shared with me his experiences of feeling tokenized in response to faculty behavior. As a biracial (African American and White) student, he explained that faculty always failed to intervene when classmates expected him to speak on behalf of African Americans. These consistent classroom experiences eventually caused him to retreat into silence and disengagement. Jackson (1999) also described a course in which African American graduate students remained silent during meetings of a course on intercultural therapeutic relationships, yet expressed many thoughts about this topic in their papers. These students later indicated that their silence in the course was a reaction to dealing with hostility from their classmates when discussing such topics in past courses. Similar episodes revealed by our interviewees suggest that sometimes students' resistance comes not from a response to intellectual content, but from their reading of the classroom context as a site of lived intergroup contact that can be unproductive, tokenizing, marginalizing, and threatening.

Keeping the concept of target group resistance in mind may help faculty members anticipate and address passive resistance that students express using absence. For example, in one of my (Kim's) graduate courses addressing intersectionality (see Part II of this volume for more on this concept), an African American female student skipped class on the day we analyzed Black feminist critiques of racism within White feminist scholarship and activism. Similarly, one faculty member interviewed described African American students who did not attend a required lecture on Black English. The faculty member initially interpreted this as reflecting students' feeling they were already experts on the topic. However, she noted it could also be the case that the topic did not feel safe for them, particularly since the White students in the course expressed very vocal negative reactions to the content.

In these instances, students may feel a need to protect themselves from possibly unsafe classroom environments. Although marginalized students may avoid the classroom or minimize engagement due to potential tokenism, others may do so due to expectations of being stereotyped or disliked. One interviewee, a faculty member teaching a course covering a variety of privilege and diversity issues, described a group of Jewish women students' responses to the course material about anti-Semitism:

> When we got to anti-Semitism they completely shut down. And I think it was, "I'm not going to participate in this because I don't want to be

seen as a targeted person, I don't want to reinforce the image on campus of, you know, the JAP [Jewish American Princess]." And there just seemed something about the motivation was just not to confront anybody or make anybody uncomfortable. "I just have to be so liked by everybody in the room."

These behaviors indicate students' beliefs that talking about anti-Semitism will result in being stereotyped. This episode suggests two important insights: first, that target group resistance might be particularly salient for students whose marginalized identities are concealable; second, this avoidance of being labeled as part of the oppressed group and feeling responsible for protecting others from the discomfort associated with confronting bigotry may reflect a gendered reaction to social niceties.

Although marginalized students' resistance may create obstacles to their own learning and the learning of their classmates, target group resistance may be essential to students' own development in that moment, and potentially to their own self-protection. In fact, initial target group resistance may occupy an important place in healthy development that leads to greater learning later in the course. Without mechanisms for self-protection, marginalized students may retreat altogether by dropping the class, avoiding reading assigned materials, and remaining silent for the entire term.

In addition, resistance in some forms may empower such students to act for social change through transformational resistance. Applying Latina/o critical race theory to student resistance, Solorzano and Delgado Bernal (2001) examined "the concept of resistance to focus on its transformational potential" (p. 308) among Chicana and Chicano students. These students organized walk outs and student strikes and empowered themselves to advocate for culturally relevant studies in education. Therefore, target group resistance may not only be essential for the development process, but may also lead to transformational learning and action for social justice. If faculty allies keep in mind that target group resistance may serve a critical purpose in learning instead of blaming them, students may find ways to return to learning rather than retreating completely.

Narrative Resistance

The third, and based on the extant literature, perhaps least familiar type of passive behavior we termed "narrative resistance." One aspect of the pedagogy involved in privilege studies can be understood as a process of arriving at shared narratives to understand the social world. However, there are times when students and teachers fail to arrive at these shared narratives and the academic conversation breaks down. This is not just a matter of rejecting particular content, but rejecting the stories we develop as co-intentional learners (Enns & Forrest, 2005; Freire, 1970) to understand this content.

Several years ago, I (Elizabeth) taught a first year seminar about how to understand and evaluate research about gender differences and similarities. I assigned Gould's (2008) "X: A Fabulous Child's Story," a fairytale-style narrative about a couple who decided to conceal their child's gender as part of an "Xperiment" to raise a child outside of gender expectations and limitations. In a playful tone, Gould described the puzzled and sometimes even angry reactions of family members, neighbors, and classmates. Eventually, most of X's peers were inspired by its example to try, and even excel at, gender-discrepant activities. I expected the theme and tone of the story to help students in my class suspend their own taken-for-granted assumptions and to imagine how their lives might be different if they, like X, lived free of gender norms. To my surprise, most of them dismissed the story outright, calling it impossible, ridiculous, and stupid. Some of them wanted to know what gender X "really was," speculating that "X" must refer to an X chromosome. They cited the fact that X gains a sibling named Y at the end of the story to support their interpretation of X as female. To my mind, this line of questioning missed the very point of the story. Rereading the story today, I recognize the students' reactions in those of the adults who surrounded X. The teachers and parents of classmates who, worried X's influence on the other children would be negative, declared, "Just because X doesn't know what it is, or what it's supposed to be, it wants to get everybody *else* mixed up, too" (Gould, 2008, p. 240). All but one student dismissed the gender critique presented in the story, but expended ample mental energy attempting to uncover the true gender of X. Their refusal to accept X as genderless illustrates a strong commitment to the gender binary and emphatic resistance of the narrative's invitation to imagine that gender could be constructed differently, or not at all.

Among our interviewees, one faculty member described teaching the Old Testament Book of Exodus as text, as the foundation for a course about liberation narratives. She then taught an article by a Native American author, Robert Warrior (2006), in which he argued that even though Exodus has been used in liberation theology in Latin America, it should not be taken up by Native Americans as a way of thinking about their own liberation because it advocates the disruption and even the murder of indigenous people. To her surprise, both Jewish and Christian students refused to consider Warrior's argument. Their response can be viewed as refusal to apply critical intellectual engagement to the cultural scope of their personal religious beliefs. More broadly, this resistance could also be viewed as a failure of the community of learners to arrive at a shared narrative. This particular early impasse colored the rest of the course. The faculty member recalled:

> When students wrote their papers ... some of them avoided discussing [Exodus] entirely. Others wrote papers in which the arguments were complicated by the fact that they could only look at the Book of Exodus from a faith-based perspective. So that, I mean, in terms of making their

arguments, it wasn't possible for them to think about the ... figure of the Old Testament God as being in any way problematic.

The faculty member recognized students' unwillingness to consider a new narrative applying critical analysis to a book of the Bible. Ironically, their commitment to a single reading of Exodus foreclosed the possibility of consideration of the implications of the fact that a religious text has multiple readings, including cultural meanings that are taken up differently by different oppressed groups. Even as their resistance confirmed the themes of the course, it rendered an important theme of the course imperceptible to them.

These examples of narrative resistance differ from simply rejecting content and have pedagogical implications for challenging privilege in the classroom. Suggestions for acknowledging resistance and minimizing these obstacles to learning are discussed below.

Pedagogical Implications and Reflections

We began this project thinking that teaching about privilege differed from most other topics particularly because of the ways it demands that students and teachers reflect on their own assumptions and social location, and consequently, often those engaged in such reflection respond with emotion. We assumed that these qualities were the roots of resistance. What can we learn if we take the perspective that resistance is part of the process of learning about privilege itself? We borrow this perspective from Tatum's (1992) conceptualization of resistance as part of the developmental learning process, but also from literature on misconceptions in science education. Campanario (2002) showed that in science education, even when students are exposed to scientific explanations, they hold on to their old ideas based on experience and intuition. Many students find scientific explanations implausible or at odds with their own experiences. As they are exposed to scientific thought, they may simultaneously hold both the intuitive belief and the new "scientific" belief. Moreover, they may experience emotional responses when existing ideas get challenged (Platt, this volume). The feeling that one's previously held beliefs were mistaken is not only powerful, but also quite difficult for many students to process. Campanario (2002) concluded that in contrast to the popular view that scientific inquiry involves the "serene analysis of contributions and the unbiased evaluation of any contribution" (p. 1099), science inherently breeds "resistance to new discovery and ... conceptual change" (p. 1099). Much of this area of science education research suggests that teachers have to learn more about their students' misconceptions and preconceptions to design pedagogy that addresses them. Similarly, Watt (2007) posits that the uncertainty that comes with learning about privilege commonly results in defensive responses, and it has been the goal of this chapter to identify some of the forms this resistance can take and strategies to address it.

Taken together with what we learned from our interviews, this insight suggests that faculty allies teaching courses about privilege need to:

- be aware of students' own identities and the classroom as a potentially threatening context;
- anticipate students' pre-existing beliefs; and
- work with students to develop shared narratives about privilege and oppression.

The classroom as a threatening context

The classroom environment may reveal threatening contexts for both privileged and marginalized students when discussions turn to identities, privilege, and oppression. These conversations and course materials may very well result in feelings of guilt, shame, fear of being stereotyped, fear of being tokenized, or feelings of personal responsibility for maintaining harmony in the classroom. For privileged students, Case and Hemmings (2005) suggested several strategies to help White women discuss racism without feeling defensive or worrying they will offend someone. They recommend a class discussion on "white talk," or the approaches that White students use to distance themselves from conversations about racism, could expose the concerns privileged students have when in a discussion of their own privilege. Providing them with a new set of linguistic tools to discuss the course concepts academically might help privileged students feel more comfortable about speaking up to confront privilege and oppression (Case & Hemmings, 2005). Along these same lines, we suggest introducing students to common forms of resistance before privilege content to allow for a more contextualized learning experience. This may even be achieved by assigning readings that address student resistance from a research perspective. For example, we have both required students to read Tatum's (2003) book on talking about race and her article (1994) focusing on White students learning about racism. If students first understand the typical or common reactions to learning about privilege, resistance may be minimized as a result of their responses being acknowledged up front by the instructor.

As faculty teaching both privileged and marginalized students within the same space, we feel it is unreasonable to expect students with oppressed social identities to do the work of bringing marginalized perspectives to the course curriculum (see also Jackson, 1999). Students should not carry the burden of teaching the course. In addition, the individual introducing potentially difficult conversations may become the target of negative emotions from classmates (LaDuke, 2009). We saw this in the interviewee's anecdote about Jewish women in the course retreating from discussions of anti-Semitism. The faculty member interpreted the students' behavior as wanting to avoid being disliked by classmates as a result of bringing up uncomfortable topics. Faculty must take responsibility for bringing a variety of voices and perspectives into the classroom via curriculum design as well as what and how questions get asked in the classroom (Case, this volume).

Students' Pre-Existing Beliefs

As an instructor, developing an awareness of the regional, local, and campus contexts may provide helpful information about students in terms of religious affiliation, cultural background, previous exposure to diversity, educational preparedness for critical thinking, etc. If faculty possess an awareness of commonly held beliefs of the broader culture, some pre-existing beliefs among students may be anticipated. For example, I (Kim) teach in Texas and encounter a diverse array of religious perspectives among students. However, some students from conservative Christian backgrounds utilizing literal interpretations of the Bible find it difficult to navigate the boundaries between their personal religious beliefs and academic critical analysis of heterosexual privilege. A proportion of students will enter the classroom with higher endorsement of Protestant work ethic, social dominance orientation, or prejudiced attitudes, while others may arrive with low or high levels of privilege awareness and intersectional consciousness (Case, 2007a; Case, 2007b; Case & Stewart, 2010; Cole et al., 2011). Instructors can also use low-stakes writing assignments (such as free writing and journal assignments) early in the term as a way to learn more about the beliefs students bring to the classroom. Awareness of social and cultural contexts, as well as of common psychological constructs that present barriers to learning about privilege, allows for pedagogical planning and stronger connections with student perspectives.

Develop Shared Narratives

When the shared narrative building in a community of learners breaks down, barriers to understanding get reinforced and sometimes fortified. In these cases, instructors need strategies for cracking the learning gridlock and clearing the path to open consideration of difficult ideas. Many instructors use *The Color of Fear* (Mun Wah, 1994) in their courses to teach about white privilege, daily encounters with racism, and institutional racism. In the film, a White man named David refuses to acknowledge racism and the lived experiences of people of color. At one point, Lee Mun Wah (producer and director of the film) asks David to consider what would happen and what it would mean to him if the incidents of racism described by the men of color were actually true. In this moment, David appears to experience a shift in his thinking due to these questions. I (Elizabeth) adapted this approach to encourage students to more fully consider difficult reading materials and research findings. Although the direct confrontation used by Lee with David in the film might cause a student to feel threatened, using these questions more generally while asking the class to reflect and perhaps even write about how they would feel or react if the arguments in their readings (or film or other course materials) were accurate, creates a space for critical analysis without requiring them to first accept the new perspectives or new information. Free from having to accept oppression and privilege as reality, students may turn their energy to critically analyzing multiple perspectives and engaging in dialogue rather than wasting that energy on defensiveness and resistance to learning.

Another way instructors can head off the impasse of narrative resistance is to consciously work to develop and sustain shared narratives in the class. Often over the course of a term in which students share the experience of common readings and frank discussions, students will pick up and repeat certain themes or phrases that can come to have particular resonance in the learning community. Such touchstones help build a sense of shared understanding that can be a resource if or when narrative resistance threatens to break down the learning community.

The Journey Back into the Community of Engaged Learners

Using in-depth faculty interviews and our own experiences, we identified world-view protection, target group resistance, and narrative resistance within courses focusing on unlearning privilege associated with social identities. If faculty members consider these forms of resistance, perhaps they can more readily identify behaviors indicating passive resistance among their own students. Awareness of students' identities and backgrounds provides essential information to instructors about the potential for privilege studies to be experienced as a threat that impairs learning. By exploring beliefs and attitudes that enter the classroom on day one, faculty may prepare exercises, readings, and targeted discussion questions to encourage critical analyses of long-held beliefs, or, at minimum, an acceptance that one's own worldview represents only one of many perspectives. As educators work to develop shared narratives in the classroom about privilege and oppression, they can effectively build a community experience and peer culture of engaged learning.

References

Armstrong, M. J., & Wildman, S. M. (this volume). "Colorblindness is the new racism": Raising awareness about privilege using color insight. In K. A. Case (Ed.), *Deconstructing privilege: Teaching and learning as allies in the classroom* (pp. 63–79). New York, NY: Routledge.

Atwood, J. (2010). Good intentions, dangerous territory: Student resistance in feminist writing classes. *Journal of Teaching Writing, 12*(2), 125–143.

Banks, C. A., Pliner, S. M., & Hopkins, M. B. (this volume). Intersectionality and paradigms of privilege: Teaching for social change. In K. A. Case (Ed.), *Deconstructing privilege: Teaching and learning as allies in the classroom* (pp. 102–114). New York, NY: Routledge.

Campanario, J. M. (2002). The parallelism between scientists' and students' resistance to new scientific ideas. *International Journal of Science Education, 24*(10), 1095–1110. doi:10.1080/09500690210126702

Case, K. A. (2007a). Raising male privilege awareness and reducing sexism: An evaluation of diversity courses. *Psychology of Women Quarterly, 31*(4), 426–435. doi:10.1111/j.1471–6402.2007.00391.x

Case, K. A. (2007b). Raising white privilege awareness and reducing racial prejudice: Assessing diversity course effectiveness. *Teaching of Psychology*, *34*(4), 231–235. doi:10.1080/00986280701700250

Case, K. A. (this volume). Beyond diversity and whiteness: Developing a transformative and intersectional model of privilege studies pedagogy. In K. A. Case (Ed.), *Deconstructing privilege: Teaching and learning as allies in the classroom* (pp. 1–14). New York, NY: Routledge.

Case, K. A., & Hemmings, A. (2005). Distancing strategies: White women preservice teachers and antiracist curriculum. *Urban Education*, *40*(6), 606–626. doi:10.1177/0042085905281396

Case, K. A., & Stewart, B. (2010). Changes in diversity course student prejudice and attitudes toward heterosexual privilege and gay marriage. *Teaching of Psychology*, *37*(3), 172–177. doi:10.1080/00986283.2010.488555

Chan, C. S., & Treacy, M. J. (1996). Resistance in multicultural courses: Student, faculty, and classroom dynamics. *American Behavioral Scientist*, *40*(2), 212–221. doi:10.1177/0002764296040002012

Cole, E. R., Case, K. A., Rios, D., & Curtin, N. (2011). Understanding what students bring to the classroom: Moderators of the effects of diversity courses on student attitudes. *Cultural Diversity and Ethnic Minority Psychology*, *17*(4), 397–405. doi:10.1037/a0025433

Dessel, A. B., Massé, J. C., & Walker, L. T. (this volume). Intergroup dialogue pedagogy: Teaching about intersectional and under-examined privilege in heterosexual, Christian, and Jewish identities. In K. A. Case (Ed.), *Deconstructing privilege: Teaching and learning as allies in the classroom* (pp. 132–148). New York, NY: Routledge.

Enns, C. Z., & Forrest, L. M. (2005). Toward defining and integrating multicultural and feminist pedagogies. In C. Z. Enns & A. L. Sinacore (Eds.), *Teaching and social justice: Integrating multicultural and feminist theories in the classroom* (pp. 3–23). Washington, D.C.: American Psychological Association.

Ferber, A. L., & Herrera, A. O. (this volume). Teaching privilege through an intersectional lens. In K. A. Case (Ed.), *Deconstructing privilege: Teaching and learning as allies in the classroom* (pp. 83–101). New York, NY: Routledge.

Freire, P. (1970). *Pedagogy of the oppressed*. New York, NY: Continuum.

Gould, L. (2008). X: A fabulous child's story. In P. Nel & J. Zipes (Eds.), *Tales for little rebels: A collection of radical children's literature* (pp. 233–242). New York, NY: New York University Press.

Helms, J. E. (Ed.). (1990). *Black and white racial identity: Theory, research and practice*. New York, NY: Greenwood Press.

Higginbotham, E. (1996). Getting all students to listen: Analyzing and coping with student resistance. *American Behavioral Scientist*, *40*(2), 203–211. doi:10.1177/0002764296040002011

Jackson, L. C. (1999). Ethnocultural resistance to multicultural training: Students and faculty. *Cultural Diversity and Ethnic Minority Psychology*, *5*(1), 27–36. doi:10.1037/1099-9809.5.1.27

LaDuke, A. E. (2009). Resistance and renegotiation: Preservice teacher interactions with and reactions to multicultural education course content. *Multicultural Education*, *16*(3), 37–44.

Mun Wah, L. (Producer/Director). (1994). *The color of fear* [Motion picture]. Berkeley, CA: Stir-Fry Productions.

Markowtiz, L. (2005). Unmasking moral dichotomies: Can feminist pedagogy overcome student resistance? *Gender and Education*, *17*(1), 39–55. doi:10.1080/0954025042000301294

Platt, L. F. (this volume). Blazing the trail: Teaching the privileged about privilege. In K. A. Case (Ed.), *Deconstructing privilege: Teaching and learning as allies in the classroom* (pp. 207–222). New York, NY: Routledge.

Solorzano, D. G., & Delgado Bernal, D. (2001). Examining transformational resistance through a critical race and LatCrit theory framework: Chicana and Chicano students in an urban context. *Urban education, 36*(4), 308–342. doi:10.1177/0042085901363002

Tatum, B. D. (1992). Talking about race, learning about racism: The application of racial identity development theory in the classroom. *Harvard Educational Review, 62*(1), 1–24.

Tatum, B. D. (1994). Teaching White students about racism: The search for White allies and the restoration of hope. *Teachers College Record, 95*(4), 462–476.

Tatum, B. D. (2003). *"Why are all the Black kids sitting together in the cafeteria?" And other conversations about race.* New York, NY: Basic Books.

Warrior, R. (2006). A Native American perspective: Canaanites, cowboys, and Indians. In R. S. Sugirtharajah (Ed.), *Voices from the margin: Interpreting the Bible in the Third World* (pp. 235–241). Maryknoll, NY: Orbis Books.

Watt, S. K. (2007). Difficult dialogues, privilege and social justice: Uses of the Privileged Identity Exploration (PIE) model in student affairs practice." *College Student Affairs Journal, 26*(2), 114–126.

Wise, T., & Case, K. A. (this volume). Pedagogy for the privileged: Addressing inequality and injustice without shame or blame. In K. A. Case (Ed.), *Deconstructing privilege: Teaching and learning as allies in the classroom* (pp. 17–33). New York, NY: Routledge.

4

TEACHING SOCIAL JUSTICE ALLY DEVELOPMENT AMONG PRIVILEGED STUDENTS

Paul B. Perrin, Sriya Bhattacharyya, Daniel J. Snipes, Rebecca R. Hubbard, Martin Heesacker, Jenna M. Calton, Ruperto M. Perez, and Jill Lee-Barber

> I felt this class was a waste of time and university resources. The class is a good idea on paper but was not practical in any way ... "Feelings" were considered OK only if you were part of a minority group.
>
> (Student course evaluation comment from Multiculturalism & Social Justice course)

A social justice movement has emerged within the social sciences whereby researchers not only empirically examine oppression, but work to alleviate it through education, advocacy, and systems-level interventions (Goodman et al., 2004; Vera & Speight, 2003). However, educators often find it challenging to educate people from privileged groups about privilege and oppression (Roades & Mio, 2000). These groups, such as Whites, heterosexuals, men, able-bodied persons, mainstream Christians, and persons of high socioeconomic status, by definition hold societal power in their domains of privilege and can play a unique role in dismantling oppression (Thompson-Miller & Feagin, 2007). Educators therefore need the skills and tools to employ when attempting to engage students from privileged groups in the transformation to becoming social justice allies. Unfortunately, multiple aspects of identity often remain invisible to privileged students, and therefore contribute to a distanced attitude toward oppression. Privileged students can become ignorant to their own privilege through distance from minority groups, often living in a social structure that reinforces and maintains their privilege. Without knowledge of oppression of other groups, this privilege remains invisible to them (Platt, this volume). Thus, making the invisible visible can help students from privileged groups understand privilege and oppression (Case, 2012). This discussion will synthesize a number of strategies for making privilege visible to students and, notably, introduce the transtheoretical model of behavior change and privilege investment as tools for this process.

Intersections of Identity

One of the sharpest tools that educators can use to make privilege visible to students from privileged groups comes from incorporating an intersectional approach to identity (Banks, Pliner, & Hopkins, this volume; Case, this volume). A major limitation of many current educational approaches aimed at students from privileged groups stems from a failure to consider the connections among different aspects of one's identity in producing allyhood. Croteau, Talbot, Lance, and Evans (2002) found that people who experienced both privilege and oppression sometimes had difficulty understanding the interplay between their multiple identities. As Banks et al. (this volume) and Case (this volume) argue, examining intersecting forms of privilege and oppression associated with different components of one's own and others' cultural identities supports efforts toward ally behavior. Many allies belong to multiple privileged and multiple minority groups, and an awareness of this intersectionality strengthens a person's sense of a global community for social justice, improving overall allyhood (Rios & Stewart, this volume). Israel (2012) asserts that "a single individual may experience intersecting privileges and oppressions that may reflect differential receipt of benefits. It's not as simple as thinking that some of us have privilege and some of us do not" (p. 169). Holding minority status in one identity domain may provide motivation for a person to become a social justice ally in an identity domain in which the person holds majority status. On the other hand, it may be difficult at times for people to remain aware of their own privileges and remain fully committed allies when they feel triggered by aspects of their minority identities (Israel, 2012). Furthermore, the teaching of privilege must not strain the experiences of one identity, as it masks the richness of intersectionality and may lead to beliefs of mutual exclusivity among identities (Ferber & Herrera, this volume).

Roades and Mio (2000) found that personal membership in a minority group represented one of the major influences on the development of social justice allies. These researchers emphasized a tendency among individuals who valued their own privileged or minority identities also to value the privileged or minority identities of other people, even those with different identities. The process of overlapping approximations (O'Brien, 2001) requires drawing an analogy between one's own experiences with oppression and oppressions of other people. In this manner, people from a majority group who also have minority identities rely on their experiences as a minority group member to understand in their domain of privilege the common experiences of minority groups (Reason, Millar, & Scales, 2005).

Other researchers also argue that intersectionality brings an important analysis to the teaching of privilege and oppression (e.g., Cole, 2009; Crenshaw, 1991;

Dill & Zambrana, 2009). Jones and McEwen (2000) created a model of integrated-identity development, wherein one's core identity consists of several intersecting demographic traits, including race, gender, sexual orientation, religion, class, and culture. Some of the demographic traits engender majority-group membership, whereas others engender minority-group membership. No single trait exists fully in isolation, and the salience of a particular trait or traits varies as a function of changing contexts and of an individual's lived experience of the trait. Marshaling this type of research, Ferber (2012) stressed the use of an intersectional approach to teach privilege in order to allow for a broader and more comprehensive understanding of privilege. However, students with one or more minority identities may be unable to see the privilege associated with their majority identities (Rios & Stewart, this volume). Some research also examined the interplay of multiple majority-group identities. For example, Borgman (2009) studied the integration of being both a Christian and heterosexual by conducting interviews with doctoral-level psychologists who identified as both Christian and lesbian, gay, bisexual, and transgender (LGBT) allies. Integrating these two identities often involved increasing awareness about the conflict between the values of these identities, experiencing dissonance and confusion, finding a way to manage and integrate multiple identities, and questioning, challenging, and redefining the self. Moradi and Subich (2003), on the other hand, argued that for people with multiple minority identities, the oppressions they face may uniquely combine at various points to create multiplicative detrimental effects greater than the sum of the effects of the separate forms of oppression.

Ferber and Herrera (this volume) provide an important review of the literature regarding identity intersections. The ideas brought forth by Banks et al. (this volume) also suggest that teaching from an intersectional lens may foster a social justice agenda among students, and thus potentially create stronger, more flexible thinking social justice allies. Despite these reviews, the research on intersections of identity has only just begun, and much more work needs to be done. The field of privilege education would benefit from shedding its heavily dichotomous conceptualizations of privilege and oppression for instead one incorporating more nuance and intersections of identity. For example, the field has hardly scratched the surface of examining the interplay of privilege and oppression in multiracial individuals, heterosexually identified individuals who experiment with same-sex behavior, transgender men, and bisexual individuals within the LGBT community or within the heterosexual community. Educators often find it more comfortable and familiar to view people of color, women, LGBT individuals, and people with disabilities as the "oppressed," or Whites, men, heterosexuals, and able-bodied individuals as the "oppressors." Unfortunately, doing so denies the holistic aspect of the human experience and stunts the potential of developing allies to have proper guidance in using multiple intersecting aspects of their identities to understand their own privilege or the life experiences of others. The research literature suggests that educators can best work with students from privileged groups by employing process-oriented content and facilitating activism that encourages exploration of the intersecting cultural backgrounds of people from privileged groups (McAllister & Irvine, 2000). This type of self-exploration naturally includes exploration of structures that engender combinations of privilege and oppression (Banks, 2001; Cochran-Smith, 2001; Wallace, 2000).

Transtheoretical Model of Behavior Change

Kim Case's introduction to this volume provides a model of privilege studies pedagogy that seeks to raise awareness of personal privilege, as well as increase and strengthen the tools that educators can employ when teaching about privilege. Her model and this overall collection offer many methods by which educators can promote social justice action in their students. As a supplement to these calls for action, we offer a framework that can simultaneously increase social justice action and help strengthen privilege education by employing behavior change theory: the transtheoretical model of behavior change (Prochaska & DiClemente, 1983). Researchers have traditionally applied it to health behaviors such as smoking cessation and other addictions (Park et al., 2003; Prochaska, DiClemente, & Norcross, 1992), exercise and nutrition changes (Lippke, Ziegelmann, Schwarzer, & Velicer, 2009), or the decision to seek regular cancer screenings (e.g., Lin & Effken, 2010). Researchers also began to employ it to enact change with regard to broader social factors, including the empowerment of women who have experienced interpersonal violence (Burke, Denison, Gielen, McDonnell, & O'Campo, 2004), readiness of communities to take action on social issues (Kelly et al., 2003), and organizational change (Madsen, Miller, & John, 2005).

Educators can also use this model to inform interventions to increase social justice behaviors and overall allyhood. The model conceptualizes behavior change in five stages. The first stage, *precontemplation*, reflects individuals who do not recognize that their behaviors are problematic. In terms of ally development, people from privileged groups in this stage are unaware of their privilege, implicit and explicit oppressive behaviors, or larger societal issues relating to social justice. In the second stage, *contemplation*, individuals experience ambivalence about wanting to change their behaviors, but will acknowledge their problematic behaviors. In this stage, people from privileged groups might acknowledge the oppressiveness of their behaviors or their privilege, but are ambivalent about changing their behaviors or working against their own privilege to benefit individuals from minority groups because of the potential costs. The *preparation* and *action* stages involve individuals preparing a new behavior and then performing the behavior. This would involve people from privileged groups preparing to act and then acting as social justice allies by, for example, speaking out against oppression, participating in demonstrations, spreading awareness of oppression, etc. The fifth stage, *maintenance*, reflects individuals' efforts to maintain changed behaviors. Here, people from privileged groups navigate obstacles in continuing to be allies, such as burnout, negative experiences with minority groups, and personal resources spent in such endeavors (Roades & Mio, 2000). Allies in this stage also continuously work on their own awareness of privilege and oppression. The transtheoretical model of behavior change applied to ally development has a cyclical nature, in that people from privileged groups often cycle back and forth between various stages.

Privilege Investment

Throughout each stage of behavior change in the transtheoretical model, students from privileged groups have extremely diverse motivations for becoming allies. These can include the protection of those they care about who experience oppression, altruism, the reduction of guilt, camaraderie or friendship with individuals from minority groups (Edwards, 2007), empathy, moral and spiritual values, and self-interest (Goodman, 2001). Considering students' motivations for becoming allies proves a vital step in the creation of approaches aimed to increase allyhood. However, not all students from privileged groups will find motivation in a higher, more "noble" purpose, such as a calling to combat oppression or adherence to humanistic principles. As a result, ally-development interventions and opportunities for ally behavior need to coincide with the potential ally's motivations and stage of development.

One initial approach involves creating opportunities for students from privileged groups to invest their privilege by engaging in social justice behavior in part to satisfy some motivation or need that they might have. We suggest that people from privileged groups can engage in privilege investment, the leveraging of privilege to work toward social justice in a manner that benefits individuals from minority groups and oneself. Educators can employ privilege investment in order to increase the general pedagogical emphasis on privilege and the effects it has on students from privileged groups, while also promoting social action to dismantle privilege as suggested in Case's (this volume) pedagogical model for privilege studies. An example of privilege investment could be using one's white privilege to educate other White individuals about privilege (Case, 2012). Privilege investment can also occur when heterosexual individuals use their heterosexual privilege to speak out against heterosexism in places where LGBT individuals may not be as readily welcomed, such as in a fundamentalist church or the U.S. military. Personal benefits of privilege investment to the heterosexual individuals in this case could involve the development of meaningful friendships with LGBT individuals and increases in their own self-esteem through adherence to their value systems. Other examples of privilege investment include a person of middle or high socioeconomic status making financial donations to a homeless shelter in order to feel good about herself or himself, a man volunteering with an anti-violence against women organization in order to put lines on his résumé, or an able-bodied person advocating to her or his boss to make an office building more wheelchair accessible in order to be able to hire a talented employee with a physical disability.

Privilege investment also gains momentum from the fact that oppression has very concrete costs to people from majority groups (Spanierman & Heppner, 2004), and, as a result, the alleviation of oppression can directly benefit individuals from minority and majority groups. Freire (1970) discussed extensively the ways in which oppressors become dehumanized in the oppression they create and perpetuate. Similarly, Goodman (2001) outlined numerous costs of oppression to people from privileged groups, including denial of one's own emotions, inability to empathize with others, limited self-knowledge, fear and pain, diminished mental health, isolation from people who are different, ostracism within one's own group, guilt and shame, spiritual emptiness, limited view of other people's culture and history, social violence and unrest, higher financial costs, waste of resources, loss of valuable employees and customers, diminished collective, and action for common concerns.

Considering the extensive costs of oppression to students from privileged groups, self-interest becomes an important component to include in educational interventions aimed at creating social justice allies. Instead of conceptualizing selflessness and self-interest as mutually exclusive, or as good or bad, it may be more effective to acknowledge that altruistic behaviors occur in part because they bring pleasure to the person engaging in them (Dawkins, 2006). Thompson (2000) wrote:

> In the long run, those of us who are motivated to end oppression out of our self-interest will be more honest with ourselves and others and less prone to burnout. Guilt does not sustain us as agents of change nor does it lead to sound decisions about resource and power sharing which will truly benefit the oppressed.
>
> (p. 482)

Goodman (2001) advocated the use of self-interest in motivating people of privilege to become allies, arguing against its pejorative connotation in favor of a more interdependent perspective. This interconnectedness, she asserts, leads to greater empathy, a morality of care, and a sense of meaning that takes one beyond oneself. Empirical research also supported these ideas, uncovering that individual enhancement predicts involvement in collective action beyond what is predicted by concerns for group enhancement (Tropp & Brown, 2004). Blumer, Green, Thomte, and Green (this volume) draw similar suggestions, identifying ways to educate heterosexuals on heteronormativity in a way that enriches understanding of the effects of anti-gay behaviors on the ingroup (heterosexuals) as well as the outgroup (LGBT individuals).

Theories of moral development (e.g., Gilligan, 1993; Kohlberg, 1984) also address self-interest's role in motivations for ally behavior, suggesting that earlier moral development occurs when people minimize their own pain and maximize their own pleasure, whereas later stages involve adherence to broad moral principles, such as altruism, justice, mercy (Kohlberg, 1984), and the interconnectedness of all people (Gilligan, 1993). In both Kohlberg's and Gilligan's models, early stages focus on the self, intermediate stages focus on rules or concepts, and later stages focus on virtues or human connection. Accordingly, increasing allyhood can result from matching privilege investment opportunities with a potential ally's developmental stage at a given moment, heavily channeling self-interest at earlier stages.

Recommendations for Interventions

Interventions that combine the transtheoretical model of behavior change and the concept of privilege investment may be useful to recruit more and better social justice allies, regardless of the identity domains of the ally. Research on the transtheoretical model of behavior change (Lin & Effken, 2010; Lippke et al., 2009; Park et al., 2003) suggested that interventions tailored to an individual's stage of readiness for change most effectively propel individuals to the next stage. In line with our proposal to catalyze ally development through behavior change, we now apply the transtheoretical model and privilege investment to interventions for developing allies who are at each stage of readiness for change. A summary of our stage-tailored suggested interventions can be found in the Table 4.1.

These types of interventions can and should be implemented in a number of different settings by a variety of people, including researchers who develop psychoeducational programs, educators, community activists, and organizational trainers, among others. Although most ally-development interventions typically occur in group formats (e.g., workshops, classrooms, or organizational trainings), the transtheoretical model of behavior change has been successful in both group (Velasquez, Stephens, & Ingersoll, 2006) and individual formats (Brogan, Prochaska, & Prochaska, 1999). People from privileged groups operate at all levels of readiness for social justice behavior change and also may have very different motivations for engaging in ally behavior (Goodman, 2001). As a result, both group and individual ally-development interventions should include opportunities for people to reflect on what they personally hope to get out of the intervention, whether it is a line for their résumé, the opportunity to meet new people, or a chance to feel good about making a difference in the world. The interventions can comprehensively include relevant material and activities for people at each stage of change, although not all material will resonate loudly with everyone.

For people from privileged groups in the precontemplation stage, educational interventions that provide information on societal manifestations of power, privilege, and oppression can effectively facilitate movement to the next stage of readiness for ally behaviors. In educational settings, students are relatively unaware of their privilege, and Sanders and Mahalingam (2012) found that most of their students entering a course on intergroup dialogues exhibited low saliency of their

TABLE 4.1

Transtheoretical Stage	Stage-tailored Intervention	Use of Privilege Investment
Precontemplation • Unawareness of privilege and oppression	Educational interventions regarding privilege and oppression (e.g., readings, personal testimony)	Social justice behaviors that heavily appeal to self-interest (e.g., fulfilling course credit, résumé building)
Contemplation • Ambivalence about social justice behavior	Reconciling new awareness with values (e.g., values assessment, discussing and processing resulting distress)	Volunteer work designed to reduce distress or guilt (e.g., making donations, working at a soup kitchen)
Preparation/Action • Preparing for or performing social justice behaviors	Building self-efficacy and confidence regarding social justice behavior (e.g., processing behaviors with other allies and educators)	Tangible and achievable opportunities to engage in social justice behavior and build self-esteem (e.g., organizing a demonstration, spreading awareness of oppression)
Maintenance • Continuing to engage in social justice work	Maintaining allies' social justice involvement (e.g., preparing for challenges to staying an ally)	Focusing on social and personal benefits of allyhood (e.g., developing forums and groups to build relationships, plan ally activism, and discuss encountered barriers)

privileged class status, or, in other words, resided in a precontemplation stage of awareness. This finding also applies to other identities as people from privileged groups entering these types of classes are usually relatively blind to unearned advantages they are experiencing (Dessel, Massé, & Walker, this volume). Educators should relay information to move students beyond a precontemplation stage via readings or videos, as testimony from individuals with minority identities, or from allies who describe their experiences becoming an ally. Many courses that incorporate privilege awareness rely on these methods, but in order to reach individuals initially most resistant to the course material, privilege investment techniques should get people to engage in social justice work in order to appeal to self-interested outcomes like fulfilling course credit, fulfilling service-hour requirements for a scholarship, or being seen by peers as an altruistic person. For example, our own courses have used mandatory "diversity experiences" in which students volunteer with an organization that serves a cultural group of which they are not a part.

The student whose end-of-semester evaluation opened this chapter was likely in the precontemplation stage and would benefit from very concrete opportunities to engage in social justice work, primarily for self-benefit. For example, the student felt that the course "was not practical in any way." More concrete opportunities for social justice behavior would have helped that student find immediate and practical self-benefit, such as being able to put a line about volunteering on her or his résumé. Concrete opportunities for social justice work would also allow cognitive dissonance to occur between her or his behaviors and worldviews, and the student's worldviews about privilege and allyhood might slowly begin to change, providing a more salient experience of learning. Social justice behaviors that fulfill these self-interested motivations will ultimately lead to a deeper awareness of privilege and oppression.

Once people from privileged groups recognize privilege and oppression, they enter the contemplation stage. Interventions in this stage should focus on highlighting and reconciling the new awareness of privilege and oppression with the individuals' value systems. People from privileged groups will benefit from conducting a values assessment and identifying which of their core values conflict with their new awareness. The cognitive dissonance resulting from the discrepancy between their values and new awareness often becomes distressing and motivates them to align their behaviors with their values. Employing privilege investment, educators will benefit from creating opportunities for people to process or discuss this discomfort, as well as behavioral opportunities to reduce it through volunteer work. Capitalizing on the alleviation of guilt or discomfort may not produce sustained allyhood, but it will likely move developing allies into the next stages of change. In our own courses, we have seen students from privileged groups display strong feelings of guilt once they become aware of systems of oppression and privilege, a natural response. Wise and Case (this volume) provide a thoughtful insight on learning about privilege and stigma, and also draw a parallel conclusion that learning about privilege can be frightening. Taking students a step further by asking them what they plan on doing with that fear or guilt can help bring them into the next stage in the transtheoretical model.

Once people have entered the stages of change that involve visible behaviors (preparation and action), an effective transtheoretical approach involves helping developing allies build self-efficacy and confidence in their abilities to engage in social justice behaviors. People from privileged groups will appreciate tangible, practical, and achievable opportunities to engage in this behavior. For example, in one of our courses, students keep a weekly journal of their experiences volunteering with diverse groups or organizations, and they specifically have to talk about the thoughts and feelings, and comfort or discomfort, that arise through their volunteering. Additional opportunities for students to process these behaviors with other students and educators help build a supportive community of allies and activists in the classroom during this critical time period. Educators can readily address issues relating to self-confidence and self-awareness through class discussion.

As allies enter the final stage of the transtheoretical model, maintenance, interventions will be most effective that maintain allies' social justice involvement.

For example, a cognitive preparation for challenges to staying an ally (challenges such as time, effort, money, resistance from others, etc.) will help offset discouragement that arises in ally work, and continued strong relationships with other allies formed in the previous stages help maintain an ally's commitment. A valuable intervention is the development of forums and groups for allies to continue to build these relationships and plan ally activism, as well as to discuss barriers they have encountered. In one of our classes, we established a course blog where students could go to discuss their experiences developing as allies and the challenges they experienced in remaining a fully committed ally. As Roades and Mio (2000) suggest, becoming an ally does not ensure that individuals from privileged groups will continue engaging in social justice behavior. The maintenance stage, and allyhood in general, includes continued self-reflection, education, growth, and active work for social justice. Another way of maintaining allyhood involves engaging in social justice research that would serve as a reinforcement of one's allyhood. These research topics vary and closely tie to the academic discipline of the individual. The mere task of engaging in social justice research helps to advance one's understanding of personal privilege (Stoudt, Fox, & Fine, 2012) and create opportunities to teach others through disseminating research findings.

Although the transtheoretical and privilege investment models can operate from an individual perspective, educators can also consider the broader social and political influences that may catalyze or inhibit social justice behavior change along this developmental trajectory. Educators will benefit from tailoring interventions employing these models in light of the research literature documenting the importance of organizational and university support for social justice behavior (Terenzini, Springer, Pascarella, & Nora, 1995), provision from universities of informational material about diversity and oppression (Broido, 2000), and the exposure of people from privileged groups to other committed allies in order to provide ally role models (Hillenbrand-Gunn, Heppner, Mauch, & Park, 2010). Additionally, educators should tailor interventions according to the combination of majority and minority groups with which a person identifies, as we discuss above in the section on intersectionality. Because personal membership in a minority group influences the development of allyhood (Roades & Mio, 2000), educators can use intersections of identity in the privilege investment model, for example, as people with minority identities feel socially empowered in a minority identity through becoming an active ally in one of their privileged domains of identity. From a transtheoretical perspective, people may be more ready to engage in social justice behaviors in one privileged domain of identity than in another, so educators can employ different stage-based techniques for each.

In addition to the transtheoretical and privilege investment models, Sherover-Marcuse (2000) offered a number of ally strategies, which include recognizing that individuals from minority groups are the experts on their own experiences and that allies have much to learn from them about being true allies. She also suggested that allies acknowledge and apologize for mistakes, refrain from trying to convince people from minority groups that the allies stand by their side or no longer assume the oppressor role, refrain from expecting gratitude from people from minority groups, and be prepared for disappointments and criticisms. Sherover-Marcuse's (2000) last point particularly relates to the transtheoretical and privilege investment models in that active allies must also navigate resistance to their work from other people of privilege. In fact, allies may draw to themselves the types of discrimination they work against or, in extreme circumstances, even encounter violence for the stances they take. Developing allies must negotiate risk taking and assess safety concerns that they may have not had to navigate in the past. As a result, allies should be wary of becoming overzealous in their fight against oppression and follow the guidance of individuals from minority groups working for justice who likely have had much more experience dealing with that form of oppression.

Conclusion

Educating students from privileged groups about privilege and oppression remains a particular challenge, even though the subject matter has gained momentum as an area of research in the last decade. In order to increase the number and quality of social justice allies among students from privileged groups, a research agenda will prove vital. Researchers should develop and rigorously test interventions that incorporate multiple intersecting aspects of privilege and oppression, that tailor activism and education to potential allies' developmental levels, and that employ the transtheoretical and privilege investment models. Researchers can also hone and empirically test the strategies described in this article, including incorporating process-oriented content and discussions about allies' self-interest. These strategies have the potential to reach a wide range of prospective allies who otherwise might continue to contribute to the system of oppression from which they benefit. These strategies, however, should not replace the current forms of education, but provide additional tools for meeting students where they are in the process of becoming effective, committed, and lasting allies.

References

Banks, J. A. (2001). Citizenship education and diversity: Implications for teacher education. *Journal of Teacher Education, 52*(1), 5–16. doi:10.1177/0022487101052001002

Banks, C. A., Pliner, S. M., & Hopkins, M. B. (this volume). Intersectionality and paradigms of privilege: Teaching for social change. In K. A. Case (Ed.), *Deconstructing privilege: Teaching and learning as allies in the classroom* (pp. 102–114). New York, NY: Routledge.

Blumer, M. L. C., Green, M. S., Thomte, N. L., & Green, P. M. (this volume). Are we queer yet? Addressing heterosexual and gender-conforming privilege. In K. A. Case (Ed.), *Deconstructing privilege: Teaching and learning as allies in the classroom* (pp. 151–168). New York, NY: Routledge.

Borgman, A. L. (2009). LGB allies and Christian identity: A qualitative exploration of resolving conflicts and integrating identities. *Journal of Counseling Psychology, 56*(4), 508–520. doi:10.1037/a0016691

Brogan, M. M., Prochaska, J. O., & Prochaska, J. M. (1999). Predicting termination and continuation status in psychotherapy using the transtheoretical model. *Psychotherapy: Theory, Research, Practice, Training, 36*(2), 105–113. doi:10.1037/h0087773

Broido, E. M. (2000). The development of social justice allies during college: A phenomenological investigation. *Journal of College Student Development, 41*(1), 3–18.

Burke, J. G., Denison, J. A., Gielen, A. C., McDonnell, K. A., & O'Campo, P. (2004). Ending intimate partner violence: An application of the transtheoretical model. *American Journal of Health Behavior, 28*(2), 122–133. doi:10.5993/AJHB.28.2.3

Case, K. A. (2012). Discovering the privilege of whiteness: White women's reflections on anti-racist identity and ally behavior. *Journal of Social Issues, 68*(1), 78–96. doi:10.1111/j.1540-4560.2011.01737.x

Case, K. A. (this volume). Beyond diversity and whiteness: Developing a transformative and intersectional model of privilege studies pedagogy. In K. A. Case (Ed.), *Deconstructing privilege: Teaching and learning as allies in the classroom* (pp. 1–14). New York, NY: Routledge.

Cochran-Smith, M. (2001). Learning to teach against the (new) grain. *Journal of Teacher Education, 52*(1), 3–4. doi:10.1177/0022487101052001001

Cole, E. R. (2009). Intersectionality and research in psychology. *American Psychologist, 64*(3), 170–180. doi:10.1037/a0014564

Crenshaw, K. (1991). Mapping the margins: Intersectionality, identity politics, and violence against women of color. *Stanford Law Review, 43*(6), 1241–1299. doi:10.1002/ir.395

Croteau, J. M., Talbot, D. M., Lance, T. S., & Evans, N. J. (2002). A qualitative study of the interplay between privilege and oppression. *Journal of Multicultural Counseling & Development, 30*(4), 239–258. doi:10.1002/j.2161-1912.2002.tb00522.x

Dawkins, R. (2006). *The selfish gene.* New York, NY: Oxford University Press.

Dessel, A. B., Massé, J. C., & Walker, L. T. (this volume). Intergroup dialogue pedagogy: Teaching about intersectional and under-examined privilege in heterosexual, Christian, and Jewish identities. In K. A. Case (Ed.), *Deconstructing privilege: Teaching and learning as allies in the classroom* (pp. 132–148). New York, NY: Routledge.

Dill, B. T., & Zambrana, R. E. (2009). Critical thinking about inequality: An emerging lens. In B. T. Dill & R. E. Zambrana (Eds.), *Emerging intersections: Race, class, and gender in theory, policy, and practice* (pp. 1–21). New Brunswick, NJ: Rutgers University Press.

Edwards, K. E. (2007). Aspiring social justice ally identity development: A conceptual model. *Journal of Student Affairs Research and Practice, 43*(4). doi:10.2202/1949-6605.1722

Ferber, A. L. (2012). The culture of privilege: Color-blindness, postfeminism, and Christonormativity. *Journal of Social Issues, 68*(1), 63–77. doi:10.1111/j.1540-4560.2011.01736.x

Ferber, A. L., & Herrera, A. O. (this volume). Teaching privilege through an intersectional lens. In K. A. Case (Ed.), *Deconstructing privilege: Teaching and learning as allies in the classroom* (pp. 83–101). New York, NY: Routledge.

Freire, P. (1970). *Pedagogy of the oppressed.* New York, NY: Continuum.

Gilligan, C. (1993). *In a different voice: Psychological theory and women's development* (6th ed.). Cambridge, MA: Harvard University Press.

Goodman, D. J. (2001). *Promoting diversity and social justice: Educating people from privileged groups.* Thousand Oaks, CA: Sage.

Goodman, L. A., Liang, B., Helms, J. E., Latta, R. E., Sparks, E., & Weintraub, S. R. (2004). Training counseling psychologists as social justice agents: Feminist and multicultural principles in action. *The Counseling Psychologist, 32*(6), 793–837. doi:10.1177/0011000004268802

Hillenbrand-Gunn, T. L., Heppner, M. J., Mauch, P. A., & Park, H. J. (2010). Men as allies: The efficacy of a high school rape prevention intervention. *Journal of Counseling & Development, 88*(1), 43–51. doi:10.1002/j.1556–6678.2010.tb00149.x

Israel, T. (2012). Exploring privilege in counseling psychology: Shifting the lens. *The Counseling Psychologist, 40*(1), 158–180. doi:10.1177/0011000011426297

Jones, S. R., & McEwen, M. K. (2000). A conceptual model of multiple dimensions of identity. *Journal of College Student Development, 41*(4), 405–414.

Kelly, K. J., Edwards, R. W., Comello, M. L. G., Plested, B. A., Thurman, P. J., & Slater, M. D. (2003). The community readiness model: A complementary approach to social marketing. *Marketing Theory, 3*(4), 411–426. doi:10.1177/1470593103042006

Kohlberg, L. (1984). *The psychology of moral development: Essays on moral development* (Vol. 2). San Francisco, CA: Harper and Row.

Lin, Z.-C., & Effken, J. A. (2010). Effects of a tailored web-based educational intervention on women's perceptions of and intentions to obtain mammography. *Journal of Clinical Nursing, 19*(9–10), 1261–1269. doi:10.1111/j.1365–2702.2009.03180.x

Lippke, S., Ziegelmann, J. P., Schwarzer, R., & Velicer, W. F. (2009). Validity of stage assessment in the adoption and maintenance of physical activity and fruit and vegetable consumption. *Health Psychology, 28*(2), 183–193. doi:10.1037/a0012983

Madsen, S. R., Miller, D., & John, C. R. (2005). Readiness for organizational change: Do organizational commitment and social relationships in the workplace make a difference? *Human Resource Development Quarterly, 16*(2), 213–234. doi:10.1002/hrdq.1134

McAllister, G., & Irvine, J. J. (2000). Cross cultural competency and multicultural teacher education. *Review of Educational Research, 70*(1), 3–24. doi:10.3102/00346543070001003

Moradi, B., & Subich, L. M. (2003). A concomitant examination of the relations of perceived racist and sexist events to psychological distress for African American women. *The Counseling Psychologist, 31*(4), 451–469. doi:10.1177/0011000003031004007

O'Brien, E. (2001). *Whites confront racism: Antiracists and their paths to action.* Lanham, MD: Rowman & Littlefield.

Park, E. R., DePue, J. D., Goldstein, M. G., Niaura, R., Harlow, L. L., Willey, C., Rakowski, W., & Prokhorov, A. V. (2003). Assessing the transtheoretical model of change constructs for physicians counseling smokers. *Annals of Behavioral Medicine, 25*(2), 120–126. doi:10.1207/S15324796ABM2502_08

Platt, L. F. (this volume). Blazing the trail: Teaching the privileged about privilege. In K. A. Case (Ed.), *Deconstructing privilege: Teaching and learning as allies in the classroom* (pp. 207–222). New York, NY: Routledge.

Prochaska, J. O., & DiClemente, C. C. (1983). Stages and processes of self-change of smoking: Toward an integrative model of change. *Journal of Consulting and Clinical Psychology, 51*(3), 390–395. doi:10.1037/0022–006X.51.3.390

Prochaska, J. O., DiClemente, C. C., & Norcross, J. C. (1992). In search of how people change: Applications to addictive behaviors. *American Psychologist, 47*(9), 1102–1114. doi:10.1037/0003–066X.47.9.1102

Reason, R. D., Millar, E. A. R., & Scales, T. C. (2005). Toward a model of racial justice ally development. *Journal of College Student Development, 46*(5), 530–546. doi:10.1353/csd.2005.0054

Rios, D., & Stewart, A. J. (this volume). Recognizing privilege by reducing invisibility: The Global Feminisms Project as a pedagogical tool. In K. A. Case (Ed.), *Deconstructing privilege: Teaching and learning as allies in the classroom* (pp. 115–131). New York, NY: Routledge.

Roades, L. A., & Mio, J. S. (2000). Allies: How are they created and what are their experiences? In J. S. Mio & G. I. Awakuni (Eds), *Resistance to multiculturalism: Issues and interventions* (pp. 63–82). Philadelphia, PA: Brunner/Mazel.

Sanders, M. R., & Mahalingam, R. (2012). Under the radar: The role of invisible discourse in understanding class-based privilege. *Journal of Social Issues, 68*(1), 112–127. doi:10.1111/j.1540–4560.2011.01739.x

Sherover-Marcuse, R. (2000). Working assumptions and guidelines for alliance building. In M. Adams, W. J. Blumenfeld, R. Castañeda, H. W. Hackman, M. L. Peters, & X. Zuniga (Eds.), *Readings for diversity and social justice: An anthology on racism, antisemitism, sexism, heterosexism, ableism, and classism* (pp. 486–487). New York, NY: Routledge.

Spanierman, L. B., & Heppner, M. J. (2004). Psychosocial Costs of Racism to Whites scale (PCRW): Construction and initial validation. *Journal of Counseling Psychology, 51*(2), 249–262. doi:10.1037/0022–0167.51.2.249

Stoudt, B. G., Fox, M., & Fine, M. (2012). Contesting privilege with critical participatory action research. *Journal of Social Issues, 68*(1), 178–193. doi:10.1111/j.1540–4560.2011.01743.x

Terenzini, P. T., Springer, L., Pascarella, E. T., & Nora, A. (1995). Academic and out-of-class influences on students' intellectual orientations. *The Review of Higher Education, 19*(1), 23–44.

Thompson, C. (2000). Can White heterosexual men understand oppression? In M. Adams, W. J. Blumenfeld, R. Castañeda, H. W. Hackman, M. L. Peters, & X. Zuniga (Eds.), *Readings for diversity and social justice: An anthology on racism, antisemitism, sexism, heterosexism, ableism, and classism* (pp. 477–482). New York, NY: Routledge.

Thompson-Miller, R., & Feagin, J. R. (2007). Continuing injuries of racism: Counseling in a racist context. *The Counseling Psychologist, 35*(1), 106–115. doi:10.1177/0011000006294664

Tropp, L. R., & Brown, A. C. (2004). What benefits the group can also benefit the individual: Group-enhancing and individual-enhancing motives for collective action. *Group Processes & Intergroup Relations, 7*(3), 267–282. doi:10.1177/1368430204046111

Velasquez, M. M., Stephens, N. S., & Ingersoll, K. (2006). Motivational interviewing in groups. *Journal of Groups in Addiction & Recovery, 1*(1), 27–50. doi:10.1300/J384v01n01_03

Vera, E. M., & Speight, S. L. (2003). Multicultural competence, social justice, and counseling psychology: Expanding our roles. *The Counseling Psychologist, 31*(3), 253–272. doi:10.1177/0011000003031003001

Wallace, B. C. (2000). A call for change in multicultural training at graduate schools of education: Educating to end oppression and for social justice. *Teachers College Record, 102*(6), 1086–1111. doi:10.1111/0161–4681.00093

Wise, T., & Case, K. A. (this volume). Pedagogy for the privileged: Addressing inequality and injustice without shame or blame. In K. A. Case (Ed.), *Deconstructing privilege: Teaching and learning as allies in the classroom* (pp. 17–33). New York, NY: Routledge.

5

"COLORBLINDNESS IS THE NEW RACISM"

Raising Awareness about Privilege Using Color Insight[1]

Margalynne J. Armstrong and Stephanie M. Wildman

Whiteness, Systemic Privilege, and Antidiscrimination Discourse

Unacknowledged white privilege pervades U.S. society and culture. As Caramanica (2012) wrote in the *New York Times*, "Whiteness is too often invisible on television, so much the norm that it no longer begs evaluation" (p. AR20). White privilege is "pervasive, structural, and generally invisible" (Law, 1999, p. 604) operating on both personal and systemic levels. Peggy McIntosh (1988) described white privilege as a knapsack of benefits of which the holder could remain oblivious. Yet the possessor of the knapsack of privilege could reliably depend on the advantages they provide, even though she or he remained unaware of them.

White privilege includes the assumption that White people define a societal norm and that people of color are "other," often considered inferior or dangerous. Because Whites represent the societal "normal" benchmark, "the White person has an everyday option not to think of herself in racial terms at all" (Flagg, 1993, p. 969). A key aspect of this unacknowledged privilege to avoid thinking of oneself as having a race is that whiteness operates as the normative foundation and reference for most discussions about race, race discrimination, and denial of equality.

With whiteness as the default assumption, Whites can claim they do not discriminate because they often do not think in racial terms. Whites may observe the discriminatory treatment of non-Whites and consider only the disadvantages that flow from being non-White without having to consider any of the benefits of appearing to be White. If a racist is a person who categorizes based on race to the detriment of non-Whites, then, Whites reason, how can they be discriminating if they do not think about non-Whites in a derogatory manner, especially when they are not thinking about race at all? Racism does not exist to Whites who reason, "Racism is not my problem because I am not someone with a race nor do I think badly about other races. I do not even usually think about race."

While the focus of this chapter is white privilege, it is important to remember that interlocking systems of privilege, across multiple identity categories, such as gender, economic wealth, sexual orientation, and physical ability, serve to mask and reinforce all forms of systemic privilege (Banks, Pliner, & Hopkins, this volume; Ferber & Herrera, this volume). Frances Ansley described this dynamic using the metaphor of a power line, a horizontal line on the blackboard (Wildman, Armstrong, Davis, & Grillo, 1996). The power line divided those who were privileged for each identity category from those who were not; those above the line are privileged with respect to those below it. Thus, most individuals have some privileges, while being excluded from privilege for other aspects of personhood. For example, a White lesbian professor might be privileged in respect to her race and education, but lack privilege based on gender or sexual orientation.

Examining privilege must become a part of discrimination discourse which rarely recognizes that race discrimination involves exclusion from privileges that are accorded to White people or others who might be above the power line. Nor does discrimination discourse analyze what those privileges are. Instead, exclusion from some specific opportunity or the denial of an unspecified, amorphous equality becomes the focus of antidiscrimination language, without an explicit examination of how or why the beneficiaries of privilege obtained their position. Efforts to dismantle inequality often beg the question of "unequal to whom or what?" Failure to examine the privileged status diverts attention from noticing and analyzing the advantages conferred by white privilege and renders any ensuing discussion of racial discrimination incomplete (Armstrong & Wildman, 2008; Case, this volume; McIntosh, 2012). The emphasis on discrimination alone, as if it existed in a vacuum, obscures the operation of privilege, thus aiding in its perpetuation. The lens that focuses exclusively on discrimination can produce only piecemeal renditions of formal equality, limiting substantive progress, while privilege still operates to the disadvantage of people of color (Case, this volume).

Public education in the United States provides one example of this process of attempts to attack privilege that serve to reinscribe it. The law prohibits segregation in public schools yet inequality in opportunity and caliber of education remains rampant (Ogletree, 2004). Efforts to equalize educational opportunity that recognize that race is still a determinative factor become bogged down by the rhetoric of colorblindness. Courts invoke colorblindness and divert attention from examining how race impacts the distribution of educational opportunity. Thus, people seeking equality are not permitted to examine, or even acknowledge, that White students are generally afforded the best educational opportunities in the United States, while these benefits elude many students of color. And because colorblindness has become the new touchstone in race discourse, it is more difficult than ever to recognize discrimination and to talk about it (Wise, 2010; Wise & Case, this volume).

In this so-called colorblind and post-racial world, educators in the classroom setting often fail to name and examine whiteness. As long as educators, particularly legal educators, and students fail to question the dynamics of whiteness and privilege in antidiscrimination law, the legal system will reinscribe that privilege and perpetuate discrimination. Identifying and understanding whiteness should be an essential component of education in the United States.

Why do many educators fail to address this normative role played by whiteness? People generally possess goodwill and truly want to see an end to discrimination. But discrimination cannot end absent an understanding of the privilege dynamic that enables discrimination to continue. This incomplete understanding of the nature of white privilege, coupled with the modern move toward colorblindness, conceals the raced nature of much law and power.

Educators and students would profit by examining the role of colorblindness against the societal background of the continued salience of race. Color insight provides an appropriate antidote to colorblindness, one that remedies the omission of context in racial discourse. The process of developing color insight requires four steps:

1. considering context for any discussion about race;
2. examining systems of privilege;
3. unmasking perspectivelessness and white normativeness; and
4. combating stereotyping and looking for the "me" in each individual.

Below, classroom exercises accompany discussion of each of these steps toward fostering color insight, providing examples for teaching and learning about each component.

Colorblindness in a Racialized World

U.S. jurisprudence and politics currently valorize colorblindness and race neutrality. The contemporary use of the term "colorblind" became prevalent through U.S. Supreme Court decisions involving challenges to affirmative action programs under the equal protection clause of the Fourteenth Amendment to the U.S. Constitution (Adarand Constructors, Inc. v. Peña, 1995; City of Richmond v. J.A. Croson Co., 1989; Regents of University of California v. Bakke, 1978). In these cases, White plaintiffs sued to end programs that had sought to promote the inclusion of people of color in education and employment opportunities that previously had been foreclosed to them. Ironically, the Court used these anti-affirmative action cases to resurrect the term colorblindness, used originally by the Court in Justice Harlan's dissent in Plessy v. Ferguson. Harlan had proposed colorblindness as a constitutional principle that would prohibit legally mandated segregation in public transportation (Plessy v. Ferguson [dissent], 1896). The Court rejected Harlan's vision of colorblindness, and instead authorized the government to recognize race to the advantage of Whites for close to a century. The contemporary use of colorblindness became an active principle only when government programs that recognized race became perceived as disadvantaging White people.

Learning about race and understanding its operation in the world is a key step for all members of society and certainly for people who will practice law or serve the public in the 21st century. It is no longer likely that any college graduate will work in a homogenous community for his or her entire career. But until educators teach about the importance of analyzing how privilege operates, students will graduate ill-equipped to work effectively in a diverse environment. If students do not grapple with issues of privilege while still in school, they may never acquire the insight or ability to recognize and combat racism and other subordination.

Society purports to prize colorblindness, and that dictate makes it hard to "see race" in public discussion. As Williams (1991) explained, race is the elephant in the room that everyone tiptoes around or claims we should avoid. The United States is a "nation of cowards," according to attorney general Eric Holder, in the face of discussing race with one another (Frieden, 2009). Yet, the failure to speak the truth about race makes it difficult to dismantle racial inequality. Since Barack Obama became president, commentators describe U.S. society as "post-racial," as if the election of a Black man to the nation's highest office meant no more conversation about race was needed. This lack of dialogue perpetuates racial separation. Three years after President Obama's inauguration, racial justice dominated the national news with stories on the killing of Trevon Martin and litigation about Arizona's Senate Bill 1070, authorizing police to require proof of immigration status.

In educational settings, faculty and students of color often carry the major responsibility for highlighting issues of racial justice. They should not shoulder the institutional work of either caring about race or the onus of educating their White colleagues. People of color know all too well that society racializes them with a race other than White. Yet, Whites often do not think about race and racial justice, except when they notice people of color are present. Whites tend not to notice that they too have a race and that their own race carries social meaning and generally positive presumptions. Whites often aspire to colorblindness, believing that colorblindness promotes equality. Most seek to emphasize that they are not prejudiced and hold egalitarian values. Seeking colorblindness means Whites fail to see how whiteness has privileged them in so many societal interactions. Endorsing colorblind ideology allows White individuals to express egalitarian principles while still enjoying a status quo that advantages them relative to people of color. This white privilege will continue because a colorblind present does not erase the modern-day effects of centuries of racism and white privilege.

White people may fear that engaging the topic of race makes them seem racist (Johnson, Olson, & Fazio, 2009). Johnson et al. (2009) suggested that even if a White person "may hold egalitarian views on racialized issues and may believe that sharing these views would create affinity with Black partners, they may also feel that they lack the appropriate self-interest or standing to raise them" (p. 559). Whites fear creating the impression that they are "insensitive or prejudiced" (Johnson et al., 2009, p. 559). It would be more helpful for everyone to notice the everyday presence of racial privilege and to think about how to combat it. Society cannot battle a phantom that it cannot recognize and name. Whites ignore race at their peril and to society's detriment. Ignoring race may cause unintended harms as the dynamics of racial hierarchy continue in people of color's daily lives.

Race remains a formative identity category that impacts the lives of both Whites and people of color, albeit in different ways. The dominant norm of colorblindness obscures and maintains that status quo of white privilege. "Colorblindness is the new racism," said one law student at a social justice event, summarizing this new so-called post-racial era. The student was not saying that all people who espouse colorblindness harbor racial animus. Rather, the student meant that the failure to acknowledge racial reality in the United States reinforces and solidifies existing racial inequality and white privilege. So seeing race for Whites must mean more than merely noticing whiteness; Whites need to learn about its accompanying privilege (Case, Iuzzini, & Hopkins, 2012). Learning about white privilege is not intuitive for Whites because "social norms of the privileged become the generalized normative expectations for marginalized groups, providing dominant group members the option of remaining ignorant and avoidant of awareness of both privilege and oppression" (Case et al., 2012, p. 3). Thus Whites must make a conscious effort to notice and learn about the operation of privilege and subordination. Society's emphasis on colorblindness sends Whites the opposite message.

Color Insight as an Antidote to Colorblindness

To draw the harmful operation of colorblindness into relief and to counter the idea of colorblindness or the notion that society is post-racial, the authors propose utilizing "color insight" (Armstrong & Wildman, 2008, 2012). Color insight admits that most of us do see race and underlines the need to understand what that racial awareness might mean (Fiske & Neuberg, 1990). For example, Fiske and Neuberg (1990) found that people form impressions of others through a variety of processes "that lie on a continuum reflecting the extent to which the perceiver utilizes a target's particular characteristics" (p. 2). While the study revealed a spectrum, the researchers found that subjects used category-based processes (quickly placing people in categories or schema) more frequently. Category-based classification serves as the "default" mode of perception. Explaining the prevalence of category-based mental processes, Fiske and Neuberg (1990) state, "If relatively category-oriented processes are successful, then the perceiver goes no further toward more attribute-oriented processes" (p. 2). Humans resort to attribute-oriented processes that collect and compile individual pieces of information and apply more careful and piecemeal analysis whenever motivation or the need for accuracy is high. As category-based perception can occur automatically and outside of conscious awareness, the study supports a conclusion that the human brain makes colorblindness unlikely.

Color insight provides a vocabulary for teaching across racial lines. It is a useful lens with which to examine societal interactions and to initiate conversations. Color insight contrasts with colorblindness by offering an alternative that better serves the purported goals of colorblindness: racial equality and justice. Color insight requires its practitioners to observe, discuss, and analyze the operation of race and privilege in contemporary society. It thus differs from other pedagogical strategies including multiculturalism and diversity studies that have been criticized as being subject to co-option such as corporate usurpation (Ladson-Billings, 2003) and over-particularization (Ravitch, 1990).

Color insight recognizes that a racial status quo exists in which society attributes race to each member. Whereas colorblindness urges us not to notice race, color insight says, "do not be afraid; notice your race and the race of others around you; racism and privilege still do affect peoples' lives; learn more about the racial dynamic." Color insight serves to promote equality and to emphasize nondiscrimination among races. As stated earlier, the process of color insight requires four steps: (1) considering context for any discussion about race; (2). examining systems of privilege; (3) unmasking perspectivelessness and white normativeness; and (4) combating stereotyping and looking for the "me" in each individual.

We suggest a classroom exercise to accompany each of these steps. Faculty participation in the exercises, along with students, ensures that students and teachers can become allies in the classroom.

Developing Color Insight

Considering Context for Discussing Race: The Racial Observation Exercise

An initial step toward applying color insight requires creating a setting to ensure that the mention and discussion of race is possible. The need for setting a productive context applies to conversations about race in any relationship, classroom, or institution. If students and faculty can understand the origins for their perceptions of race, they may be more willing consciously to move from endorsing colorblindness to supporting color insight. Observing race and racialization and also acknowledging these observations is key. We all have much to learn from meaningful discussions examining race, racialization, and the operation of systemic privilege (McIntosh, 2012). Because color insight requires observation and reflection, students must necessarily observe race operating in the "real world." Many colleges and universities provide service-learning classes involving "organized service activity that meets identified community needs" (Bringle & Hatcher, 1996, p. 222) combined with opportunities for the students to reflect on their service in a manner that enhances the course. Applying color insight to assignments such as directed writing, small group discussion, and class presentations compels students to notice the operation of race rather than ignoring or obscuring contemporary manifestations of racial privilege.

Race has had different meanings over time and its significance continues to fluctuate. Even word usage has evolved and keeps changing. Thus, color insight begins by considering the different contexts that participants in a discussion of race bring to the table. Individual concepts of race may differ and cause concern that one's views may offend others. This fear leads to a tendency to avoid discussing race altogether. Color insight requires a commitment not to sweep race under the rug, but rather to name its presence and to examine its attributes from multiple perspectives, including the operation of privilege. One classroom activity for opening this dialogue is a racial observation exercise. For this project, we instruct students that they must start the assignment more than 24 hours prior to submission. We also give them instructions that state:

> Society sends many messages favoring colorblindness; do these messages further social justice? This assignment asks you to notice the racial composition of your environment for a 24-hour period and to record your observations. What are the apparent races of the people you view? How do you know? Note their jobs and/or the activities in which they are engaged. Note the kinds of interactions you observe and your position. Are you privileged in the interaction? Where are you in relation to Professor Fran Ansley's (Wildman et al., 1996) "power line?" [The exercise refers to *Privilege Revealed* and the discussion of the power line that appears earlier.] Make sure that you are in several different localities during the day (not just at home or the law library, although time spent in these places is pertinent). Conclude by sharing your reactions about what you have observed.

We also give them a sample observation:

> I [Stephanie] found myself, several weeks ago, stranded at Dulles airport with a cancelled flight and eight hours until I could depart. So I used some of the privileges I have to walk into one of those red carpet lounges, purchase a day pass, and settle in to work. In the eight hours I spent, I found that all the airline employees who worked at computers and talked with clientele were White; all the clientele, with the exception of one African American man, (based on just my looking) were White; the bartender was White; and all the service employees, who put out food, cleaned it up, and cleaned the bathrooms, were people of color. I exercised my white privilege by my silence, just doing my work. When I got on the airplane, the fasten

seatbelt sign had white hands. The day after I came home, I went to the gym (mostly White), where a young, apparently White man—probably high school age—was working out in a t-shirt with an Indian mascot on it. I didn't know the young man and I said nothing.

Students share their observations in electronic format with other class members; the observations are available only to students enrolled in the class through a class email list. Here are some excerpts from student observations:

I reached my sister's apartment building, a nice high-rise, which requires a key to enter or to be buzzed in. I tried to call my sister several times, but she did not answer the phone. As I waited, a Caucasian couple walked in and held the door for me to come in. I couldn't help but wonder if they would have easily let me into the apartment building if I weren't a young Caucasian woman. When I entered the building, an African American women sitting at the front desk smiled and didn't say anything about me being let in this way.

(White woman student)

As I approached the entrance of the Federal Building, a Caucasian male security guard met me at the security line, and asked for my ID. The man in front of me in line for security was an African American male, and his backpack was being searched as I grabbed my bag and continued on.

(Asian woman student)

None of the other White women in the nail salon spoke to the Vietnamese women who serviced their hands and feet. This lack of interaction bothered me because both my mom and I made sure to learn the names of the women working on us and to try to start conversations with them. However, even the nail ladies at times looked down and seemed to not want to talk to us, like they were used to being treated as inferior. Not enough people in the world actually pay attention to the individuals who help them or do work for them.

(White Latina student)

By writing their own observations and reading the work of others, students discover examples of privilege in their daily lives and reinforce their own and their classmates' learning how to recognize privilege in operation. Students may not have understood why Indian mascots are offensive, given their prevalence in society, or noticed searches applied unequally to Black co-workers. For some Whites, noticing race is uncomfortable and they are surprised to learn that their classmates of color state that noticing race is familiar to them. Observation does not end the racialized reality in which we live, but the exercise provides a shared context that the class can return to in later discussion. Through reading and discussing the observations, students learn a bit more about privilege. Students report that they notice more in the weeks following the exercise.

Examining Systems of Privilege: The Power Line Exercise

Both Whites and people of color need to recognize their own and one another's individual privileges. Systems of privilege based on identity categories, such as gender, heterosexual orientation, economic wealth, language or accent, physical appearance and ability, education, and religion, in addition to race, continue as impediments to equality. Crenshaw's (1989) path-breaking work on intersectionality focused on the multiplicity of subordination at the crossroad of two paths. But imagine a multidimensional intersection, with strands for every imaginable identity category. Picture a "Koosh ball," a toy that resembles a wad of multicolored rubber bands tied in the middle and cut open to reveal loose, moving ends. This dynamic postmodern ball changes shape as it sails through the air, as one color then others dominate (Wildman et al., 1996). We all reside at the center of a Koosh ball of strands that mark our identity. No person is purely privileged or unprivileged; we are privileged in respect to some categories and not privileged in respect to others. Sometimes one strand is dominant, sometimes another. This experience of both privilege and subordination in different aspects of our lives causes the experience of privilege to be further obscured; the presence of privilege may be further hidden from our vocabulary and consciousness if we focus only on the ways in which we face disadvantage.

The power line exercise provides a valuable tool for identifying and discussing privilege and subordination. This classroom exercise, inspired by the work of Kendall (2006) and Ansley (Wildman et al., 1996), asks each student to consider themselves in relation to a power line that separates privileged and non-privileged categories. The exercise is useful for facilitating student understanding of the existence of systemic privilege in relation to identity categories. While it could be done prior to the observation project discussed above, it teaches more effectively after the observation project. Students are more open to examining their own privileges having built the trust with classmates that the observation project engendered.

For this exercise, teachers should provide a printed sheet with characteristics based on the context of the classroom. Descriptive characteristics above the line might include White, middle class, heterosexual, Christian, and male. Listings below the line might include non-White, working class, lesbian, non-Christian, and female. Tell students they may add their own boxes; for example, a transsexual student might prefer to list her own box. A power line chart, such as that shown in Figure 5.1, might be given to students to illustrate potential identity categories for class members to examine and discuss privilege and subordination.

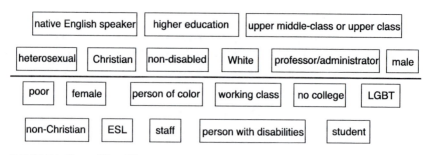

FIGURE 5.1 Power Line Chart

Students work alone for about five minutes and circle the descriptions, based on identity, career, or any other categories, that apply to each of them. The professor should also identify her categories. In a group discussion, either small groups or with the entire class, students can share what characteristics they chose and whether they regard their choices as reflecting privilege (above the line) or lack privilege (below the line). Ideally, students would discuss first in pairs and then in the large group. Discussion can also reflect upon categories not named and a consideration of why they were not present. Teachers should take particular care not to require students of color to "testify" as to their experience, particularly if there are few of them in the class. The class should then focus on only the "above the line attributes" that each person possesses. To break the ice, the professor may want to share first. In a class that is largely White, this focus will necessitate a discussion of whiteness. Ask students how often they talk about these privileged (above the line) attributes and what it would mean for their lives to keep those systemic privileges in the forefront of their consciousness most of the time. Paying attention to the privileges many people in the classroom have ensures that the subordinated Koosh ball strands do not receive all the attention. Inequality cannot end absent recognition of the privilege dynamic that allows discrimination to continue.

Unmasking Perspectivelessness and White Normativeness: Naming Race

Color insight requires recognition of the myth of perspectivelessness and unmasking white normativeness, discussed earlier. A theoretically neutral lack of perspective permeates most classrooms, particularly law school classroom environments, and diverts students and professors from examining how whiteness and many other factors inform academic culture generally and law school culture particularly. Perspectivelessness operates by teaching cases and statutes in a manner that disassociates them from the people and institutions that make law. The lack of attribution makes the law appear organic and universal, as if springing from some font of absolute truth. This theoretical neutrality actually masks a majoritarian, white racial perspective, suggesting that all students must share the same view, for example, of slavery, when that institution had a differential impact on different races and cannot be studied as a "neutral" exercise of legal power. The idea that students of law should ignore its human and societal origins erases perspective with potentially debilitating results. Students can miss seeking answers to important questions that might affect the outcome of a case.

Considering race in classroom hypotheticals that appear to be race neutral reveals the partial picture of reality painted by white normativeness and underlines the need to recognize perspective for a deeper educational experience. What are the implications for failing to state race in examples in the classroom? Should the classroom really be colorblind or does the failure to mention race prevent a learning opportunity? Imagine you are teaching medical malpractice, a field that concerns the possible negligence of a physician (Perea, Delgado, Harris, Stefancic, & Wildman, 2000). You tell your students that their firm represents the injured person, who is considering suing the doctor because of an improper dose of anesthesia administered before surgery. A litigation attorney in the firm comes to tell you about the case.

At this point, ask students to consider: "Did you picture the plaintiff and the doctor? Stop and picture them. Do they have a race? A gender? Do you imagine them with any other characteristics? Will you ask the attorney about the race of the parties or any other characteristics?" Many students of all races assume the parties are White; that default to whiteness is part of white privilege. This exercise illustrates how white privilege excludes the identity of people of other races, so some cannot even see themselves reflected in quotidian reality.

Continue the exercise by disrupting the operation of white normativeness, asking: "Now consider this same example with a Black plaintiff suing a White doctor. Do you want to ask questions about race on voir dire [questions to prospective jurors, asked before empanelling the jury that will sit in judgment at trial]? Why or why not? Does it change your answer if a White plaintiff is suing a Black doctor?" Ask the students if the attorney in this example can adequately represent her client if she does not consider race. Attorneys have an obligation to learn about race and strategize about how it could affect each case.

This exercise, racing classroom hypotheticals, can be used in any discipline where teaching examples often rely on the default assumption of whiteness. By exploding that default assumption, teachers help students make privilege visible and deepen their understanding of its operation.

Combating Stereotyping by Looking for the Me in Each Individual

Color insight requires combating racial stereotypes. Urging students to see the "me," the individual who transcends those stereotypes, reveals multiple intersections of privilege and lack of privilege in each person. This recognition enables the construction of bridges between individuals across identity categories and deeper recognition of the role of privilege in all of our lives.

Culp (1991), an African American law professor at Duke University School of Law, reported that his students asked him, "Where did you attend law school?" (p. 543). He later realized that this question was a subterfuge for students asking, "What gives *you* the right to teach this course to *me*?" (Culp, 1991, p. 543). He told them he had attended the University of Chicago and Harvard Law School. Seeking to impact the way the students viewed race within his classroom, he also told them he was the son of a coal miner. Culp (1991) explained that he wanted to say to his Black students that "they too can engage in the struggle to reach a position of power and influence" (p. 539). He also wanted his White students to see that "Black people have to struggle" (Culp, 1991, p. 539). Yet, Culp found that the reaction from students of both races when he told them his history was often incredulity. He was facing the students' stereotyped views of him and his background.

Culp (1991) explained that his use of autobiography conveyed more than an effort to put his students at ease about his qualifications. He wrote:

> My autobiographical statement—I am the son of a poor coal miner—has informational content that has a transformative potential much greater than my curriculum vitae. Who we are matters as much as what we are and what we think. It is important to teach our students that there is a "me" in law, as well as specific rules that are animated by our experiences.
>
> (p. 543)

Culp was combating stereotypes by urging students to see the "me," the individual who transcends those stereotypes and resides at the intersection of multiple identity categories, privileged as to some and not privileged as to others. Culp's view of the importance of the "me" in law and his memorable message about where he came from can inspire us all to teach about race, socioeconomic background, and other identity categories in the classroom.

A number of different exercises, done in writing and shared with the class or done orally either "around the room" or in small groups, can help students to see the "me" in one another. These exercises include sharing stories about one's maternal grandmother, about how one's ancestors came to be in the United States, recalling one's first memory of having a race, or asking "what is your race and how did you learn what it was?" Here is an example of the grandmother exercise[2] (from Stephanie):

> I would like to go around the room and have each of you introduce yourself, so say your first name and last name, and tell us a few sentences about your maternal grandmother. If you really cannot speak about your maternal or paternal grandmother, pick another relative or someone close to you from that generation or earlier.
>
> I hope, from doing this exercise, we can begin the process of appreciating our differences as well as our commonalities as individuals. Throughout the

semester, I expect strong disagreements to emerge, but we can all learn from respectfully listening to and commenting on our disagreements as well as our commonalities.

I will go first. My maternal grandmother Lena Sokol died in 1995 at the age of 96. My grandmother was part of that generation of Jewish women who fled from the Ukraine to escape pogroms. Her mother died when she was young and her father and brothers left her and emigrated to America. She was raised by an aunt [whom she called the mima] and her family. I guess there was some money there, because she tells of arriving at the mima's house and being afraid to walk on the wood floor, fearing that she would fall in. She was used to dirt floors. She too left Russia in her late teens or early twenties after World War I and after her marriage with my grandfather. Her first child, who was a son, died during this journey. Her second child, my mother, was born in Romania. My grandmother came to New York and worked in a mattress factory. She always had bad knees from pushing the pedals. She had two more daughters, and all of them became teachers.

By the time I knew her in Los Angeles, she didn't work outside the home, but she cooked for all her daughters and sent food to their houses. I think she believed that the most important thing I ever did was to get married and have children. So we saw the world differently in terms of life choices and priorities, but I do miss her.

Here is an example of the grandmother exercise from a student:

In 1932, when she was six years old, my paternal grandmother Neva left her small village outside of Lucca, Italy, to meet her father Enrico in San Francisco. Her mother had just died of tuberculosis and she made the journey with her uncle. She remembered nothing about the trip across the Atlantic other than it was the first time she had strawberry jam; she thought it was the best thing she had ever tasted and loved it ever since.

She lived in San Francisco with Enrico who remarried a wonderful woman, Yolanda, my bisnonni. My nonni's aunt and uncle, however, were unable to have children. They told her stepmothers can be horrible and offered to raise her as their own in Sparks, Nevada. Nonni decided to live with her aunt and uncle. When I was older, I asked Nonni why, and she explained what a difficult decision it was; she loved both families very much, but she had relied on her uncle when she left Italy, and she felt like a stranger in Enrico and Yolanda's life.

I loved Nonni very much, but only as an adult did I truly appreciate her fire. She was extremely opinionated and had no time for hurt feelings, especially if she was telling the truth. Her three children were everything to her, and her grandchildren meant even more ... More than anything, she wanted to see me get married. Her husband and family meant everything to her, and she wanted the same for me. When she died she told me she was sorry she wouldn't get to see my wedding, but she was happy knowing that one day I would be an attorney. She was very proud of that.

Here is another example (from Margalynne) of the exercise on how one's ancestors came to the United States:

> Two of my grandparents died before I was born, the other two died when I was still quite young. What I know of my grandparents' backgrounds derives from researching the census. My paternal grandfather Jacob was born around 1859 in Tennessee and was very likely born a slave, given that in 1860 less than 1% of the Black population in Tennessee was free. My grandmother Mary was Jacob's second wife (I learned this fact from my mother) and Mary was more than twenty years younger than my grandfather. She gave birth to my father in 1922. I find it amazing that I, a law professor in the 21st century, can be one generation removed from a man who was probably born enslaved.

Most people today are very removed from the realities of their grandparents' lives, and students are often beneficiaries of the progress that has occurred since their grandparents were young. Listening to one another's histories enables students to overcome assumptions and to share the personal in a context that does not reflect judgment on any individual, while helping White students to recognize that they too possess a racial categorization. The grandparent and ancestor exercises introduce a larger historical framework that can expand the focus of discussions of privilege from personal attributes to more systemic analysis. The emphasis on the personal, the "me," underlines the different perspectives that racialization in society causes. Thus, the exercises help students to see that their own racial perspective is not the only one.

Conclusion

In this chapter, we advocate for the application of color insight rather than colorblindness as an approach to thinking about race. Color insight does not provide a magic wand that dispenses with racism, but it does offer a vocabulary and some significant points of entry for deeper conversations. This chapter also provides suggestions for classroom techniques utilizing color insight to foster a more complete understanding of the function of race and whiteness in the classroom and in law. These exercises include a "racial observation exercise," in which students focus on race in the surrounding world for a 24-hour period to establish a context for the discussion; a power line exercise to make privilege and subordination explicit; consideration of the race of the parties in classroom hypotheticals when no race is mentioned, discussing the relevance of perspective to the exploration of knowledge;

and making sure students see the "me" in one another with exercises to combat stereotyping. Faculty can adopt two additional techniques:

1. extracurricular discussion sessions within the school that introduce racial awareness into the institutional culture and cultivate an attitude about the importance of this learning; and
2. student reflections, throughout the semester, shared with the whole class, as they process reading and discussion in the course.

Extracurricular brown-bag sessions can include relevant films, such as *The Color of Fear* (Mun Wah, 1994) or *Mirrors of Privilege: Making Whiteness Visible* (Butler & Butler, 2006), or discussion of essays such as those detailed in the references for this chapter. Student reflections on assigned reading or class conversations and exercises remain a significant method for extending class discussion time on complex issues. These techniques can enhance both institutional and classroom learning while providing an enriched context for ongoing exploration of racial justice issues. Faculty participation in all of these activities illustrates the power of collaboration as students and faculty learn together. Student reactions to these exercises and techniques suggest they do make a difference both to students who already see a racialized reality and to those who are just learning that one exists.

Notes

1 The authors thank Elizabeth Hollis, for outstanding research assistance, Ellen Platt, for superlative library support, and Kim Case, for thoughtful editorial comments.
2 Charles Lawrence and Mari Matsuda originally told the authors about this exercise.

References

Adarand Constructors, Inc. v. Peña, 515 U.S. 200 (1995).

Armstrong, M. J., & Wildman, S. M. (2008). Teaching race/teaching whiteness: Transforming colorblindness to color insight. *North Carolina Law Review, 86*(3), 635–672.

Armstrong, M. J., & Wildman, S. M. (2012). Working across racial lines in a not-so-post-racial world. In G. Gutiérrez y Muhs, Y. F. Niemann, C. G. González, & A. P. Harris (Eds.), *Presumed Incompetent: The intersections of race and class for women in the academy* (pp. 224–241). Logan, UT: Utah State University Press.

Banks, C. A., Pliner, S. M., & Hopkins, M. B. (this volume). Intersectionality and paradigms of privilege: Teaching for social change. In K. A. Case (Ed.), *Deconstructing privilege: Teaching and learning as allies in the classroom* (pp. 102–114). New York, NY: Routledge.

Bringle, R. G., & Hatcher, J. A. (1996). Implementing service learning in higher education. *Journal of Higher Education, 67*(2), 221–239. doi:10.2307/2943981

Butler, S. (Producer), & Butler, S. (Director). (2006). *Mirrors of privilege: Making whiteness visible*. United States: World Trust Educational Services, Inc.

Caramanica, J. (2012, April 29). Broadcasting a world of whiteness. *New York Times*, pp. AR20.

Case, K. A. (this volume). Beyond diversity and whiteness: Developing a transformative and intersectional model of privilege studies pedagogy. In K. A. Case (Ed.), *Deconstructing privilege: Teaching and learning as allies in the classroom* (pp. 1–14). New York, NY: Routledge.

Case, K. A., Iuzzini, J., & Hopkins, M. (2012). Systems of privilege: Intersections, awareness, and applications. *Journal of Social Issues, 68*(1), 1–10. doi:10.1111/j.1540-4560.2011.01732.x

City of Richmond v. J.A. Croson Co., 488 U.S. 469 (1989).

Crenshaw, K. (1989). Demarginalizing the intersection of race and sex: A Black feminist critique of antidiscrimination doctrine, feminist theory, and antiracist politics. *University of Chicago Legal Forum, 1989,* 139–167.

Culp, J. M. (1991). Autobiography and legal scholarship and teaching: Finding the me in the legal academy. *Virginia Law Review, 77,* 539–559. doi:10.2307/1073361

Ferber, A. L., & Herrera, A. O. (this volume). Teaching privilege through an intersectional lens. In K. A. Case (Ed.), *Deconstructing privilege: Teaching and learning as allies in the classroom* (pp. 83–101). New York, NY: Routledge.

Flagg, B. J. (1993). "Was blind, but now I see": White race consciousness and the requirement of discriminatory intent. *Michigan Law Review, 91*(5), 953–1017. doi:10.2307/1289678

Fiske, S. T., & Neuberg, S. L. (1990). A continuum model of impression formation, from category-based to individuating processes: Influences of information and motivation on attention and interpretation. In M. P. Zanna (Ed.), *Advances in experimental social psychology,* (Vol. 23, pp. 1–74). San Diego, CA: Academic Press, Inc.

Frieden, T. (2009, February 18). Holder: U.S. a "nation of cowards" on race discussions. *Articles. CNN.com.* Retrieved from http://articles.cnn.com/2009–02–18/politics/holder.race.relations_1_holder-affirmative-action-black-history-month?_s=PM:POLITICS

Johnson, C. S., Olson, M. A., & Fazio, R. H. (2009). Getting acquainted in interracial interactions: Avoiding intimacy but approaching race. *Personality and Social Psychological Bulletin, 35*(5), 557–571. doi:10.1177/0146167208331160

Kendall, F. E. (2006). *Understanding white privilege: Creating pathways to authentic relationships across race.* New York, NY: Routledge.

Ladson-Billings, G. (2003). New directions in multicultural education: Complexities, boundaries, and critical race theory. In J. Banks & C. Banks (Eds.), *Handbook of research on multicultural education* (pp. 50–65). San Francisco, CA: Jossey-Bass.

Law, S. A. (1999). White privilege and affirmative action. *Akron Law Review, 32*(3), 602–627.

Mun Wah, Lee. (Producer/Director). (1994). *The color of fear* [Motion picture]. Berkeley, CA: Stir-Fry Productions.

McIntosh, P. (1988). *White privilege and male privilege: A personal account of coming to see correspondences through work in women's studies* (Working Paper No. 189). Wellesley, MA: Wellesley Centers for Women.

McIntosh, P. (2012). Reflections and future directions for privilege studies. *Journal of Social Issues, 68*(1), 194–206. doi:10.1111/j.1540-4560.2011.01744.x

Ogletree, C. (2004). *All deliberate speed.* New York, NY: W.W. Norton.

Perea, J. F., Delgado, R., Harris, A. P., Stefancic, J., & Wildman, S. M. (2000). *Race and races: Cases and resources for a diverse America* (2nd ed.). St. Paul, MN: Thomson/West.

Plessy v. Ferguson, 163 U.S. 537 (1896).

Ravitch, D. (1990) Diversity and Democracy: Multicultural education in America. *American Educator, 14*(1), Spring, 16–20, 46–48.

Regents of University of California v. Bakke, 438 U.S. 265 (1978).

Wildman, S. M., Armstrong, M. J., Davis, A. D., & Grillo, T. (1996). *Privilege revealed: How invisible preference undermines America.* New York, NY: New York University Press.

Williams, P. J. (1991). *The alchemy of race and rights: Diary of a law professor.* Cambridge, MA: Harvard Press.

Wise, T. (2010). *Colorblind: The rise of post-racial politics and the retreat from racial equity.* San Francisco, CA: City Lights Books.

Wise, T., & Case, K. A. (this volume). Pedagogy for the privileged: Addressing inequality and injustice without shame or blame. In K. A. Case (Ed.), *Deconstructing privilege: Teaching and learning as allies in the classroom* (pp. 17–33). New York, NY: Routledge.

PART II

Intersectional Privilege Studies Pedagogy

6

TEACHING PRIVILEGE THROUGH AN INTERSECTIONAL LENS

Abby L. Ferber and Andrea O'Reilly Herrera[1]

In the fields of women's and ethnics studies, intersectionality has not only become the latest buzzword, but is also shaping the trajectory of current research (Davis, 2008). Over the past two decades, research that employs an intersectional approach to social justice issues proliferated (Collins, 2004; Kang, 2010; McCall, 2001; Moore, 2011; Villalón, 2010). Growing out of critiques by women of color, such as Audre Lorde (1984), Barbara Smith (1993), Angela Davis (1983), and Gloria Anzaldúa (2007), as well as international activists and scholars, including Chandra Mohanty (1991) and Trinh T. Minh-ha (2009), academics increasingly acknowledged the idea that social justice advocacy cannot be effectively advanced by separating out issues such as race, gender, and class and focusing on only one of these at a time. An intersectional approach acknowledges that individuals and groups are multidimensional and multiply constituted and that their experiences and concerns are not mutually exclusive. For example, while lesbians of color may face common barriers in terms of being denied certain rights and legal protections, the "coming out" process, as well as the way in which they encounter discrimination and support in their local communities, is often very different from the experiences of White lesbians (Moore, 2011). An intersectional approach prevents overlooking, eliding, or marginalizing the needs and concerns of those who are directly impacted by the negative, interactive effects of categories such as race or ethnicity, class, gender, sexuality, religion, citizenship, ability and age, etc. (Davis, 2008; Dill & Zambrana, 2009; Villalón, 2010; Zerai, 2000).

As Keating (2007) and Luft and Ward (2009) found, failing to adopt an intersectional approach to social justice interventions may further marginalize individuals and groups and may also lead to increased backlash. Ultimately, as the African American Policy Forum (n.d.) (an organization co-founded by Kimberlé Crenshaw) pointed out, intersectional theory provides "a critical lens for bringing awareness and capacity to the social justice industry in order to expand and deepen its interventions" (p. 3).

Despite the burgeoning of theoretical and empirical analyses using an intersectional approach, and the widespread embrace of intersectionality among feminist scholars (Berger & Guidroz, 2009; Gilkes, 2001; Ken, 2010; Luft & Ward, 2009; Pratt-Clarke, 2010; Wing, 2003), there remain two key areas where intersectionality is under-applied. The first is the relative dearth of research that examines issues of privilege and intersectionality, particularly when it comes to white privilege (Coston & Kimmel, 2012; Ferber, 1998, 2007; Kimmel & Ferber, 2010). Despite a few recent notable exceptions, the origins of intersectionality in the work of the multiply oppressed has, to some extent, trained academic eyes to focus on those who suffer at the margins of multiple systems of oppression, rather than on those who are privileged (Case, 2012; Coston & Kimmel, 2012; Ferber, 2012; Frankenberg, 1993; Kimmel & Ferber, 2010). The second area identified as needing further development is the teaching of intersectionality. As highlighted in the introduction to this collection (Case, this volume), few scholarly works provide specific strategies regarding effective teaching from an intersectional perspective (Banks, Pliner, & Hopkins, this volume; Berger & Guidroz, 2009; Case & Lewis, 2012; Goodman & Jackson, 2012). We address both of these issues and argue that the intersectional examination of privilege is essential to successful intersectional teaching. More specifically, we review recent publications that focus on the pedagogy of intersectionality and that argue for the effectiveness of a single-dimension or single-axis approach. We then advance our own pedagogical method, which highlights and integrates both privilege and intersectionality.

Intersectionality: Moving from Theory to Practice

In their critical work, Goodman and Jackson (2012) pointed out the many challenges that arise when teaching about racial identity through the prism of intersectionality. Based on the claim that learners possess varying degrees of racial consciousness or readiness to handle cognitive complexity, we urge educators to adopt an incremental framework, which puts a race-centered, single identity focus at the center of inquiry and only gradually incorporates an intersectional paradigm. Such an approach is both useful and appropriate and more accurately captures people's lived experiences.

Luft and Ward (2009) put forward a similar argument regarding intersectionality. They caution against what Luft (2009) described as the flattening of difference, or the idea that all differences carry equal weight. They emphasize the unintended consequences of a blanket application of intersectionality, as well as the detrimental results when "intersectional politics are claimed, but intersectional methods are not used" (Luft & Ward, 2009, p. 17). Luft and Ward succinctly highlighted many of the problems that arise when intersectionality is embraced at the theoretical level, but not put into action in politics and teaching. The contemporary tendency toward deemphasizing or decentering race, they argued, in the current climate in which the notion of colorblindness is widely embraced (Armstrong & Wildman, this volume), demands a direct, single-focus approach to racial privilege and oppression. In other words, they warned that, once an intersectional perspective is introduced, the focus on race ends up getting lost in the discussion, as privileged White people tend to shift the discussion to other identities such as sexuality or class. Like Goodman and Jackson (2012), Luft and Ward (2009) urged faculty to focus on only one primary status at a time, and proposed a race-only method for anti-racist results. They also documented the lack of guidance and research available on effectively teaching from an intersectional perspective.

Teaching Intersectionally? Yes, It's Possible!

For the past 15 years, we (Andrea and Abby) have worked to develop and refine a method for intersectional pedagogy. In the Women's and Ethnic Studies program that we co-founded at the University of Colorado, Colorado Springs, we consistently apply an intersectional approach in all of our courses. Given the overwhelming success we have experienced in our classrooms, we are inspired by the belief that all students are cognitively capable of understanding their own subject positions from an intersectional perspective and consequently can apply this knowledge to the experience of others. In our view, a silo approach to the study of social identity, inequality, and social activism oftentimes perpetuates the idea that the primary statuses are discreet or mutually exclusive, which is one of the fundamental concepts we seek to dismantle. Moreover, a single-focus approach tends to reify, rather than dismantle, essentialist and monolithic notions regarding identities, cultures, and social problems. Spelman (1990) used a "pop bead" analogy of multiple identities, in which race, gender, class, and other categories are envisioned like big, colorful pop beads for children, where each bead can be connected to the next one to form a chain. This additive approach to social identities suggests that, like individual beads, individual social identities can merely be "popped on and off" depending upon the focus of our research. For example, in a study of women's experiences of domestic violence, a professor with a diverse classroom of students may choose to focus solely on the subject of gender. In the process, the ways in which some women's experiences may be differently shaped due to race, class, disability, sexual orientation, etc., are left unanalyzed, as though these social identities can be removed from the chain in order to focus on just one pop bead at a time.

A single-axis approach to teaching about privilege may also prevent many students from understanding the interdependent, complex interaction between privilege and oppression. Rather than thinking about identity as a pop-bead necklace, a tapestry serves as a more useful metaphor, in which each thread may represent a different aspect of social identity. Like a tapestry, identities are the product of the interwoven patterns of multiple threads. If an individual thread is removed for examination, the tapestry itself comes apart, and comprehension of the whole is lost (Ferber, 2007). Ken (2010) provided a theoretical fleshing out of the concept of intersectionality, providing useful culinary metaphors for thinking about intersectionality. Ken asked the reader to imagine race as sugar, gender as flour, and class as baking soda, and then poses the question: What happens when one mixes them together? The response she anticipates is that they become something else, their very nature changes, and they are no longer distinguishable on their own. Ken (2010) argued that the combination produces "something new—something that would not exist if that mixing had not occurred" (p. 156). Like race, class, gender, and sexuality, when these various ingredients are combined, they are changed in the process.

Coston and Kimmel (2012) provided an empirical examination of this dynamic in their research on marginalized men:

> Gender is the mechanism by which the marginalized are marginalized. That is, gay, working-class, or disabled men are seen as "not-men" in the popular discourse of their marginalization. It is their masculinity—the site of their privilege—that is specifically targeted as the grounds for exclusion from privilege.
>
> (p. 98)

As they observed, reverting to a single-axis approach while considering issues of masculinity results in consciously or unconsciously reinforcing a normative concept of privilege. Focusing solely on gender leaves out race, class, ableism, sexuality, etc. By default, the focus shifts to White, middle-class, heterosexual women. Similarly, strictly focusing on race highlights the experiences of middle-class, heterosexual men of color. In other words, ignoring the intersectional relationship among categories, such as race, class, gender, ableism, sexuality, etc., may result in reifying and perpetuating privilege. This occurs even when people focus on issues of privilege. For example, much of the research on white privilege fails to employ an intersectional perspective, thereby reinforcing male privilege, heterosexual privilege, and other systems of privilege in addition to race (Ferber, 2007). This is ironic, given the roots of much recent work on white privilege in McIntosh's (1988) foundational essay in which she compared the operations of white, masculine, and heterosexual privilege.

Even if the eventual goal of teaching about privilege is to incrementally build toward an intersectional approach, we found that teaching about any social identity from a single-lens perspective is not as efficient as an intersectional approach when it comes to learning outcomes. Though it may seem preferable and perhaps easier (as some colleagues have told us) to approach issues of privilege from a single-focus perspective, attempting to train students to analyze issues of social justice from a narrow perspective can present its own set of obstacles to learning. More often than not, it further reinforces students' preconceived, stereotypical notions about categories such as race or ethnicity, gender, class, sexuality, etc., consequently making it more difficult for them to abandon this framework of analysis. Moreover, teaching about social inequality from a single-axis perspective may delay the learning process, for it initially encourages new learners to become conversant with a single-framed rubric, and then later asks them to undo that same learning in order to adopt a more complex, holistic, intersectional application. Finally, we find that an intersectional approach decreases student resistance to examining white privilege.

In spite of its many advantages, approaching social justice issues and advocacy from an intersectional perspective is not an easy task. I (Andrea) see it as something akin to teaching beginners to play chords on a guitar rather than single notes. Though it is a formidable challenge, the obstacles presented when teaching about privilege from this perspective can be overcome with patience and practice.

The Matrix Framework: Privilege as Key to Intersectional Teaching

The concept of privilege is core to our approach to teaching intersectionally. We believe that, by bringing privilege to the fore, the obstacles identified by Goodman and Jackson (2012) and Luft and Ward (2009), respectively, can be avoided. We focus on the dynamics of privilege and oppression and advocate adopting an intersectional framework from the outset in all of our classes, including those that ostensibly focus on one primary category.

We refer to our pedagogical approach as the "Matrix of Privilege and Oppression Framework" (Ferber, 2010). Other scholars have referred to the operations of oppression, inequality, and intersectionality as a "matrix." Like the tapestry analogy mentioned above, the idea of a matrix evokes images of intersecting dynamics. For example, Hardiman and Jackson (1997) depicted the "Social Oppression Matrix" as a series of stacked boxes, and explain:

> In our model, social oppression is maintained and operationalized at three levels: the individual, the institutional, and the societal/cultural [and] illustrates the dynamic workings of these three levels along three dimensions that operate to support and reinforce each other: the context, the psychosocial processes, and the application.
>
> (p. 18)

They use the term "matrix" to demonstrate the complicated ways in which systems of oppression operate across all sectors and dimensions of society. Their concept of the matrix refers specifically to the context and intersecting levels where inequalities operate.

Our use of the term "matrix" is more directly inspired by Collins' (2000) concept of the "Matrix of Domination." In this work, as well as others, she demonstrated that the entire paradigm for thinking about race, gender, and class shifts when Black women are placed at the center of analysis. The new paradigm is an intersectional one, which eschews additive approaches or attempts to hierarchize oppressions, and instead reveals a much broader politics of domination in which systems of race, class, gender, sexuality, etc., all participate. Collins (2000, 2004) argued that everyone experiences privilege and oppression in varying degrees and that our experiences of privilege and oppression shift according to where we are physically located at any given time and in any given social, political, or historical context. Her concept of the matrix refers specifically to the intersecting axes of oppression and privilege, such as race, class, gender, disability, and other categories, which all operate as systems of domination and subordination.

Our Matrix Framework is not a theoretical model, but rather a method for teaching that puts into practice the insights of intersectional theorists, such as Collins (2000), and connects these with an emphasis on the importance of explicitly examining privilege. The laboratory for testing our own Matrix Framework has always been our classrooms. As scholars conducting intersectional research and committed to intersectional theory, we have worked together over many years building a framework for intersectional teaching. The Matrix of Privilege and Oppression Framework centrally informs our annual curriculum transformation workshop, "The Knapsack Institute: Transforming Teaching and Learning," which is offered to faculty across the country. Several of us also edited an intersectional reader informed by our Matrix Framework (Ferber, Jiménez, Herrera, & Samuels, 2008).

The overarching features of the Matrix of Privilege and Oppression Framework emphasize many of the points discussed thus far. The Matrix Framework centrally informs our course development, curriculum, activities, and objectives across disciplines in any course that addresses one or more social identities, such as race or gender.

Components of the Matrix of Privilege and Oppression Framework

Social Identity Classifications are Socially Constructed

Our Matrix of Privilege and Oppression Framework is grounded in the well-established assumption that basic social identity group classifications (including race, gender, sexuality, disability, and other primary statuses) are socially constructed classification systems subject to change and that everyone's life is shaped by these constructed categories and statuses (see Ferber et al., 2008). Proof of the constructed nature of a category such as race is the fact that definitions of race vary cross-culturally and historically and reveal the interaction of biology and culture (Omi & Winant, 1994). A constructivist approach emphasizes the idea that discriminatory behavior and attitudes are learned through a process of socialization and acculturation. Social change is possible specifically because these classifications are constructed and discriminatory behavior is learned. This approach also points out that difference in itself is not the problem. The problem, as Johnson (2006) observed, is the meanings imposed on these perceived differences.

Integration of Privilege and Oppression

The Matrix Framework stresses the idea that privilege and oppression are interdependent; one cannot exist without the other (Kimmel & Ferber, 2010).

Inclusive and Connectionist

The Matrix Framework also advocates a connectionist, non-divisive approach, which is relational and begins by focusing on something that ties students together (Keating, 2007). In our classrooms, we emphasize that all students share the experience of some form of privilege, and consequently, all possess the potential to become change agents (as discussed below). We approach issues of privilege based on the assumption that White people have a race, men have a gender, and these factors affect their life experiences and opportunities. We also emphasize that virtually everyone has, at one time or another, experienced some form or degree of privilege. When we examine privilege intersectionally, and bring race, gender, class, sexuality, nationality and citizenship, dis/ability, and age into the big picture, we find that the experience of some form of privilege is something we all share.

Inequality as Harmful to All

In the same vein, our Matrix Framework emphasizes that narrow or single-focus group identities can be harmful (in varying degrees) to everyone, even those in privileged groups. For example, boys experience many negative effects from our culture's narrow definition of masculinity, which in turn, can be a central factor in bullying (Klein, 2012). In addition, even White people are inadvertently damaged by privilege (Goodman, 2011).

Proactive

The Matrix Framework highlights the conviction that individuals can choose to become social change agents and thereby actively become part of the solution. We make an effort to provide students with specific examples of role models from both privileged and oppressed groups fighting to end inequality. We also introduce them to social justice organizations that enact a practice of social justice that is intersectional (e.g., Incite! Women of Color Against Violence, www.incite-national.org). In addition, we provide examples of social justice movements that initially failed to adopt an intersectional approach, such as the Chicano Movement

(Ruiz, 1999) and the Civil Rights Movement (Robnett, 1999), both of which virtually ignored issues of gender. The idea that individuals can make a difference can be empowering for students who often feel overwhelmed and discouraged once they begin to understand the breadth and depth of inequality in the nation and in the world.

Does not Blame Individuals

Finally, the Matrix Framework emphasizes that privilege and oppression are not characteristics of individual people, but rather of society and institutions at large. According to Johnson (2006), "oppression and dominance name social realities that we can participate in without being oppressive or dominating people" (p. 13). Nevertheless, we are all enmeshed in these systems, and we cannot "opt out."

Praxis in the Classroom

Faculty in our Women's and Ethnic Studies program introduce students to the concepts of privilege and intersectionality early on in all of their courses. We focus on the idea that the various axes of inequality that shape our identities are inextricably related and interacting, and each one of us experiences privilege based on one or several of our social identities or primary statuses. I (Andrea) ask students to imagine that each person is like a barrel filled with bobbing apples of various sizes, which represent various social identities. All of the apples are present in the barrel all of the time, though some are submerged while others bob to the surface of the water. In the same way, all of our social identities are always present, though some become more salient or visible than others depending upon the given social, political, or historical context.

We employ a variety of strategies to train students to approach issues of social justice from an intersectional perspective. Pedagogical approaches offered by Adams, Bell, and Griffin (1997) and the teaching guide for *The Matrix Reader* (Samuels, 2009) provided many concrete activities that aid students in recognizing their own multiple social identities, both privileged and oppressed. Once students begin to look at their own lives intersectionally, they spend time examining which identities they are most aware of and why. This usually leads into a discussion of the invisibility and, to borrow Johnson's (2006) term, obliviousness of privilege.

We also encourage our students to consider their own social positioning in terms of models of social identity development to provide them with an opportunity to further consider the ways in which their understandings of their various social identities may differ. A wide variety of social identity models exist (see Helms, 1993; Wijeyesinghe & Jackson, 2012). Some models focus specifically on oppressed identities, others highlight specifically privileged identities, and several focus on single identities such as sexual orientation, race, or multiracial identity. While these types of developmental models have implicit limitations and can be reductionist, they provide a useful tool for asking students to consider their own positioning in terms of specific identities, as well as to personally connect with the subject matter. They also allow them to gain insight into the complexity of their identities by examining the ways in which they or others may be at different points developmentally in terms of the process of identity formation. This, in turn, provides them with insight into the range of emotions they and their classmates may experience or exhibit in the classroom. We (Andrea and Abby) have each developed specific activities using social identity development models that we have successfully implemented in our classrooms.

"Moving from the Other to the Self": Andrea's use of Social Identity Development Models

I (Andrea) provide students with a handout I created that summarizes Cross's (1991) "Model for Black Racial Identity Development" and Helm's (1993) "Model for White Racial Identity Development," drawn from the work of Tatum (1992). I ask students to analyze characters in films or fictional works or actual persons in small group discussions in order to determine where these individuals are located in these developmental models. Depending on the specific course, I alternately choose novels or films in which characters or persons can be easily placed in the various stages of development outlined in the handout. As a follow-up journal activity, I ask students to determine the placement of family and friends in the various stages. Finally, as a second journal assignment, students place themselves within a model. As a result of this exercise, students are initially able to distance themselves from the process as they analyze characters or persons in films or narratives. Then, they are gradually encouraged to consider the experience of family and friends as well as their own lived experience. By approaching the subject of identity development incrementally, students are able to intellectualize the process and thereby avoid becoming defensive or overly emotional. They are also introduced to the idea that racial identity development is a process that can result in integration and internalization once they become conscious. Finally, the student feedback I have received indicates that this particular activity encourages students to be more patient and understanding when dealing with friends and relatives. In effect, it allows them to intellectually comprehend where their friends and family members are coming from, and thereby better strategize regarding how to discuss issues of privilege with them, with the hope of helping them come to increased consciousness about the dynamics of inequality.

"Coming Face to Face with Privilege": Abby's use of Social Identity Development Models

As mentioned previously, our faculty and affiliates in Women's and Ethnic Studies often teach courses with titles that focus on one specific category, yet they still incorporate an intersectional approach. I (Abby) teach a course on the sociology of race relations. While this class is focused primarily on race, I utilize an intersectional lens. Students may be reading a text that examines the historical construction of Asian American identity, but I ask them to also consider the ways in which Asian American men and women's experiences have differed historically. For example, U.S. immigration policy often invited Asian men to come to the United States as laborers, and restricted Asian women from immigrating in order to prevent whole families from migrating to and staying in the United States. The class examines the impact this had on the social organization of immigrant men's lives, as well as on the families they often left behind. We also discuss the intersections of race and gender in immigration policy. In this manner, the course emphasizes the ways in which systems of racial inequality intersect with other systems of inequality both historically and currently, as well as the ways in which an individual's experience of race is always shaped by other significant social identities in varying contexts.

"Coming Face to Face with Privilege," the activity I (Abby) developed using a social identity development model, plays an important role in this class. Specifically, it is one way in which I implement our Matrix Framework and bring both privilege and intersectionality to the forefront. I developed a handout that provides a summary, as follows, of the more generic social identity development model provided by Goodman (2011).

Stage I: Naïve or No Social Consciousness

In this stage, individuals in both privileged and oppressed groups are some-what naïve and just becoming aware of differences between themselves and members of other social groups. In effect, individuals are still learning what it means to be a member of their social identity group. Numerous events transform children from naïve to accepting of their social dominance or subordination.

Stage II: Acceptance

The stage of acceptance represents some degree of internalization of the dominant culture's norms and ideology. The acceptance stage is described as ranging from passive to active, depending upon the relative consciousness and intentionality with which a person holds to the dominant belief system.

Stage III: Resistance

The resistance stage is one of increased awareness of the existence of privilege and oppression and their impact.

Stage IV: Redefinition

The focus of the redefinition stage is on creating an identity independent of the hierarchical system of oppression and privilege.

Stage V: Internalization

The main task in this stage is to incorporate the identity developed in the redefinition stage into all aspects of daily life. The process of refining identity can be ongoing as new sources of history, past feelings, or thoughts characteristic of earlier stages reemerge or are triggered. There is essentially no exit phase for this stage. The ongoing task is one of lifelong exploration and nurturance.

Students conduct this assignment outside of class. I (Abby) ask all students to carefully read the handout, and then to locate themselves in the model using *two* specific identities. At least one of the two identities must be race, and at least one must be a privileged identity. In this way, I ensure that all students are focusing on their racial identities, the subject of the class, while also focusing on the ways in which they experience some form of privilege. The focus on shared privilege serves to build connections and community among the students when we discuss this activity in the following session. I ask them to write up a two-page reflection on why they located themselves in the specific stages they selected for each of the two identities they chose. In the subsequent class meeting, we discuss the activity and I ask volunteers to share their answers. I never have a problem getting students to volunteer to do so, especially after one or two get the discussion started.

This activity serves to connect the students in their recognition that they are all selecting an advantaged identity to examine. It leads to the recognition that all of their classmates can relate to the experiences of privilege. The class consequently spends a great deal of time addressing the differences in these experiences (i.e., the fact that all oppressions are not the same and do not have the same impact or limitations).

This particular social identity activity has a number of specific effects. First, it disarms majority students' resistance, a frequently encountered obstacle (Case, this volume). Given the instructions, for example, White students are required to examine their whiteness as one of the two identities. More often than not, they select an oppressed (as opposed to privileged) identity as their second identity. This allows them to acknowledge an oppressed identity while, at the same time, preventing them from shifting the focus away from their white privilege. In this manner, I (Abby) directly avoid the problem of "the race to innocence" (Pierce, 2003, p. 199) that many teachers and facilitators experience when trying to examine race intersectionally. The race to innocence describes the tendency for White people to quickly shift their focus to an oppressed identity when utilizing an intersectional approach. The parameters placed on this activity prevent that from occurring. It implements what Collins (2000) referred to as a "both/and" approach, in that it asks students to examine both an oppressed identity and also requires White students to examine their white privilege. As many of my students have confirmed, by acknowledging that White people may experience various forms of oppression or discrimination based on gender, class, etc., White students feel more fully "seen," and are able to let down their resistance to examining their white privilege. This activity increases students' empathy, patience, and compassion for each other.

In respect to first-generation White students, some of whom come from families whose income is below the poverty line, it is understandable that they may feel resistant when they are told that they are the beneficiaries of white privilege. The reality is that they often do not feel privileged (Wise & Case, this volume). For example, I have taught a number of White male students who experienced homelessness as youths, and consequently, were resistant and felt attacked by the notion that they are privileged because they are White. In each case, they became angry and outspoken in class, arguing that they grew up in dire poverty and did not see any privilege in their lives. An intersectional approach was very successful in helping these students grasp the ways in which class and race intersected to shape their lives and opened up a space for them to recognize the many ways they have benefited from whiteness. For example, they were able to reexamine specific instances where they saw the differences in how White and Latino families were treated by the welfare system, shelter agencies, etc. They opened up to exploring the ways in which the lives of people in poverty in the United States are impacted by race and developed an interest in the dynamics of racism in the history of U.S. welfare programs.

For students of color, on the other hand, this activity counterbalances the experience of feeling victimized or targeted in courses on race. While they must examine where they are in terms of their racial identity, they are also required to select and examine a privileged identity. For some students, principally women of color, it may be the first time they have been asked to examine a privileged identity. This has been a particularly powerful experience for many students of color, who may be examining their heterosexual privilege, for example, for the first time.

While this activity is completed privately, students are invited to share their insights with the class in our follow-up conversation. "Coming Face to Face with Privilege" never fails to produce a richly nuanced discussion. Students of color often share their insights into the ways in which they are thinking about ways their privileged identities (in regard to heterosexuality, class, nationality and citizenship, or ability) impact their experiences of race. One African American woman, who focused on race and class for this activity and initially displayed vocal resistance in the first few class sessions, shared her epiphany that she could now see the ways that her upper-middle-class background shielded her from many of the forms of structural racism we were reading about. This recognition of intersectionality in her own life helped her to move beyond her resistance to seeing much of the racial inequality that exists. She was able to stop blaming other people of color for their failure to succeed and recognize that her own experiences of race and racism had been impacted by her social class status.

A second illustrative example is the experience of a Latina student, who chose to examine her race and her heterosexual privilege for this activity. At the end of the semester, she shared that this was the first time she had ever taken a class on race in which she did not feel angry, defensive, and disheartened. She said that when issues of race come up in most classes, she is usually one of the only people of color and feels forced to represent her race and play the role of educator. According to Blackwell (2010), this pattern is familiar to many students of color. In my (Abby's) class, while the focus was still on race, this student examined the ways in which her own heterosexual privilege shaped her organizing work in the local Latino/a community and the ways her work had inadvertently excluded LGBT Latinos/as. She grasped an opportunity to learn and grow in her understanding of the dynamics of exclusion within minority communities.

Seeing Beyond Binary Categories: Practicing Intersectional Analysis

Like Abby, I (Andrea) have developed specific strategies for encouraging students to read the world from an intersectional perspective. When teaching entry-level students in courses such as the Introduction to Race and Gender, I open the semester by introducing several core concepts, beginning with privilege as approached by Johnson (2006). Students are then asked to explore additional foundational concepts such as the constructed nature of primary statuses (Omi & Winant, 1994) and Collins' (2000) matrix of domination.

Once students have grasped these basic concepts and contemplated the complexity of their own social identities, I shift the focus away from the personal by assigning groups of three students to four interlinked essays, all of which treat specific topics or themes. In this manner, I attempt to minimize students' tendency to hijack or reframe (Gorski, 2011) the conversation according to their own personal experiences, privilege, or concerns. In a unit titled "Seeing beyond binary categories," for example, all students are required to read the following essays:

- Alsultany's (2002) "Los intersticios: Recasting moving selves," which addresses the conundrum of being caught on the hyphen and categorized in monolithic, cultural, ethnic or national categories;
- Martinez's (2005) "Seeing more than black and white," which takes up the subject of biracial identity;
- Rowan's (2001) "Sleeping with the enemy and liking it," which addresses bisexuality and the continuum of sexuality; and

- Smith's (1993) "Homophobia: Why bring it up," which discusses the phenomenon of homophobia within the Black community and the potentially negative effects of a race-centered approach to privilege and oppression.

After dividing the class into small discussion groups, I assign a single essay to each set of students. After about 20 minutes, the class reconstitutes as a single group. A lead learner from each group opens the general discussion by summarizing the main points of each respective essay and reporting on the group's conversation. I then ask the class why they think I clustered these particular essays. In responding, they are encouraged to consider the links among the essays. Then I ask the class to identify issues or historical or political circumstances that distinguish the essays. Throughout the conversation, students are urged repeatedly to consider what social statuses or categories are omitted or ignored in the assigned readings. For example, issues such as ageism, ableism, and class are not addressed in the "Seeing beyond binary categories" unit in general. In the same vein, Smith's (1993) essay did not treat the subject of gender in any depth, and Rowan's (2001) did not consider race. Influenced by a strain of feminist literary theory that originated in France in the early 1970s (commonly referred to as *écritoire féminine* or women's writing), I encourage students to pay particular attention to the silences and the gaps in the texts, a strategy I also employ in my literature classes. Clearly, the overarching connective tissue among the essays in the "Seeing beyond binary categories" unit is the tendency to treat the various social statuses as mutually exclusive categories. In addition to becoming aware of the shortcomings of a binary or single-axis approach to issues of privilege, students begin to consider the consequences of omitting social categories from a discussion of social equity.

The students continue this exercise for the remainder of the semester, treating alternating unit themes or subjects such as "citizenship" or "body image." Although they may not make easy connections among the essays from the very outset, with practice, the majority of my students to date managed to develop the capacity to critically analyze the assigned reading materials from an intersectional perspective in spite of the fact that all of the essays they are considering are not always intersectional. Because they are often working together in groups, they learn to see these connections from each other as well.

As the Introduction to Race and Gender course draws to a close, we conclude by analyzing social issues, such as poverty, or institutions, such as education, and proposing concrete solutions. At that point in the semester, a preponderance of students begin to independently identify the groups, categories, or issues that are silenced, marginalized, or omitted entirely from the discussion. Their demonstrated ability to approach these topics and issues in such a complex manner implies that they are contemplating group experiences and social interventions according to interactive factors such as race, ethnicity, class, gender, sexuality, religious orientation, citizenship, ableism, age, etc.

Conclusion: Not Just Wide, but Deep

One of the myths about intersectionality is that it asks us to focus on "everyone and everything." This is a fear we encountered when building our intersectional program. Many faculty members who had been previously housed in our stand-alone Women's Studies or Ethnic Studies programs feared that the curriculum would be watered down if we integrated these programs and that the focus on gender or race (respectively) would be lost. These fears, we discovered, were based on a misunderstanding of intersectionality. Rather than asking us to examine everyone and everything, an intersectional approach encourages us to consider whatever issue or category we are treating in a deeper, more inclusive manner. Sometimes, intersectionality may be implemented to provide a wider perspective, while other times it encourages us to go deeper. As these classroom examples clearly highlight, an intersectional approach does not have to distract attention away from race, but can instead provide more profound insights into its operations. Examining race intersectionally promotes consideration of every member within a particular racial group. It encourages questions about how the experiences of people in a specific racial group vary by age, gender, sexuality, class, or ability (e.g., the work of Evelyn Nakano Glenn, bell hooks, Andrea Smith, and Mary Romero). Rather than flattening difference, it opens up an exploration of internal-group differences and provides a check against homogenizing assumptions about "all Blacks" or "all women," for example.

It is not an exaggeration to say that the Matrix of Privilege and Oppression Framework has transformed our classrooms. Over the years, we have witnessed students' progress firsthand both in our classrooms and beyond. It is our consistent experience that a single-axis analysis artificially puts into relief a single identity and suggests that the various factors or primary statuses that shape experience are mutually exclusive. Ultimately, such an approach fails to address subjects such as the manner in which individuals are simultaneously members of many groups that are distinct yet interact to impact their lives simultaneously. As the African American Policy Forum (n.d.) suggests, employing an intersectional approach to privilege provides a prism through which to effectively analyze social problems and consequently shape more inclusive public policy and enact coalitional interventions and advocacy. In our experience, utilizing an approach that centers upon the concepts of connectivity, inclusion, privilege, and intersectionality helps preempt student resistance and hostility while facilitating transformational learning. Because our approach starts from the position of examining privilege, it avoids the pitfalls and problems encountered by other intersectional approaches that often lead to "escapism," whereby students may avoid examining their positions of privilege by focusing only on their oppressed identities. As Luft and Ward (2009) highlighted, "Nearly 20 years after its emergence, intersectionality remains one of the most vital and widely used concepts within feminist studies" (p. 100). Nevertheless, there are few resources available to guide educators in teaching intersectionally. Each year at our Knapsack Institute, we work directly with faculty from a wide range of disciplines who are able to successfully transform their pedagogical practice and empower students to connect with the concepts of intersectionality and privilege. It is our hope that the Matrix of Privilege and Oppression Framework can serve as a useful resource for other educators as well.

Note

1 Author order was determined alphabetically given that co-authors contributed equally to this work.

References

Adams, M., Bell, L.A., & Griffin, P. (Eds.). (1997). *Teaching for diversity and social justice*. New York, NY: Routledge.

African American Policy Forum. (n.d.). *A primer on intersectionality* [Online resource]. Retrieved from http://aapf.org/our-work/intersectionality/

Alsultany, E. (2002). Los intersticios: Recasting moving selves. In G. E. Anzaldúa & A. Keating (Eds.), *This bridge we call home* (pp. 106–109). New York, NY: Routledge.

Anzaldúa, G. (2007). *Borderlands/La frontera* (3rd ed.). San Francisco, CA: Aunt Lute Books.

Armstrong, M. J., & Wildman, S. M. (this volume). "Colorblindness is the new racism": Raising awareness about privilege using color insight. In K.A. Case (Ed.), *Deconstructing privilege: Teaching and learning as allies in the classroom* (pp. 63–79). New York, NY: Routledge.

Banks, C.A., Pliner, S. M., & Hopkins, M. B. (this volume). Intersectionality and paradigms of privilege: Teaching for social change. In K. A. Case (Ed.), *Deconstructing privilege: Teaching and learning as allies in the classroom* (pp. 102–114). New York, NY: Routledge.

Berger, M. T., & Guidroz, K. (2009). *The intersectional approach: Transforming the academy through race, class and gender*. Chapel Hill, NC: University of North Carolina Press.

Blackwell, D. M. (2010). Sidelines and separate spaces: Making education anti-racist for students of color. *Race Ethnicity and Education, 13*(4), 473–494. doi:10.1080/13613324.2010.492135.

Case, K.A. (2012). Discovering the privilege of whiteness: White women's reflections on anti-racist identity and ally behavior. *Journal of Social Issues, 68*(1), 78–96. doi:10.1111/j.1540-4560.2011.01737.x.

Case, K.A. (this volume). Beyond diversity and whiteness: Developing a transformative and intersectional model of privilege studies pedagogy. In K. A. Case (Ed.), *Deconstructing privilege: Teaching and learning as allies in the classroom* (pp. 1–14). New York, NY: Routledge.

Case, K. A., & Lewis, M. (2012). Teaching intersectional LGBT psychology: Reflections from historically Black and Hispanic serving universities. *Psychology and Sexuality, 3*(3), 1–17. doi:10.1080/19419899.2012.700030

Collins, P. H. (2000). *Black feminist thought: Knowledge, consciousness, and the politics of empowerment* (2nd ed.). New York, NY: Routledge.

Collins, P. H. (2004). *Black sexual politics: African Americans, gender, and the new racism*. New York, NY: Routledge.

Coston, B., & Kimmel, M. (2012). Seeing privilege where it isn't: Marginalized masculinities and the intersections of privilege. *Journal of Social Issues, 68*(1), 97–111. doi:10.1111/j.1540-4560.2011.01738.x.

Cross, W. E. (1991). *Shades of Black: Diversity in African-American identity.* Philadelphia, PA: Temple University Press.

Davis, A. Y. (1983) *Women, race, and class.* New York, NY: Vintage Books.

Davis, K. (2008). Intersectionality as buzzword: A sociology of science perspective on what makes a feminist theory successful. *Feminist Theory, 9*(1), 67–85. doi:10.1177/1464700108086364.

Dill, B. T., & Zambrana, R. E. (Eds.). (2009). *Emerging intersections: Race, class and gender in theory, policy and practice.* New Brunswick, NJ: Rutgers University Press.

Ferber, A. L. (2012). The culture of privilege: Color-blindness, postfeminism, and Christonormativity. *Journal of Social Issues, 68*(1), 63–77. doi:10.1111/j.1540-4560.2011.01736.x.

Ferber, A. L. (2010). Dismantling privilege and becoming an activist. In M. S. Kimmel & A. L. Ferber (Eds.), *Privilege: A reader* (2nd ed.). Boulder, CO: Westview Press.

Ferber, A. L. (2007). Whiteness studies and the erasure of gender. *Sociology Compass, 1*(1), 265–282. doi:10.1111/j.1751-9020.2007.00014.x.

Ferber, A. L. (1998). *White man falling: Race, gender and white supremacy.* Lanham, MD: Rowman & Littlefield.

Ferber, A. L., Jiménez, C., Herrera, A., & Samuels, D. (Eds.). (2008). *The Matrix Reader: Examining the dynamics of oppression and privilege.* New York, NY: McGraw-Hill.

Frankenberg, R. (1993). *White women, race matters: The social construction of whiteness.* New York, NY: Routledge.

Gilkes, C. T. (2001). *If it wasn't for the women: Black women's experience and womanist culture in church and community.* Maryknoll, NY: Orbis Books.

Goodman, D. J., & Jackson, B. (2012). Pedagogical approaches to teaching about racial identity from an intersectional perspective. In C. Wijeyesinghe & B. W. Jackson (Eds.), *New perspectives on racial identity development: Integrating emerging frameworks* (2nd ed., pp. 216–240). New York, NY: New York University Press.

Goodman, D. J. (2011). *Promoting diversity and social justice: Educating people from privileged groups* (2nd ed.). Thousand Oaks, CA: Sage.

Gorski, P. C. (2011). *Class, race, and images of Wilma: Complicating "white privilege."* Retrieved from www.counterpunch.org/2011/12/30/complicating-white-privilege/

Hardiman, R., & Jackson, B. W. (1997). Conceptual foundations for social justice courses. In M. Adams, L. A. Bell, & P. Griffin (Eds.), *Teaching for diversity and social justice: A sourcebook* (pp. 16–29). New York, NY: Routledge.

Helms, J. E. (Ed.). (1993). *Black and white racial identity: Theory, research, and practice.* Westport, CT: Praeger.

hooks, b. (1984). *Ain't I a woman: Black women and feminism.* Boston, MA: South End Press.

Johnson, A. G. (2006). *Privilege, power, and difference* (2nd ed.). New York, NY: Mayfield.

Kang, M. (2010). *The managed hand: Race, gender, and the body in beauty service work.* Berkeley, CA: University of California Press.

Keating, A. (2007). *Teaching transformation: Transcultural classroom dialogues.* New York, NY: Palgrave Macmillan.

Ken, I. (2010). *Digesting race, class, and gender: Sugar as a metaphor.* New York, NY: Palgrave Macmillan.

Kimmel, M. S., & Ferber, A. L. (Eds.). (2010). *Privilege: A reader* (2nd ed.). Boulder, CO: Westview Press.

Klein, J. (2012). *The bully society: School shootings and the crisis of bullying in America's schools.* New York, NY: New York University Press.

Lorde, A. (1984). *Sister outsider: Essays and speeches.* Freedom, CA: Crossing Press.

Luft, R. E. (2009). Intersectionality and the risk of flattening difference: Gender and race logics, and the strategic use of antiracist strategy. In M. Berger & K. Guidroz (Eds.), *The intersectional approach: Transforming the academy through race, class, and gender* (pp. 100–117). Chapel Hill, NC: University of North Carolina Press.

Luft, R. E., & Ward, J. (2009). Toward an intersectionality just out of reach: Confronting challenges to intersectional practice. In V. Demos & M. T. Segal (Eds.), *Perceiving gender locally, globally, and intersectionally* (*Advances in gender research,* Vol. 13) (pp. 9–37). Bingley, England: Emerald Group Publishing Limited. doi:10.1108/S1529-2126 (2009)0000013005.

Martinez, E. (2005). Seeing more than black and white. In M. L. Andersen, K. A. Logio, & H. F. Taylor (Eds.), *Understanding society* (2nd ed., pp. 178–183). Belmont, CA: Thomson Learning, Inc.

McCall, L. (2001). *Complex inequality: Gender, class, and race in the new economy.* New York, NY: Routledge.

McIntosh, P. (1988). *White privilege and male privilege: A personal account of coming to see correspondences through work in women's studies* (Working Paper No. 189). Wellesley, MA: Wellesley Centers for Women.

Minh-ha, T. T. (2009). *Woman, native, other: Writing postcoloniality and feminism.* Bloomington, IN: Indiana University Press.

Mohanty, C. T. (1991). *Third World women and the politics of feminism.* Bloomington, IN: Indiana University Press.

Moore, M. (2011). *Invisible families: Gay identities, relationships, and motherhood among Black women.* Berkeley, CA: University of California Press.

Omi, M., & Winant, H. (1994). *Racial formation in the United States: From the 1960s to the 1990s* (2nd ed.). New York, NY: Routledge.

Pierce, J. L. (2003). "Racing for innocence": Whiteness, corporate culture, and the backlash against affirmative action. *Qualitative Sociology, 26*(1), 53–70. doi:10.1023/A:1021404020349

Pratt-Clarke, M. A. E. (2010). *Critical race, feminism, and education: A social justice model.* New York, NY: Palgrave Macmillan.

Robnett, B. (1999). *How long? How long? African-American women in the struggle for civil rights.* Oxford: Oxford University Press.

Rowan, R. (2001). Sleeping with the enemy and liking it: Confessions of a bisexual feminist. In L. Karaian, A. Mitchell, & L. B. Rundle (Eds.), *Turbo chicks: Talking young feminisms* (pp. 238–244). Toronto, Canada: Sumach Press.

Ruiz, V. L. (1999). *From out of the shadows: Mexican women in twentieth-century America.* Oxford: Oxford University Press.

Samuels, D. R. (2009). *Teaching race, gender, class, and sexuality: A teaching guide to accompany The Matrix Reader.* New York, NY: McGraw-Hill.

Smith, B. (1993). Homophobia: Why bring it up? In H. Abelove, M. Barale, & D. Halperin (Eds.), *The lesbian and gay studies reader* (pp. 99–102). New York, NY: Routledge.

Spelman, E. (1990). *Inessential woman.* Boston, MA: Beacon Press.

Tatum, B. D. (1992). Talking about race, learning about racism: The application of racial identity development theory in the classroom. *Harvard Educational Review, 62*(1), 1–24.

Villalón, R. (2010). *Violence against Latina immigrants: Citizenship, inequality, and community.* New York, NY: New York University Press.

Wing, A. K. (Ed.). (2003). *Critical race feminism: A reader* (2nd ed.). New York, NY: New York University Press.

Wijeyesinghe, C. L., & Jackson, B. W. (2012). *New perspectives on racial identity development: Integrating emerging frameworks* (2nd ed.). New York, NY: New York University press.

Wise, T., & Case, K. A. (this volume). Pedagogy for the privileged: Addressing inequality and injustice without shame or blame. In K. A. Case (Ed.), *Deconstructing privilege: Teaching and learning as allies in the classroom* (pp. 17–33). New York, NY: Routledge.

Zerai, A. (2000). Agents of knowledge and action: Selected Africana scholars and their contributions to the understanding of race, class, and gender intersectionality. *Cultural Dynamics, 12*(2), 182–222. doi:10.1177/092137400001200205.

7

INTERSECTIONALITY AND PARADIGMS OF PRIVILEGE

Teaching for Social Change

Cerri A. Banks, Susan. M. Pliner, and Morgan B. Hopkins

The concept of privilege examines the ways social inequality actualizes in everyday lived experiences, systems, and institutions. Privilege theory recognizes that race, class, gender, ability, and other markers of identity are "socially constructed spaces with biological connections" (Banks, 2009, p. 11) and that those occupying the most valued markers (e.g., White, male, heterosexual, able-bodied) have lived experiences saturated with opportunities that translate into economic, social, and political power. McIntosh (1988) provided groundbreaking access into discussions about the everyday ways unearned advantages confer economic, social, and political power to White people and to men. This dialogue from McIntosh, a cornerstone of privilege theory, continues to offer a compelling point of entry into teaching and learning opportunities that analyze social inequity.

In recent years, scholars expanded the discourse of privilege by using it in conversation with other theoretical frameworks that contest inequality. This resulted in academic discussions about the lack of usefulness of privilege hierarchies, "mental processes associated with privileged group members" (Case, Iuzzini, & Hopkins, 2012, p. 2), the limitations of single identity analysis, the elucidation of pedagogies that challenge and reinforce privilege, and the impact of student learning about privilege (Banks, 2009; hooks, 2010; Kendall, 2006; Rothenberg, 2008; Wildman & Davis, 2008). We argue that the theory of intersectionality provides a critical framework for teaching and learning about privilege.

Dill and Zambrana (2009) recognized intersectionality as a critical field of study, claiming that the theory provides an analytic lens to interrogate identity disparities and that it contests existing ways of looking at structures of inequality, thus "transforming knowledge as well as the social institution in which they have found themselves" (p. 1). Along the same lines, additional scholars explained that the theory of intersectionality includes the understanding of race, class, and gender as well as other markers of identity as "mutually constructing features of social organization" (Collins, 2000, p. 299) that impact privilege and oppression in daily life on both individual and systemic levels (Brewer, 1999; Collins, 1995; Crenshaw, 1991; McIntosh, 2012).

While the discourse of privilege advanced the work of equity and social justice, academic conversations about privilege stayed in the realm of individual identity constructs or "-isms" language (Collins, 2009; Harro, 2000). Most of the existing work on privilege still centers the discussion on white skin privilege and male privilege (Adams, Bell, & Griffin, 1997; Kendall, 2006; Wise, 2008). Further, most privilege dialogue situates conversations about power into binaries and dichotomies, which articulates power dynamics as "oppressor and oppressed," "agent and target," or "dominant and subordinate" (Adams et al., 2010). This practice positions people into either/or categories and flattens the discussion about the ways identity, privilege, and power rule social structures (Brewer, 1999). In addition, this hinders learners from examining lived experiences in simultaneous ways. When teaching about privilege, such discursive limitations make it a challenge to help students understand that individuals can experience oppression related to identity (e.g., race or gender) while also experiencing or exercising privilege related to another identity (e.g., class, ability, or sexuality). Intersectionality is a critical concept when teaching about privilege that challenges binaries and dichotomies and makes the complex consequences of interconnected identities visible (Collins, 2000; Crenshaw, 1993).

Intersectional pedagogy addresses classroom equity and encourages teachers and students to acknowledge the complex ways identity and power inform teaching and learning. Intersectional theory forces students to analyze privilege outside of individual identity spaces and to consider broader discourse that includes political, social, and economic power structures. Educators can deepen classroom conversations about privilege by using intersectionality as a framework with which to explore the interplay of all features of identity and the ways they are connected to a continuum of privilege and oppression.

What follows is a discussion of ways to use the theory of intersectionality to advance the teaching of privilege. This model of privilege studies pedagogy (Case, this volume) includes strategies and assignments that help students understand their connections to privilege and how comprehending the concept of intersectionality deepens that connection. It will address how to overcome challenges related to this way of teaching and learning and use undergraduate student voices to illustrate how learning in this way moves them toward social justice activism. The students quoted herein (using pseudonyms) represent a range of identities. We made the purposeful choice of not describing the students using these markers. Instead, each student, in their comment, identified the features of identity that are salient in their individual process of learning about systemic privilege and intersectionality. This approach creates a focus on the student

learning process and reinforces that each person must recognize and acknowledge
the ways systemic privilege and oppression occur simultaneously.

Making Connections through Self-Reflection

> I never really spent much time considering how my race, religion, sexuality,
> and class affected me and others; these were positions where I held privilege
> and power. Instead, I identified myself more along the lines of positions in
> which I was oppressed, such as gender. Discovering the intersectionality of
> my race, class, gender and other positions has allowed me to view myself as
> an actor in the world both as a perpetuator and challenger of the systems
> which hold power structures in place.
>
> (Angela)

Establishing a personal connection to privilege engages students with the theoretical
concept and provides a foundation from which to enter the discussion. Kendall
(2006) encouraged all educators and students to do this reflective work and described
this initial stage of understanding privilege as "beginning with ourselves." As social
justice educators, we believe it is important, before introducing any course content,
that students must be prompted to identify and take ownership of their knowledge,
beliefs, and experiences related to identity and privilege. This includes articulating
their current thinking about their own identity, and those of others, and a discussion
of how they make meaning of that articulation. We also require them to discuss how
they determine their position in the larger political, institutional, and social structures,
how they recognize their biases within the systems of which they are a part, and
what this means for their daily lives. This common entry point allows all students to
claim an initial position and readies them to participate in the course content from
a solid sense of individual accountability prior to exploring the intersections of
identity and structural and systemic inequality.

Assignment: The Self-Interview

We invite students to enter into this discussion through an assignment that requires
them to conduct a tape-recorded self-interview. Using a guide purposefully
designed to incorporate an intersectional framework, students ask themselves
questions as if they were being interviewed. Students must record the interview
and they are assured that their answers are kept confidential. We do not listen to
the recording or share the recording with others, so students can respond honestly
and without feeling pressured to defend or feel embarrassed about their
experiences, positions, or beliefs. The interview protocol covers:

* *Experience and Contact* (e.g., When did you first notice that people were
  different? What did you notice? What was your neighborhood like? Where
  did you go to school?).

- *Viewpoints and Perspectives* (e.g., Do wealthy people have advantages in our society? How are people of different faiths perceived? How do the media portray people with disabilities? How do these perspectives inform your life?).

This broad protocol allows students to review a wide range of experiences they have had related to identity, including occurrences that they may not have connected to identity at the time. They then begin to explore their feelings and perspectives about those events, how they developed those ideas, and the impact that has had in their lives.

Once students complete the interview, they write a reflective essay on the process and answer questions (e.g., What were the points of comfort or discomfort? What questions came up for you during the self-interview? What would you like to know more about? Where do you think your beliefs come from?). This self-reflection gives students glimpses into their relationship with identity and privilege in complex ways. It positions them in both attitude and knowledge, helps confirm their relationship with these ideas, and prepares them for course content that includes a broader intersectional approach to systemic and structural inequality. At the end of the semester, the students listen to their recordings again and write another final reflection. This allows them to track and document their learning and its impact on their beliefs.

Engaging the Individual with the Systemic

The most uncomfortable I felt during the interview was when addressing issues of race. I am aware that I carry the "invisible backpack," as a professor once referred to it, of the privilege of being White. I am aware that this will give me unfair advantages in the world. I don't like to talk about it because I'm ashamed that I have this leg up without having to do anything to obtain it. I like to work hard for what I have, and race isn't something I can control or choose. The question "Is your race a sense of pride for you?" especially made me uncomfortable, because I am often not proud to be White. Historically, White people have been terribly prejudiced and hateful of other races, and that does not represent who I am at all.

(Donna)

The questions that asked what it meant to be a part of my racial and class group provided discomfort for me. This is because I am not quite sure of the answer to these questions. I have always classified myself based on my personality, ideas, beliefs, morals, and backgrounds. I never really thought of thinking of myself in terms of race or class, so I did not know what it meant to be a part of that group because I never thought of myself in those terms.

(Barb)

Donna and Barb's reflections demonstrate that learning about the theory of privilege comes with its own set of challenges. Privilege theory requires learners to examine the ways privilege confers unearned advantages on dominant identities in society and how those advantages manifest in everyday social, political, and economic structures (McIntosh, 1988; Wildman & Davis, 2008). Specifically, challenges frequently surface when examining one's role in maintaining inequitable power structures and how one benefits from systemic privilege, whether intentional or not. For many students, this recognition about privilege bumps aggressively up against their sense of self, conflicts with their upbringing, and challenges their overall position in the world. Such dissonance can cause confusion, denial, and even pain as students begin to acquire a lens that allows them to see systemic privilege (i.e., privilege is unearned, privilege is often invisible, privilege and oppression happen simultaneously) and work to understand it in their individual lives (Kimmel & Ferber, 2003; Perrin et al., this volume). Though teaching about privilege invites difficult conversations with students, intersectionality can mitigate student discomfort by moving the conversations from strictly individual to more systemic dialogue.

Assignment: The Concept List

In order to help students begin to think of privilege systemically, we ask students to keep a concept list in our courses. Each time we present new theory, students must:

- list the theory;
- keep track of the discussions and readings that explain and define the theory;
- discuss the theory in conversation with the concept of intersectionality;
- explain the impact of the theory on discussions of identity; and
- jot down any questions they have about the theory and its application.

Assigning readings that show the interplay of these theoretical spaces and having students engage beyond their definitions sets the stage for critical and analytical thinking, writing, and dialogue. It also helps students begin to understand their relationship to privilege and identity as systemic. For example, in order to comprehend privilege, students must understand concepts of social location and dominance (two of the concepts included on the list). A typical theoretical question might be, "What is the relationship between social location, privilege, and dominance?" An intersectional framework alters the question to ask, "In what ways does an understanding of multiple social locations inform conversations about dominance and privilege?"

For Donna, quoted earlier, the answer to this intersectional question would allow her to understand that privilege and oppression occur at the same time and expand her discussion of "shame about having a leg up" to one that includes the complexities of being able-bodied, heterosexual, White, and a woman. This intersectional approach provides a fuller representation of the continuum of privilege and oppression that allows her to use her privileged identities to understand systemic inequalities and challenge the oppression and dominance that comes with marginalized social locations. For Barb, the intersectional approach could motivate her to think about the complexities of her own identity. It would help her realize that all of our "personality, ideas, beliefs, morals and backgrounds" (Barb) exist within a complex structure that outside forces shape and evaluate (Harro, 2000). Whether intended or not, her race, class, and other markers of identity do matter. Those identity markers shape the way people and institutions place her in the world, how society determines when to confer privilege or oppression, and the way she responds to imposed social expectations, either deliberately or instinctively.

Assignment: Privilege List

After students engage in self-reflection through the self-interview and begin creating and utilizing a concept list in class discussions and in their writing assignments, we ask them to create a privilege list following McIntosh's model (1988) and take an extra step to make the list reflect their intersecting identities. This process helps students begin to connect individual experiences with identity to larger social structures that both shape and reflect those experiences. The process also unearths some of the challenges students face when grappling with understanding the definition of systemic privilege.

Recently, one student's privilege list included the statement: "I have privilege as a woman because when I get pulled over by a male police officer I can cry and get out of a speeding ticket, but a man who cries is thought of as weak and still gets a ticket." For this student, crying to get out of a speeding ticket is a privilege related to gender because her current critique of the world tells her that a man would face ridicule for attempting the same thing and would ultimately not be successful. Since we discuss systemic privilege and intersectionality together in our courses, the class can collectively test the merits of her assertion with questions such as:

- What are the implications of a woman crying? What are the implications of a man crying? Why?
- Where does the power lie in this scenario? Why?
- What other theoretical concepts may apply and what do they add to this discussion?
- What if the officer is female? What if the driver were a gay male?
- Are women of all races afforded the same vulnerability?
- How does race and class inform this interaction?

As students move through the questions, it becomes clear, for example, that the stereotype of women as weak and in need of protection, an example of benevolent sexism, is prominent in terms of being a perceived benefit (Glick & Fiske, 1996). They recognize that this stereotype derives from a system of male dominance, most often specific to White women and women of color deemed pretty by European beauty standards. They ultimately concluded that the described benefit does not qualify as unearned advantage for women, and occurs as a result of systemic marginalization and oppression. They also see that the systemic marginalization and oppression due to male dominance also harms men, who cannot cry without fear of being read as weak, gay, or mentally ill. This analysis demonstrates a sophisticated and nuanced understanding of privilege using an intersectional lens. This process fosters critical thinking and analytical reasoning to help students understand the systemic implications of individual experiences and move past the kind of discomfort, guilt, and shame that Donna and Barb discussed earlier and that scholars have identified as a barrier to learning about privilege (Pliner & Banks, 2012; Wise & Case, this volume).

Helping students understand the difference between privilege at the systemic level and its connection to dominance and intersecting social locations advances their knowledge and understanding of the complexities of their own beings. It also allows them to confront their feelings of shame, guilt, or blame within an academic context that has compelling real-world application. As Donna learned more about her intersecting social identities and their relationship to privilege, her comments reflected a movement from an individual analysis to a more systemic one. Later in the course, in response to a reading, she stated:

> I did not have an easy time with this reading. To be told that as a White woman I am systematically and unknowingly oppressing those around me was not an easy thing for me to digest. Privilege is not something that you choose, and it also is not something you can give back. It is, however, a tool you can use to work toward change.
>
> (Donna)

From our experience, the severity of oppression makes it a challenge for students from marginalized backgrounds to understand the ways they may have privilege. For example, as Jarrid explains below, intersectionality provides a framework for students to understand the ways most people received some form of unearned advantage and accept the responsibility to use it to challenge oppression. He stated:

> Now that I have had the experience of learning about intersectionality, it has broken me out of that mentality that I am just being held down by the "White man" and that I am being picked on. Now I realize I am much more than a Black man in the world, but I am also an educated, able-bodied

Black man. I have learned not to take for granted the things I am privileged to have. But I have also learned that along with my privilege I have the influence to help make a difference for those who are not as privileged as I am. I have now realized that my job as a middle class, straight, Christian, able-bodied male is that I have the authority to help make change. No longer am I ignorant to the beliefs about the LGBT community . . . now I am more respectful to women and have a sense of urgency when hearing or witnessing women being oppressed on an individual or systemic level.

(Jarrid)

Using intersectionality to help students move from the individual analysis of privilege to a systemic analysis of privilege deepens their understanding of the ways the concept informs social inequity and gives them a framework for thinking about actions for social justice.

Outcomes: Student Learning and Social Change

I think the most important thing is becoming aware of the systems of oppression that we unknowingly help to maintain. As long as we recognize the ways in which we are privileged, we can work to get rid of them. The way to do this would most likely be to inform others about their own unearned privileges. The more people are informed about their role in systems of oppression, the less power these systems will have.

(Justin)

In our courses, we are clear with students that our work as educators has a larger agenda that includes teaching for social change. Thus far, we described a teaching and learning process that outlines the following steps:

• self-questioning and self-reflection;
• the acquisition of theoretical knowledge through course content; and
• skills and strategies that help apply advanced understandings to everyday life.

On its own, this process has intellectual merit. The ideal learning outcome is when students, like Justin, recognize the significant role that understanding systemic privilege can have on how they move in the world and make choices to address systemic inequity with social justice activism. Addressing social action defines an additional step in the process.

Analyzing students' written coursework, class participation, and conversations with them after graduation demonstrated to us that students moved through a process. In other words, learning about privilege through an intersectional lens and moving towards working for social change. We recognize that every student moves through the learning process differently and will manifest the application of learning about privilege in distinct ways. Morgan (co-author), who shares her story below, took classes with both Cerri and Susan as an undergraduate student. When we began to work on this chapter together, it became clear that her story was a direct representation of the process we described above.

Morgan's Story

Entering my (Morgan's) first year of college, I felt drawn to Women's Studies. In my high school Women's Studies course, most of the women we learned about were second-wave feminists such as Gloria Steinem, the mother of feminism and a pioneering force that inspired historical activism. While these [White] women are irreplaceable figures within the feminist movement, they do not represent the complexities of identity, power, privilege, or systemic social inequalities within the movement. Although the theoretical content intrigued me enough to take Introduction to Women's Studies in my first semester of college, I still felt nervous to claim the label "feminist." In retrospect, my first two Women's Studies classes lacked both a term and an analytical lens that might speak to my experience growing up. For example, I only know one half of my ethnicity. Because of my physical appearance, I often received many questions about my racial and ethnic background. As I got older, I realized that White people assumed I was White, while people of color would ask more questions as they tried to determine my racial identity and, thus, my place, group membership, or social position, especially as I navigated multiple college spaces. When I took courses with Susan and Cerri, I learned about intersectionality and used this approach to dissect my own experiences as well as systemic structures of oppression and privilege. Susan and Cerri challenged students to examine their identities and how identity has affected experiences, behaviors, and attitudes.

Learning about intersectionality completely shifted my feminist paradigm and identity. As a sophomore, I took a bi-disciplinary course that incorporated psychology and education called Race, Class, and Gender in Everyday Life. In this course, we learned about privileged identities through the acronym "SCWAMP" (Grinner, 2010). As Grinner (2010) explains, "SCWAMP is an intersectional framework that helps us understand that ideological positions are interconnected and relational and that these relationships are shaped and affected by the society in which they are embedded" (p. 181). Each letter in SCWAMP stands for a social location in our society afforded unearned privileges (straight, Christian, White, able-bodied, male, property-owning). The students in the class also suggested that we could add ["E" for] "English-speaking" to the end of the acronym. This exercise required students to apply intersectional theory to our own and our peers' experiences to develop deeper understandings about one another. For example, we would choose the social location "able-bodied" and list all the ways the able-bodied benefit from unearned advantage. We did this for each identity represented by SCWAMP. We then looked at all of the locations SCWAMP represents at once and discussed ways privilege changed if one or more features of SCWAMP changed (i.e., the different experiences of a *straight*, Christian, White, able-bodied, property-owning male and a *gay*, Christian, White, able-bodied, property-owning male). Participating in these exercises gave me a new understanding of the complexity of my identities and how they constantly shift and affect each other over time. I also learned that I could not just cry oppression because of my status as a woman in a patriarchal society without recognizing the ways I am afforded privilege through my other identities and social locations, such as being able-bodied and formally educated.

By the spring semester of my senior year, my awareness of privilege and intersectionality sometimes felt like a burden. My intersectional awareness helped me realize that my racially ambiguous physical appearance allowed me to navigate various spaces on campus. I started to use the privilege of being light-skinned to push back on injustices within the undergraduate institutional structures in ways that other students of color, those with more visible black and brown statuses, may not be able to do so successfully or feel safe doing so. I often felt I had to be the spokesperson for issues of identity in other courses and spaces on campus, which led to resentment due to my uncertainty about applying my academic under-standing of intersectional identities to create large-scale structural social change. I also felt frustrated because I had gained an understanding of intersectionality but struggled to apply it to my primary field of study. This discrepancy showed up when writing my honors thesis in social psychology, which also incor-porated intersectional theory. I found it difficult to keep an intersectional lens throughout my honors process because my psychology courses failed to effectively address the use of intersectionality in research methods or data analysis (Case et al., 2012).

Learning about the intricate system of privilege and oppression woven into our society can be really overwhelming and shake students' foundations. As an undergraduate student, I craved the bridge between the theory I learned in the classroom and the practical application of those theories. I struggled a lot with the questions of "What do I do now? What can I do?" after being confronted with my own privilege.

After graduating, I moved to the politically conservative state of Texas for graduate school. My understanding of privilege and intersectionality informed my approach to my graduate studies, as well as my activism and community organizing. In graduate school, I realized that my learning about the theory of intersectionality laid important groundwork for practice when I became more directly and purposefully involved in grassroots activism. For example, as an organizer of SlutWalk Houston, I found it impossible to ignore the widespread critiques of the "SlutWalk movement." Many women of color refused to participate in the event in their respective cities because of the lack of awareness among White organizers about the historical meanings of the word "slut" to women in communities of color. I brought this critique to my fellow (all White) organizers, and not one of them knew anything about the critiques. I attribute this to a lack of an intersectional lens. The group of core organizers of one of the largest SlutWalks in the United States, SlutWalk New York City, splintered after the march because of similar issues. Privilege and intersectionality continue to affect my activism in complex ways. This presents a constant challenge to look beyond my own identity and privilege and aim for inclusiveness in my own activism.

Throughout the second year of my graduate career, my passion deepened for issues regarding women's bodily autonomy. The growing political polarization around those issues pushed me to become directly engaged in grassroots organizing around legislation. As I began to learn more about the reproductive rights framework, I felt there were certain narratives missing from the discourse. The reproductive justice framework, which the SisterSong Women of Color Reproductive Justice Collective developed, focused on issues like the disparate access to health care for women of color and poor women in ways that the reproductive rights framework did not. In other words, if certain groups of people cannot access their legal rights to reproductive and health care services, then those rights are essentially useless. For me, this significant paradigm shift gave me an additional opportunity to apply the concept of intersectionality to my activism and to help others do so as well.

My intellectual knowledge of intersectionality makes me a more effective activist. My ongoing awareness of coexisting privileged and oppressed identities often takes difficult self-reflective work, but it allows me to organize in a more inclusive and intersectional way. It offers me a lens to manage the complexities of my experience, as well as the experiences of others, as I work toward social justice.

Privilege and Intersectionality as Empowering Pedagogy

Teaching privilege with an intersectional lens requires educators to engage in the process of understanding their own social identities within an intersectional framework and providing opportunities for students to do this also. This ongoing process occurs both inside and outside of the classroom. It allows both students and teachers to understand "the ways relations of power intersect with oppression" (Russo, 2009, p. 313) and allows for greater accountability for exercising privilege in the classroom and the world. Issues of social inequity and unearned privilege infiltrate every educational space, and all students deserve access to quality education and freedom from oppression as they pursue their degrees (Hale, 2004; Hurtado, Milem, Clayton-Pederson, & Allen, 1999). Intersectional pedagogy supports a learning environment with a range of opportunities to engage all students and to encourage student participation (Harper, 2008). This inclusive approach can dismantle resistance in the classroom and move students past the master narratives of guilt, shame, and blame in ways that binaries and dichotomies cannot (Pliner & Banks, 2012).

As educators, we acknowledge our own non-neutrality and openly share our worldviews and expectations with students. We do not demand that students subscribe to our way of thinking or share our values. We do, however, remain adamant that they become critical and analytical thinkers and writers. This includes gaining the skills to articulate multiple approaches and ideas and recognize the societal consequences to all beliefs. These conversations may be difficult, but utilizing intersectional pedagogy to teach privilege helps students develop a sophisticated and empowering sense of self and better understand the lives of others (Nash, Bradley, & Chickering, 2008). It empowers students to move towards an increasingly complex understanding of how privilege fits in structural and systemic inequity. Teaching privilege intersectionally stimulates purposeful conversations about social justice that can help students develop the capacity for action.

References

Adams, M., Bell, L. A., & Griffin, P. (Eds.). (1997). *Teaching for diversity and social justice*. New York, NY: Routledge.

Adams, M., Blumenfeld, W. J., Castañeda, C., Hackman, H. W., Peters, M. L., & Zúñiga, X. (Eds.). (2010). *Readings for diversity and social justice* (2nd ed.). New York, NY: Routledge.

Banks, C. A. (2009). *Black women undergraduates, cultural capital, and college success*. New York, NY: Peter Lang.

Brewer, R. M. (1999). Theorizing race, class, and gender: The new scholarship of Black feminist intellectuals and Black women's labor. *Race, Class, and Gender, 6*(2), 29–47.

Case, K. A., Iuzzini, J., & Hopkins, M. (2012). Systems of privilege: Intersections, awareness, and applications. *Journal of Social Issues, 68*(1), 1–10. doi:10.1111/j.1540–4560.2011.01732.x

Case, K. A. (this volume). Beyond diversity and whiteness: Developing a transformative and intersectional model of privilege studies pedagogy. In K. A. Case (Ed.), *Deconstructing privilege: Teaching and learning as allies in the classroom* (pp. 1–14). New York, NY: Routledge.

Collins, P. H. (1995). Symposium: On West and Fenstermaker's "Doing and difference." *Gender and Society, 9*(4), 491–494. doi:10.1177/089124395009004006

Collins, P. H. (2000). *Black feminist thought: Knowledge, consciousness, and the politics of empowerment* (2nd ed.). New York, NY: Routledge.

Collins, P. H. (2009). Emerging intersections: Building knowledge and transforming institutions. In B. T. Dill & R. E. Zambrana (Eds.), *Emerging intersections: Race, class, and gender in theory, policy, and practice* (pp. vii–xiii). New Brunswick, NJ: Rutgers University Press.

Crenshaw, K. (1991). Mapping the margins: Intersectionality, identity politics, and violence against women of color. *Stanford Law Review, 43*(6), 1241–1299. doi:10.2307/1229039

Dill, B. T., & Zambrana, R. E. (2009). Critical thinking about inequality: An emerging lens. In B. T. Dill & R. E. Zambrana (Eds.), *Emerging intersections: Race, class, and gender in theory, policy, and practice* (pp. 1–21). New Brunswick, NJ: Rutgers University Press.

Glick, P., & Fiske, S. T. (1996). The Ambivalent Sexism Inventory: Differentiating hostile and benevolent sexism. *Journal of Personality and Social Psychology, 70*(3), 491–512. doi:10.1037/0022–3514.70.3.491

Grinner, L. A. (2010). Hip-hop sees no color: An exploration of privilege and power in "Save The Last Dance." In R. Lind (Ed.), *Race/gender/media: Considering diversity across audiences, content, and producers* (pp. 180–187). Boston, MA: Allyn & Bacon.

Hale, F. (2004). *What makes racial diversity work in higher education? Academic leaders present successful polices and strategies.* Sterling, VA: Stylus Publishing.

Harro, B. (2000). The cycle of socialization. In M. Adams, W. J. Blumenfeld, R. Castañeda, H. W. Hackman, M. L. Peters, & X. Zúñiga (Eds.), *Readings for diversity and social justice: An anthology on racism, anti-Semitism, sexism, heterosexism, ableism, and classism* (pp. 15–21). New York, NY: Routledge.

Harper, S. (2008). *Creating inclusive campus environments for cross-cultural learning and student engagement.* Washington, D.C.: National Association of Student Personnel Administrators.

hooks, b. (2010). *Teaching critical thinking: Practical wisdom.* New York, NY: Routledge.

Hurtado, S., Milem, J., Clayton-Pedersen, A., & Allen, W. (1999). Enacting diverse learning environments: Improving the climate for racial/ethnic diversity in higher education. *ASHE–ERIC Higher Education Report, 26*(8). Washington, D.C.: The George Washington University Graduate School of Education and Human Development.

Kendall, F. E. (2006). *Understanding white privilege: Creating pathways to authentic relationships across race.* New York, NY: Routledge.

Kimmel, M. S., & Ferber, A. L. (Eds.). (2003). *Privilege: A reader.* Boulder, CO: Westview Press.

McIntosh, P. (1988). *White privilege and male privilege: A personal account of coming to see correspondences through work in women's studies.* Working Paper No. 189. Wellesley, MA: Wellesley Centers for Women.

McIntosh, P. (2012). Reflections and future directions for privilege studies. *Journal of Social Issues, 68*(1), 194–206. doi:10.1111/j.1540–4560.2011.01744.x

Nash, R., Bradley, D. L., & Chickering, A. (2008). *How to talk about hot topics on campus: From polarization to moral conversation.* San Francisco, CA: Jossey-Bass.

Perrin, P. B., Bhattacharyya, S., Snipes, D. J., Hubbard, R. R., Heesacker, M., Calton, J. M., Perez, R. M., & Lee-Barber, J. (this volume). Teaching social justice ally development among privileged students. In K. A. Case (Ed.), *Deconstructing privilege: Teaching and learning as allies in the classroom* (pp. 49–62). New York, NY: Routledge.

Pliner, S. M., & Banks, C. A. (2012). *Teaching, learning, and intersecting identities in higher education.* New York, NY: Peter Lang.

Rothenberg, P. S. (Ed.). (2008). *White privilege: Essential readings on the other side of racism* (3rd ed.). New York, NY: Worth Publishers.

Russo, A. (2009). The future of intersectionality: What's at stake? In B. T. Dill & R. E. Zambrana (Eds.), *Emerging intersections: Race, class, and gender in theory, policy, and practice* (p. 313). New Brunswick, NJ: Rutgers University Press.

Wildman, S. M., & Davis, A. D. (2008). Making systems of privilege visible. In P. S. Rothenberg (Ed.), *White privilege: Essential readings on the other side of racism* (3rd ed., pp. 109–115). New York, NY: Worth Publishers.

Wise, T. (2008). *White like me: Reflections on race from a privileged son.* Berkeley, CA: Soft Skull Press.

Wise, T., & Case, K. A. (this volume). Pedagogy for the privileged: Addressing inequality and injustice without shame or blame. In K. A. Case (Ed.), *Deconstructing privilege: Teaching and learning as allies in the classroom* (pp. 17–33). New York, NY: Routledge.

8

RECOGNIZING PRIVILEGE BY REDUCING INVISIBILITY

The Global Feminisms Project as a Pedagogical Tool

Desdamona Rios and Abigail J. Stewart

> As psychologists, feminists, and activists, we must ask who is not here, and
> how does that affect, shape, comfort, or define those of us in the room.
>
> (Fine, 2002, p. 19)

In the introduction to this collection, Kim Case describes an emotional outburst by a student about people of color being "animals" (Case, this volume). In the instance of Case's student, the high visibility of people of color as criminals represents a stereotype not easily challenged because of a lack of positive representations of people of color. Invisibility secures privilege because it allows for discrimination against others based on limited information about them. Invisibility differs from absence because privileged group members use invisibility as an exclusionary tool in educational curricula (among other domains). The absence of representations or information about marginalized groups may also be interpreted by privileged persons as a lack of participation, interest, or contribution by marginalized (and invisible) groups. Understanding invisibility as an act of exclusion provides privileged group members with an understanding of the power of representation for all groups of people across political and social domains. Invisibility is either absolute or relative, with absolute invisibility meaning that no representations of a particular group exist, whereas relative invisibility implies limited representation, including misrepresentations and negative representations of a particular group (Fryberg & Townsend, 2008). Additionally, intersectional invisibility renders some groups invisible at intersections of more than one subordinated status (Purdie-Vaughns & Eibach, 2008), as experienced by Black feminists and documented in the book *All the Women are White, All the Blacks are Male, But Some of Us are Brave* (Hull, Scott, & Smith, 1982). Groups who see limited or no representations of their group face the difficult task of resisting negative stereotypes because of a lack of positive examples with which to identify (Steele, 1997). Without knowledge of positive counter examples, privileged group members may not challenge negative stereotypes about marginalized groups (Hegarty & Pratto, 2001; Stewart, Latu, Branscombe, Phillips, & Denney, 2012). In the worst case, people who do not fit the implicit prototype of their identity groups, such as women of color or women with disabilities, may be rendered totally invisible in the imagination of students. Asking students to list the names of famous people of color or persons with disabilities often results in a list of mostly men of color and only men with disabilities, indicating gender privilege in both instances.

Peggy McIntosh (1988) cautioned against imagining privilege as an achievement to be coveted. Privilege operates within an invisible system that normalizes the dominance of one group over another regardless of their intention or desire. In this system of power, those with unearned privilege reinterpret basic human rights, such as access to education, safe housing, health care, and reproductive freedom, as privileges earned under the assumption that everyone has equal access to the same resources (Wise & Case, this volume). Our particular focus includes these unearned privileges, including those that accrue to some groups simply because they belong to socially dominant or high-status groups.

The following sections offer strategies for teaching students about the ways in which invisibility maintains unearned privilege, as well as interventions for making the invisible visible. We use examples from the Global Feminisms Project (GFP), an archive of interviews with women activists and scholars from China, India, Poland, Nicaragua, and the United States, to illustrate these points. Key questions for teachers include:

- Without consistent and frequent examples from instructors of groups who are invisible to some degree, how will students fill these knowledge gaps (if they seek the information at all)?
- How does invisibility of information facilitate students imagining that they earned their privilege when, in many cases, privilege gets granted rather than earned?

Working on the GFP, we learned much about the role of invisibility in our own lives. Even as feminists who consider ourselves to be allies to most groups of people, we discovered some social issues remained invisible to us. For example, the invisibility of disability in mainstream contexts as well as the absence of disability in my (Desdamona's) family rendered the disabled invisible in my imagination. After participating as an audience member for the taping of disability rights activist Adrienne Asch's interview, I recognized disability as a marginalized and invisible identity. As a result, I now include disability issues across my curricula to reduce the invisibility of this marginalized group. Providing diverse exemplars in curricula moves privileged students away from stereotypes or fragmented ideas about "other" groups, provides marginalized students with exemplars with which they can identify (Rios, Stewart, & Winter, 2010), and illuminates the corners in which groups with intersecting subordinate identities become invisible (Purdie-Vaughns & Eibach, 2008).

The Global Feminisms Project

The GFP is an archive of interviews with 53 women activists and scholars from China, India, Poland, Nicaragua, and the United States, and two additional interviews with women born in India now residing in the United States (for overviews of the project, see Lal, McGuire, Stewart, Zaborowska, & Pas, 2010; Stewart, Lal, & McGuire, 2011). Although maintained by the Institute for Research on Women and Gender at the University of Michigan, each country's GFP project team selected their interviewees and developed their interview protocols based on their own criteria. Interviews include background information about the interviewee's life, her work, and reflections on her work as it relates to feminism. While interview questions varied across each interview, site coordinators video-recorded all interviews, which spanned 1 to 3 hours. The interviews are available in both written and video form on the GFP website (www.umich.edu/~glblfem). Contextual materials about each site and interviewee are also available on the website.

The archive offers a wide range of interviewees for each site. For example, the India site includes the founders of the academic fields of women's studies and women's history in India (Neera Desai and Vina Mazumdar); a women's rights attorney (Flavia Agnes), a performance artist (Mangai) and writer (Mahasweta Devi), as well as activists in opposition to dowry (Shahjehan Aapa), the legalization of prostitution (Jarjum Ete), a women's mosque (D. Sharifa), and environmental issues (Lata Pratibha Madhukar). Some of these women had educated parents, and have advanced degrees from Western institutions; others had parents with no education, and they themselves have very little education. Some are from relatively privileged castes and others from under-privileged castes. They come from several regions in India and grew up in different religions and speak different languages. This diversity characterizes the women interviewed for the China, Nicaragua, Poland, and United States sites.

How Do I Teach about What Students Can't See?

Invisibility operates at many levels and across many domains to create and maintain privilege (Fryberg & Townsend, 2008). In educational contexts, social representations promote positive possible selves for privileged students, such as discussing only White male presidents of the United States as examples of leadership (Ruvolo & Markus, 1992), while rendering invisible other information that might inform positive possible selves for marginalized students, such as the leadership of women and people of color who have led social movements. Making some groups invisible reinforces an understanding of who matters in a given context. Privileged group members learn to expect the unearned privilege of consistent representation of identity-matched exemplars, whereas marginalized group members imagine earning the privilege of representation by participating or contributing in a noteworthy way. At the most general level, the GFP offers multiple examples of different types of women in different roles who can serve as positive exemplars for both recognizing and challenging unearned privilege. Additionally, the archive provides marginalized students identity-matched exemplars with which to identify, thus providing a privilege that all students should have.

The GFP interviewees identify examples of the use of visibility and invisibility to create and maintain privilege, especially at specific intersections such as feminists of color, young feminists, anti–capitalist U.S. feminists, and Christian Indian feminists. Additionally, the topics covered in the archive provide multiple contexts with which to ground conversations about diverse groups of women involved in various types of activist work. For example, the narratives include a prominent theme of education, including examples of women who had access to education and, subsequently, access to knowledge or professions that empowered them to pursue key goals in their activism. An important point to make for students is that these women acknowledge and use their privilege to champion for others who do not enjoy the same access to the opportunities they have. Privileged students may believe that education is accessible to all people, and that all groups of people enjoy the same quality of education. Asking students to consider their own assumptions about educational access helps them to reflect on educational privileges they have but do not recognize. Beyond this example, the GFP archive provides a rich source of illustrative examples of invisibility in terms of creating and maintaining privilege across multiple contexts.

"I'm Privileged? I Don't See It": Overlooking Privilege at the Intersection of Identities

Teaching Goals and Main Concepts

In her introduction, Case (this volume) offers a model of privilege studies that includes the need to recognize multiple intersections of privilege and oppression. Intersectionality (Cole, 2009; Crenshaw, 1991; Hurtado, 1996) is a standard analytic tool taught in gender and women's studies, psychology of women, and ethnic studies courses. The theory of intersectionality highlights the ways in which individual persons occupy multiple social locations (gender, race or ethnicity, social class, ability, occupational role, etc.) at the same time, rather than a single category. Intersectionality offers a way to recognize intragroup differences by highlighting experiential differences at the intersection of multiple social identities located in a hegemonic structure (thus, a middle-class White woman's and a poor White woman's life experiences differ because of social class; Crenshaw, 1991). The results of a system that differentially grants power and privilege to different groups of people include a person experiencing more or less visibility based on holding one or more subordinate identities (Coston & Kimmel, 2012). Possessing multiple subordinate-group identities renders a person "invisible" relative to those with a single subordinate-group identity (Purdie-Vaughns & Eibach, 2008). Arguably, groups with privileged identities, including White people, heterosexuals, people without disabilities, and men, will implicitly interpret their standpoint as representative of a universal standard, norm, or experience. People define those who hold multiple subordinate identities as non-prototypical members of their respective identity groups, thus rendering them marginalized members within an already marginalized group (Purdie-Vaughns & Eibach, 2008). Holding one subordinate identity may render some people highly visible and therefore targets of discrimination (e.g., African American males when driving, White women in U.S. electoral politics; Coston & Kimmel, 2012). Emphasizing the point that being invisible may have different and sometimes worse consequences than being highly visible facilitates an opportunity for students to reflect on important intersections of more or less privileged identities.

Students who hold one or more marginalized identities may overlook the privilege that their non-marginalized identities hold (Wise & Case, this volume). For example, White women or White gay men may not acknowledge the race privilege they have, or heterosexual men of color may not acknowledge their heterosexual and gender privilege. Holding some privilege, albeit context specific, means that prototypical members of a subordinate group enjoy being perceived as credible in both knowledge production and leadership status compared with members who hold a non-prototypical status, such as women of color or gay men of color (Purdie-Vaughns & Eibach, 2008).

Teaching Examples from the GFP Archive

Using GFP interviews to compare women's experiences, whether in different national settings or within a single setting (e.g., McGuire, Stewart, & Curtin, 2010), provides students with opportunities to imagine groups in more complex ways. For example, although many of the interviewees from India are Hindu, among the scholar activists represented in the group of Indian feminists, D. Sharifa is a Muslim feminist actively engaged in efforts to create a female-friendly mosque. Equally, Flavia Agnes describes her struggle within Indian feminist circles to be recognized and accepted as Christian. In contrast, among the mostly Christian Polish interviewees, Bożena Umińska discusses the intersection of her Jewish identity and her feminism within an anti-Semitic and misogynist context. Examining the experience of religious minorities in these different contexts can illuminate commonalities across very different identities and experiences, as well as differences between feminists in a single context.

Less routinely discussed intersectional invisibilities are described by other scholar-activists in the GFP. For example, Li Huiying (China site) talks about the difficulty of being a single woman in Communist China with no way to make a claim for private domestic space, and Grace Lee Boggs (U.S. site) defines herself at the intersection of her ethnicity and gender (an Asian American woman), but also describes herself as old, one of the most invisible subordinate identities in the United States.

Classroom Application

Recognizing the dynamic nature of intersectional invisibility includes highlighting the point that even one privileged identity offers a respite from negative experiences that people who hold multiple marginalized identities cannot access. This pedagogical strategy depends on examples of the way that women in the GFP use their own privilege in one sense (e.g., class privilege) to challenge unearned privileges they recognize elsewhere. Students are often resistant to thinking about their own intersectional identities and identifying their privileged and marginalized identities. In an exercise of this nature, they are challenged to think about their experiences and the experiences of others they assume to be similar to themselves. This reflection promotes an important step toward recognizing privileges held by some and the invisible status held by others. Assigning a final paper or writing an exam question that asks students to apply key concepts or research findings to a GFP interview allows them to apply the theory to someone's real-life experiences. Contextual information about the interviewee and the video-recorded interview and transcript can be accessed on the GFP website. Encouraging students to use both formats allows them to refer to the text while viewing the video-recording, with the transcript serving as a reference for direct quotes for identifying:

1. intersectionality or intersectional invisibility as discussed by the GFP interviewee;
2. privileges related to some identities held by the women and the use of this privilege to challenge unearned privilege held by others; and
3. their own privilege even among assumptions that have none.

This exercise encourages students to practice identifying privilege at the intersection of identities in the life of another person and directs them toward reflection of their own invisible privileges.

Invisibility as a Tool for Heterosexism and Homophobia

Teaching Goals and Main Concepts

Sexual identity and heterosexism commonly receive coverage in courses taught in disciplines that explore feminist, queer, and critical race theory. However, the way students learn about non-heterosexual identities varies, including the maintenance of heterosexual privilege via the invisibility of sexual minorities. Importantly, students should understand activism and coalitional work as central to many area studies, including gender and women's studies, queer studies, and ethnic studies. The GFP contains four interviews with women who self-identify as lesbians and who offer accounts of both absolute and relative invisibility in academic settings as well as in the context of their activist work: Cathy Cohen and Holly Hughes (United States), Anna Gruszczyńska (Poland), and Ruth Vanita (India/United States; see Shapiro, Rios, & Stewart, 2010). In their narratives, Cohen, Hughes, Gruszczyńska, and Vanita affirm the relative invisibility experienced by non-heterosexual students and challenge heterosexual students to consider their own invisible heterosexual privilege.

Teaching Examples from the GFP Archive

These four interviews lend themselves to comparative analysis by highlighting each woman's location as a citizen of a particular nation, in the academy, and as a participant in a social justice movement. The invisibility of lesbian, gay, bisexual, transgender, and queer (LGBTQ) issues is described by the women as a means to maintain heterosexual privilege and homophobic perspectives in their educational experiences. For example, Hughes and Gruszczyńska both discussed the invisibility of lesbians as role models and scholarship by lesbians in their education. Holly Hughes describes her early education as extremely conservative until her teacher, Anita Wendt, gave her "forbidden books ... like *The Autobiography of Malcolm X*, *I'm Okay, You're Okay*, [and] *Jonathan Livingston Seagull*" that informed Hughes of alternative political viewpoints. In her GFP interview, Hughes recalled that her feelings of romantic love for her teacher inspired her to seek out information about lesbians. However, the relative invisibility of lesbians in any scholarly texts reinforced the idea of same-sex love as abnormal.

> So, I went to the most important sexual authority of that time ... Dr. David Reuben's *Everything You Always Wanted to Know About Sex But Were Afraid To Ask* ... I noticed that male homosexuals had their own chapter, but the females were just a footnote under prostitution ... I thought that homosexuality had something to do with, you know, attraction between two people of the same sex, but not according to David Reuben, oh no ... the most important part of a homosexual experience, male or

female, is their compulsive erotic relationship to household appliances. This is not fiction.

(Holly Hughes)

Using Hughes' example encourages heterosexual students to reflect on the unearned privilege of seeing their lives validated by positive representations of heterosexuality in the media (movies, television, magazines) and in their academic curricula (McIntosh, 1988).

Anna Gruszczyńska made a similar point in her GFP interview when she describes the absolute invisibility of women writers, more generally, and lesbian writers in particular in her Spanish Language and Literature graduate study program, pointing out that, "For the whole year, my mentor didn't even pronounce the word 'lesbian.'" Hughes' experiences of seeking alternative information sources about lesbians and Gruszczyńska's experience with exclusionary practices are good starting points for encouraging student reflection about the relationship between positive social representations of your group and a positive self-construal (Blumer, Green, Thomte, & Green, this volume). More importantly, why are lesbian, gay, bisexual, and queer persons denied the privilege of positive representations and information about themselves in mainstream educational curricula? And, finally, do heterosexual students earn the privilege of seeing exemplars with whom they identify each day they attend school?

Cohen and Vanita experienced invisibility in their often-overlapping social and activist circles. In response to making lesbian and gay rights visible, Cathy Cohen experienced resistance from the African American community. Through this process, she grew to understand invisibility as a powerful tool for marginalizing a subset of people within a larger marginalized group. Here she described her coalitional work as graduate student:

> I also learned lessons about divisions in community, because there were times when ... other black students kind of attacked us for ... working in collaboration with Whites. There were certain students on campus that attacked us for having women leadership, for addressing issues of lesbian, gay, bisexual, and transgender concerns in terms of student body. So, you know, you learn from both ... the victories that you have and the battles that you engage in ... and it was really in undergrad and then in graduate school that I started to have what I think is a feminist analysis that talks about power and oppression at multiple sites.
>
> (Cathy Cohen)

In this comment, Cohen emphasized the importance of developing a politically useful analysis of social structure to address social issues within the activist community. Ruth Vanita described the self-imposed public invisibility of sexuality for lesbian and bisexual feminist activists in India as a double-edged sword that may have protected them from homophobic backlash while simultaneously suppressing a support system for lesbian and bisexual women. In her GFP interview, she explained:

> Yeah, I would say two things were missing. One was sexuality and the other was depth ... lesbianism was ... I now know that many of the leaders of those autonomous women's groups were either lesbian or bisexual and were actively talking about it among themselves. But in the public, when we came together as groups, you would never talk about it ... that has still not been acknowledged, the amount of lesbian energy that went into the movement in the '70s and '80s. And now in the '90s it began to be acknowledged, and now some of the groups are talking about it.
>
> (Ruth Vanita)

By focusing on changes in public discourse over time, Vanita articulated clearly the invisibility of lesbians in the earlier period.

Cohen and Vanita described experiencing intersectional invisibility and pointed to members of their respective groups who enjoy privileges based on one majority status, such as African American men and heterosexual Indian feminists. Through these examples, students understand invisibility as a tool used across contexts (Poland, India, or the United States, educational settings, activist forums) and across modes of communication (scholarly texts, activist meetings) to maintain a heterosexist culture. The way each woman experienced invisibility informed her of her own privilege, or lack of it. The absence of information distorted their own understanding of lesbian and gay lives, including same-sex love as abnormal or LGBTQ persons as hypersexual or pathological, which prompted them later to engage in anti-homophobia movements.

Classroom Application

These examples illustrate key concepts such as sex, gender, sexuality, sexual identity, sexual orientation, heterosexuality, and heterosexism. Identifying these concepts in video-recorded excerpts from each interview provides a starting point for further discussion about the relationship between binary terms (heterosexual vs. homosexual; normal vs. abnormal) and the invisibility of sexual orientation in educational contexts. Explicitly highlighting the values placed on being on the "right" side of the binary helps students consider other binary categories in their lives, such as white vs. of color, men vs. women, and the unearned privileges that come with identifying with the more powerful category.

Denying Everyday Privileges to the Hidden Minority: The Invisibility of Disability

Teaching Goals and Main Concepts

Identifying invisibility in the curriculum engages students in discussions about visibility as a privilege more generally. Although the field of psychology has diversified in terms of topics and populations studied, relatively little information is included about people with disabilities as a group in the psychology canon or in psychology curricula (Asch & McCarthy, 2003), and even less information is included about women with disabilities. Authors often render the disabled invisible to some degree by devoting little attention to them in psychology textbooks. In particular, most psychology of women courses cover many topics important to most women's lives, yet the experiences and needs of women with disabilities are summed up in one or two paragraphs (Garland-Thomson, 2002). Limited teaching resources make it difficult to incorporate women with disabilities in a meaningful way into a course such as psychology of women, yet this absence of information begs the question, "How does invisibility of people with disabilities encourage negative or limited perceptions of women (and men) with disabilities?" The meaning of special accommodation differs for people with and without disabilities, such that those without disabilities enjoy the privilege of defining "accommodation" in a way that ignores the everyday accommodations made for the non-disabled while defining special accommodations for the disabled as non-normative and a costly inconvenience to the majority.

Teaching Example from the GFP Archive

Adrienne Asch is a social justice activist and scholar interviewed for the U.S. site of the GFP. Her scholarship examines issues of bioethics, reproduction, and disability. In her interview, Asch challenged the viewer to acknowledge assumptions about people with disabilities and issues of identity centrality, sexuality, parenthood, and activism. Asch argued that maintaining the illusion that only persons with disabilities require special accommodation allows non-disabled persons to deny their own privilege while denying special accommodations to disabled persons. Asch described examples of unmarked and unearned special accommodations such as typewriters (now computers) as an aid to writing quickly, and strollers as help to move children more quickly or for longer distances.

Additionally, people who hold one or more subordinate statuses are often denied the privilege of claiming an identity for themselves and the privileged overlook the consequences for imposing an identity onto another person. Highlighting the privilege of self-identification for students provides them with the space to reflect on identity as a source of empowerment. Asch explained in her GFP interview:

It has been very difficult to force my identity apart from disability, because people … my whole life, have been trying to tell me that that's the most important thing about me. And so when I say that it actually isn't, and that the most important things about me as far as I'm concerned are that I do bioethics or that I'm a leftist or that I went to Swarthmore, or that I love Renaissance music, people really often don't like that. They want me to tell them that I'm blind.

(Adrienne Asch)

Students who hold privileged identities may not understand the relevance of self-identification because of its invisibility. Non-disabled persons often define persons with disabilities by their disability and often assume that persons with disabilities are incompetent to some degree (Asch & McCarthy, 2003).

Classroom Application

Some scholars refer to individuals with disabilities as the hidden minority (Kleinfield, 1979). Increasing the visibility of this group recognizes them as whole persons rather than as persons with disabilities. We have found it useful to teach about disability in separate learning modules as well as integrated across the curriculum. To demonstrate for students the social construction of disability, we use contextual information, such as definitions of disability and the number of people with disabilities in the United States, along with Asch's interview. This approach guides students to identify the role invisibility plays in maintaining the privilege of special accommodations for those without disabilities while denying needed accommodations to those with disabilities. Equally, it is useful to point out that some individuals are not defined as "persons with disabilities" even though they mention various constraints and limitations on their activities, particularly those associated with aging. Thus, some disabilities are normalized and accommodated, while other disabilities are pathologized and marginalized. Asch argued that everyone will be disabled at some point in their lifetime, many of us from the aging process. For students currently without disabilities, reflection on their temporary ability status and stereotypes related to the disabled community encourages them to use their current position of privilege to advocate for social services for the disabled and re-evaluate their own worldviews about what defines a person with a disability.

Who Makes a "Good" Leader? Based on What We See, It's Being a Man

Teaching Goals and Main Concepts

The GFP disrupts the stereotype of women as ineffective leaders (Rudman & Glick, 2001), as well as associations between masculine traits and good leadership

(Carroll, 2009; Eagly, 2007). A curriculum that includes gender analysis has positive benefits for women students and their possible future selves in terms of careers in male-dominated fields (Rios et al., 2010; Weisgram & Bigler, 2007), and the GFP provides multiple topics related to leadership. Students hear from the activists/scholars themselves about their feminist activism in ways that challenge assumptions about women's relative invisibility in male-dominated fields of practice and study (e.g., politics and political science). Erasing, or making invisible, the participation of female leaders creates the impression that only men possess the agentic traits associated with social and political change. For students who enjoy the privilege of seeing frequent leadership exemplars like themselves, the GFP narratives provide insight into the consequences of being blocked from holding a leadership position and rendering issues invisible that marginalized groups deem important.

Teaching Examples from the GFP Archive

Although Indian activist Lata Pratibha Madhukar (Lata P. M.) played a leading role in an environmental movement, the media failed to recognize her as a leader. In particular, the producers of the internationally acclaimed documentary that chronicled this particular movement, *A Narmada Diary* (Patwardhan & Dixon, 1995), excluded her presence entirely. Lata explained:

> In Anand's film I'm nowhere. I'm there only for half a second in Hutatma Chowk. This has happened not only with me but with many full timers despite second rank leadership positions. . . . A lot has been written about male activists.
>
> (Lata Pratibha)

Lata's narrative highlighted the assumptions about men as legitimate leaders, a privilege denied to women through erasure of their presence and contributions to these movements.

American activist Loretta Ross has held key organizer and participant roles in the March for Women's Lives in Washington, D.C., one of the largest demonstrations in the history of the United States (National Organization for Women, n.d.). However, the demonstration received little media attention compared to smaller demonstrations in Washington, D.C. In these instances, examples of disproportionate coverage of men's leadership and participation in movements compared with women's relative invisibility in media coverage reinforces ideas of who makes a good leader and relevant social issues.

Classroom Application

The stereotype that men have natural leadership abilities facilitates their holding positions of power. The stereotypes imposed upon women, such as being natural caregivers, are often incongruent with characteristics associated with good leadership, such as being aggressive, ambitious, and analytic (Eagly, 2007; Rudman & Glick, 2001). Thus, the high visibility of men in leadership positions secures their unearned privilege under the assumption that they are natural leaders. In Lata's interview, students learn to identify when stereotypes about motherhood (i.e., gender-congruent role) are imposed upon Lata to delegitimize her as a leader (i.e., gender-incongruent role). Additionally, students learn to identify good leadership characteristics in Lata and the invisibility of women's issues. These exercises expose male students to the ways that gendered perceptions of legitimate leadership falls in their favor as well as the relationship between those who lead and the issues addressed in a given context. What issues might men miss based on their limited life experience, or more specifically, not having a woman's perspective? Encouraging students to share their own experiences with leadership positions and perceptions of men and women can facilitate or block access to leadership opportunities.

In the case of Loretta Ross, a comparative approach can be accomplished by providing students with information about a well-publicized demonstration, such as the Million Man March and the March for Women's Lives. Although the Million March did not actually include one million male participants, the March for Women's Lives reached close to that number. Comparing media coverage of these two marches allows students to examine why the media widely covers certain events while ignoring others. The inverse relationship between privilege and invisibility is easily demonstrated in this example because the march that focused on the concerns of people with one key privileged identity (maleness) received much more media attention than a march in which women with privileged identities (White women) allied with women with subordinate identities (women of color).

Making Global Feminisms Visible by Exposing a Privileged Standpoint

Teaching Goals and Main Concepts

Even within a field whose goals include exposing systems of power, privileged standpoints often remain invisible. According to standpoint theory, all persons or groups differentially experience the dominant culture in which all groups exist. In any society, dominant group members enjoy the privilege of having their views validated more often than those held by subordinate groups (Collins, 2000; Harding, 1991; Hartsock, 2003). Chandra Mohanty (1988) cautioned Western feminists against gazing at "Third World women" through "Western eyes," through which global feminism is interpreted as global sisterhood (Morgan, 1984). Accordingly, students may also endorse the idea that gender oppression unites all women, with global feminism being a transfer of Western feminist ideals to Third World women who are assumed to have no experience in organizing their own political movements (Mohanty, 1988). The GFP interviews disrupt stereotypes of Chinese, Indian, Nicaraguan, and Polish feminists by providing narrative accounts of each woman's participation in various political movements in their countries. Additionally, the diversity of U.S. feminists challenges assumptions that all American feminists are White and middle class. Exposure to women of color like the members of the Sista II Sista collective, and women working on behalf of poor women in Michigan like Maureen Taylor and Marian Kramer, brings the diverse history of feminist activism in the United States to life. Moreover, exposure to these examples shows that gender oppression as the exclusive focus of feminist activism reflects a privileged social position because many women from China, India, Nicaragua, Poland, and the United States experience oppressions as interlocking rather than in isolation from one another (Cole, 2009; Crenshaw, 1991; Hurtado, 1996).

Reflection on the intersection of multiple social identities, including race, gender, sexual orientation, ability status, and social class, helps students think about the privilege of having their basic needs met daily. Although some students may have experience with poverty, many do not. Taylor and Kramer's work focuses on day-to-day struggles faced by the poor. Using Taylor and Kramer's interview (U.S. site) as a basis for discussion, students can reflect on the last time their families worried about where they would sleep each night.

Teaching Examples from the GFP Archive

Many of the U.S. site interviews demonstrate the intersection of gender oppression with other types of oppression. Taylor and Kramer expressed passionate views in opposition to capitalism ("Make no mistake: we hate capitalism. Hate it. It's no good."), often thought of as a defining feature of U.S. life. Through their account, students learn about the differential effects of capitalism for groups of people based on their position in a hegemonic structure. Equally, it would be impossible for students to stereotype all "Third World women" when they are faced with a range of women who work to improve their own lives. Through these examples, students reflect upon why stereotypes persist about the "salvation" of Third World women being dependent on First World intervention (Mohanty, 1988). Similar to the example of men being presumed legitimate leaders and creators of knowledge, First World women hold the unearned privilege of believing they can decide what issues matter most for all women (Mohanty, 1988).

Classroom Application

Teaching materials including transcripts and videotaped interviews and contextual materials are available on the GFP site for each interviewee (www.umich.edu/~glblfem/teaching.html). These materials contextualize feminism in each of the sites and for each woman, and provide rich examples of women organizing based on the needs of their communities, which often includes many issues rather than solely gender oppression (Mohanty, 1988). Comparing historical contexts and a topical example from each site, students can identify commonalities and differences in feminist organizing. To address invisible privileges, this diversity within each site challenges students' stereotypes about U.S. feminists and women from the countries represented in the project. The invisibility of this privileged standpoint relies on the assumption that Third World women need to be saved from their oppressive cultures and makes it difficult for U.S. students to imagine the possibilities of coalition and alliance with women in other countries (Mohanty, 1988). By making visible the diversity of global feminisms, new possibilities open up.

Reducing Invisible Privileges with the GFP Archive

The women in the GFP not only identified invisibility in their lives, they also offered strategies for exposing invisibility as a tool for creating, perpetuating, and maintaining privilege. Screening the interviews, assigning students papers that require comparative analysis across national contexts, and analyzing the lives of individual women help students gain insight into the way that invisibility operates to maintain privileges for different groups of people. D. Sharifa, from the India site, identified privileges that she feels entitled to, regardless of her gender, and flags the invisibility of men's privileged access to what McIntosh (1988) referred to as positive privileges to which everyone should feel entitled. Sharifa explained:

> My action is informed by feminist thinking ... A girl must consider her self-respect, her mind, her thoughts, and decisions to live her own life, as her responsibility. Likewise, her life and all happenings are within the framework of this society. "I have the right to all the privileges and recognition accorded in the society. I have to demand it." That feeling should be there.
>
> (D. Sharifa)

Sharifa emphasized here that basic human rights, such as access to education, safe housing, health care, and reproductive freedom, are entitlements all people should claim. However, many persons who enjoy the privilege of whiteness, maleness, heterosexuality, a non-disabled status, and middle- or upper-class social status, reinterpret access to most privileges as something to be earned, often under the assumption that they themselves have earned these privileges, or that all groups of people have equal access to the resources needed in order to "earn" these privileges.

The narratives in the GFP provide opportunities for students to identify the privilege within a system that normalizes the dominance of one group over another regardless of their intention or desire. Additionally, students learn to identify their own privilege by considering the way invisibility protects unearned privileges while simultaneously denying their benefits to others.

References

Asch, A., & McCarthy, H. (2003). Infusing disability issues into the psychology curriculum. In P. Bronstein & K. Quina (Eds.), *Teaching gender and multicultural awareness: Resources for the psychology classroom* (pp. 253–269). Washington, D.C.: American Psychological Association. doi:10.1037/10570–018

Blumer, M. L. C., Green, M. S., Thomte, N. L., & Green, P. M. (this volume). Are we queer yet? Addressing heterosexual and gender-conforming privilege. In K. A. Case (Ed.), *Deconstructing privilege: Teaching and learning as allies in the classroom* (pp. 151–168). New York, NY: Routledge.

Carroll, S. J. (2009). Reflections on the gender and Hillary Clinton's presidential campaign: The good, the bad, and the misogynic. *Politics and Gender, 5*(1), 1–20. doi:10.1017/S1743923X09000014

Case, K. A. (this volume). Beyond diversity and whiteness: Developing a transformative and intersectional model of privilege studies pedagogy. In K. A. Case (Ed.), *Deconstructing privilege: Teaching and learning as allies in the classroom* (pp. 1–14). New York, NY: Routledge.

Cole, E. R. (2009). Intersectionality and research in psychology. *American Psychologist, 64*(3), 170–180. doi:10.1037/a0014564

Collins, P. H. (2000). *Black feminist thought: Knowledge, consciousness, and the politics of empowerment* (2nd ed.). New York, NY: Routledge.

Coston, B. M., & Kimmel, M. (2012). Seeing privilege where it isn't: Marginalized masculinities and the intersectionality of privilege. *Journal of Social Issues, 68*(1), 97–111. doi:10.1111/j.1540–4560.2011.01738.x

Crenshaw, K. (1991). Mapping the margins: Intersectionality, identity politics, and violence against women of color. *Stanford Law Review, 43*(6), 1241–1299. doi:10.1002/ir.395

Eagly, A. H. (2007). Female leadership advantage and disadvantage: Resolving the contradictions. *Psychology of Women Quarterly, 31*(1), 1–12. doi:10.1111/j.1471–6402.2007.00326.x

Fine, M. (2002). 2001 Carolyn Sherif award address: The presence of an absence, *Psychology of Women Quarterly, 26*(1), 9–24. doi:10.1111/1471–6402.00039

Fryberg, S. A., & Townsend, S. S. M. (2008). The psychology of invisibility. In G. Adams, M. Biernat, N. R. Branscombe, C. S. Crandall, & L. S. Wrightsman (Eds.), *Commemorating Brown: The social psychology of racism and discrimination* (pp. 173–193). Washington, D.C.: American Psychological Association. doi:10.1037/11681–010

Garland-Thomson, R. (2002). Integrating disability, transforming feminist theory. *NWSA Journal, 14*(3), 1–32. doi:10.2979/NWS.2002.14.3.1

Harding, S. (1991). *Whose science? Whose knowledge? Thinking from women's lives.* Ithaca, NY: Cornell University Press.

Hartsock, N. (2003). The feminist standpoint: Developing the ground for a specifically feminist historical materialism. In S. Harding & M. B. Hintikka (Eds.), *Discovering reality: Feminist perspectives on epistemology, metaphysics, methodology, and philosophy of science* (2nd ed.). London: D. Riedel Publishing Company. doi:10.1007/978–94–010–0101–4

Hegarty, P. J., & Pratto, F. (2001). The effects of social category norms on explanations for intergroup differences. *Journal of Personality and Social Psychology, 80*(5), 723–735. doi:10.1037/00223514805723.

Hull, G. T., Scott, P. B., & Smith B. (Eds.) (1982). *All the women are White, all the Blacks are men, but some of us are brave: Black women's studies.* Old Westbury, NY: The Feminist Press.

Hurtado, A. (1996). *The color of privilege: Three blasphemies on race and feminism.* Ann Arbor, MI: University of Michigan Press.

Kleinfield, S. (1979). *The hidden minority: A profile of handicapped Americans.* Boston, MA: Little, Brown, and Company.

Lal, J., McGuire, K. M., Stewart, A. J., Zaborowska, M., & Pas, J. (2010). Recasting global feminisms: Towards a comparative historical approach to women's activism and feminist scholarship. *Feminist Studies, 36*(1), 13–39.

McGuire, K. M., Stewart, A. J., & Curtin, N. (2010). Becoming feminist activists: Comparing narratives. *Feminist Studies, 36*(1), 99–125.

McIntosh, P. (1988). *White privilege and male privilege: A personal account of coming to see correspondences through work in women's studies* (Working Paper No. 189). Wellesley, MA: Wellesley Centers for Women.

Mohanty, C. (1988). "Under Western eyes": Feminist scholarship and colonial discourse. *Feminist Review, 30*(1), 61–88. doi:10.1057/fr.1988.42.

Morgan, R. (1984). *Sisterhood is Global.* New York, NY: The Feminist Press.

National Organization for Women. (n.d). *History of marches and mass actions.* Retrieved from www.now.org/history/protests.html

Patwardhan, A., & Dhuru, S. (1995). *A Narmada diary* [DVD]. New York, NY: First Run/ Icarus Films.

Purdie-Vaughns, V., & Eibach, R. P. (2008). Intersectional invisibility: The distinctive advantages and disadvantages of multiple subordinate-group identities. *Sex Roles, 59*(5–6), 377–391. doi:10.1007/s11199–008–9424–4

Rios, D., Stewart, A. J., & Winter, D. G. (2010). "Thinking she could be the next President": Why identifying with the curriculum matters. *Psychology of Women Quarterly, 34*(3), 328–338. doi:10.1111/j.1471–6402.2010.01578.x

Rudman, L. A., & Glick, P. (2001). Prescriptive gender stereotypes and backlash toward agentic women. *Journal of Social Issues, 57*(4), 743–762. doi:10.1111/0022–4537.00239

Ruvolo, A. P., & Markus, H. R. (1992). Possible selves and performance: The power of self-relevant imagery. *Social Cognition, 10*(1), 95–124. doi:10.1521/soco.1992.10.1.95

Shapiro, D. N., Rios, D., & Stewart, A. J. (2010). Beyond stage theories: Socializing structures and individual choices in lesbians' sexual identity development. *Feminism & Psychology, 20*(10), 491–510. doi:10.1177/0959353509358441

Steele, C. M. (1997). A threat in the air: How stereotypes shape intellectual identity and performance. *American Psychologist, 52*(6), 613–629. doi:10.1037/0003–066X.52.6.613

Stewart, A. J., Lal, J., & McGuire, K. (2011). Expanding the archives of global feminisms: Narratives of feminism and activism. *Signs, 36*(4), 889–914. doi:10.1086/658683

Stewart, T. L., Latu, I. M., Branscombe, N. R., Phillips, N. L., & Denney, H. T. (2012). White privilege awareness and efficacy to reduce racial inequality improve White Americans' attitudes toward African Americans. *Journal of Social Issues, 68*(1), 11–27. doi:10.1111/ j.1540–4560.2012.01733.x

University of Michigan (n.d.) 'Welcome to the Global Feminisms Project!' Retrieved from www.umich.edu/~glblfem/

Weisgram, E. S., & Bigler, R. S. (2007). Effects of learning about gender discrimination on adolescent girls' attitudes towards and interest in science. *Psychology of Women Quarterly, 31*(3), 262–269. doi:10.1111/j.1471–6402.2007.00369.x

Wise, T., & Case, K. A. (this volume). Pedagogy for the privileged: Addressing inequality and injustice without shame or blame. In K. A. Case (Ed.), *Deconstructing privilege: Teaching and learning as allies in the classroom* (pp. 17–33). New York, NY: Routledge.

9

INTERGROUP DIALOGUE PEDAGOGY

Teaching about Intersectional and Under-examined Privilege in Heterosexual, Christian, and Jewish Identities

Adrienne B. Dessel, Johanna C. Massé, and Lauren T. Walker

Teaching about social identity privilege, or the unearned societal advantages conferred upon someone based on their social group identity (race, social class, gender, sexual orientation), provokes controversy in many higher education classrooms (Bell, Love, & Roberts, 2007). Challenging oppression and reducing bias require critical understanding of institutional and structural forms of social identity-based privilege (Adams, Bell, & Griffin, 2007). An examination of the intersection of various social identities as they relate to power and privilege may provide a more nuanced understanding of the socially constructed nature of power imbalances (Zúñiga, Nagda, Chesler, & Cytron-Walker, 2007).

Intergroup dialogue presents a method of social justice education that is increasingly used in higher education settings to raise awareness about privilege, oppression, and social identity inequalities. Academics across fields of social work, psychology, student affairs, and communications utilize dialogic methods to enhance discussions and awareness about the relationship between social identities and power, privilege, and oppression (Dessel, Woodford, Routenberg, & Breijak, in press; Kivlighan & Arseneau, 2009; Maxwell, Nagda, & Thompson, 2011). This awareness, along with fostering relationships, promotes commitments to social action and the pursuit of a more equitable society (Nagda, Gurin, Sorensen, & Zúñiga, 2009).

Teaching and learning about heterosexual, Jewish, and Christian privilege proves particularly challenging. Intergroup dialogue courses on sexual orientation address heterosexual privilege, religion dialogues aim to teach about Christian privilege, and dialogues on the Arab–Israeli conflict promote learning about Jewish privilege in relation to Arab communities. A review of the literature provides an overview of the use of intergroup dialogue pedagogy for teaching about privilege, with specific attention to the intersectionality of identities. Intergroup dialogue pedagogy provides a model that uses intergroup dialogue methods to teach about privilege

(Maxwell, Nagda, et al., 2011; Zúñiga et al., 2007). Course materials illustrate a focus on the intersectionality of identities with regard to learning about privilege and offer practical teaching applications. Qualitative research on learning about heterosexual, Jewish, and Christian privilege from these three intergroup dialogue course topics illustrates a pedagogical approach to intergroup conflict. Lessons learned and recommendations for research and pedagogy further the learning about intergroup dialogue as a method of teaching and learning about privilege.

Intergroup Dialogues in Higher Education

Intergroup dialogue provides a key pedagogy used in higher education settings to teach about identity privilege and related social power (Maxwell, Nagda, et al., 2011). This teaching method uses a curriculum that focuses on social identities such as race, gender, or religion. Undergraduate and graduate dialogue courses engage equal numbers of students from two different identity groups who have a history of conflict with the goal of balancing social power (Zúñiga et al., 2007). Two trained student facilitators who belong to the two identity groups, one representing a more privileged group and one representing a marginalized group, co-lead the courses. Readings, experiential exercises, journals, and other assignments promote critical thinking about privilege and social justice, and foster commitment to redressing social inequalities. Participation in intergroup dialogue courses promotes relationship building, exploration of differences and commonalities of experiences, engagement with controversial hot topics, alliance building, and action planning (Zúñiga et al., 2007).

Co-facilitators make important contributions to the intergroup dialogue process. Facilitators balance social power in the dialogue with regard to air time, support and guide the flow of the discussion, and employ an array of "questioning methods" that help participants reflect on their own and others' privilege (Maxwell, Fisher, Thompson, & Behling, 2011; Zúñiga et al., 2007). These facilitator methods promote learning about privilege, oppression, and social justice.

The critical-dialogic model of intergroup dialogue focuses on both promoting an understanding of identity-based inequality and building affective relationships among participants (Nagda & Maxwell, 2011). Students gain a deeper understanding of the connections among individual, institutional, and structural oppression and privilege through activities such as personal narrative sharing and the development of empathy. Intergroup dialogue pedagogy builds on this knowledge and these relationships and develops individual and collective responsibility for reducing social inequalities and oppression and promoting social justice (Nagda & Maxwell, 2011). Students' participation in experiential learning activities such as role-playing and simulations helps to raise awareness of oppression and privilege and supports engagement in uncomfortable self-examination (Goodman, 2001).

Intergroup dialogue courses explore the nature of privilege in an in-depth manner. The pedagogy emphasizes multiple and intersecting identities as an important aspect of learning about privilege (Cole, 2009; Ferber & Herrera, this volume). Applying intersectional theory, students learn about the ways in which their unique combination of identities influence their experiences of oppression and privilege (Case & Lewis, 2012; Case, Miller, & Jackson, 2012; Hardiman, Jackson, & Griffin, 2007).

Intergroup dialogue courses also aim to engage students in a critical analysis of the negative effects of power and privilege imbalances on everyone and encourage them to re-envision and reconstruct change (Zúñiga et al., 2007). Members of privileged dominant groups often fail to recognize their unearned privilege, while some members of marginalized groups express a keen awareness of the social inequities associated with their identities (Hardiman et al., 2007). Some members of privileged groups may feel uninformed, guilty, or attacked when discussing or thinking about privilege (Case & Cole, this volume; Case, Iuzzini, & Hopkins, 2012; Stewart, Latu, Branscombe, Phillips, & Denney, 2012). Other members of oppressed groups feel frustrated at the lack of knowledge or consideration given to power differences (Hardiman et al., 2007). Previous research indicated dominant groups prefer to examine commonalities between groups with disparate power access, while marginalized groups push to recognize power imbalances (Saguy, Pratto, Dovidio, & Nadler, 2008). Intergroup dialogue pedagogy places social identity conflicts within the framework of power and privilege differences. Dialogic interactions that involve safety, sharing, and the development of critical consciousness can lead to bridge building across these differences (Zúñiga et al., 2007). Intergroup dialogue seeks to build alliances between members of privileged and oppressed groups, encourages privileged groups to share power, and empowers all participants to create change.

Most intergroup dialogue research in higher education settings has focused on race and gender (Nagda et al., 2009). Miller and Donner (2000) describe racial dialogues and the tendency of White students to focus on their oppressed identities rather than acknowledging racial privilege. Miller and Donner found more learning about privilege occurred for White students than students of color. Learning about privilege can also lead to negative reactions for White students (Cole, Case, Rios, & Curtin, 2011). Authentic sharing of personal life stories in intergroup dialogue courses allows privileged and marginalized groups to come to greater understanding of outgroup members (Rozas, 2007). Participation in intergroup dialogues can raise self-awareness about one's own privilege and promote a heightened sense of responsibility to end racism (Rozas, 2007).

Results of intergroup dialogue participation indicate students gain a greater understanding of the structural nature of identity privilege and the influence of structural inequalities on intergroup interactions as compared to students in a standard social science course or control group (Nagda & Gurin, 2007; Nagda et al., 2009). Nagda and colleagues' (2009) national study demonstrated that with regard to race and gender dialogues, all groups regardless of societal privilege evidenced significantly higher learning on outcomes of intergroup understanding about group based inequality, development of positive relationships, and commitment to actions that promote social justice.

More scholarship on privilege focused on white privilege (Case, this volume). Other areas of privilege receive less attention in the intergroup dialogue literature, such as heterosexual privilege, Christian privilege, and Jewish privilege in the U.S. context of Arab–Jewish relations. This study examines intergroup dialogue courses on sexual orientation, religion, and the Arab–Jewish conflict using data from student final papers and post-dialogue interviews. We discuss curriculum examples, pedagogy successes and challenges, and outcomes of learning about privilege.

Undergraduate Intergroup Dialogue Courses

The Program on Intergroup Relations at the University of Michigan is a social justice education program with a particular focus on teaching about power, privilege, and oppression. These dialogues employ a critical-dialogic approach with three primary educational goals:

1. consciousness-raising about social power inequality;
2. building relationships across differences and conflict; and
3. strengthening capacity for social justice action (Zúñiga et al., 2007).

These two-credit undergraduate dialogue courses run a full semester and follow the highly structured model.

The course curriculum recognizes that social identities fall on a continuum. However, social identity power gets ascribed in a binary fashion by cultural and institutional forces, with certain social identities (e.g., White, heterosexual) awarded more social power than others (Case, Iuzzini, et al., 2012). Therefore, each course focuses on a single identity, such as race/ethnicity, gender, social class, or sexual orientation. We assign roughly equal numbers of students from two identity groups representing the privileged and marginalized identity groups in each course in order to balance power in the dialogue (Allport, 1954). These assignments occur via student enrollment in a psychology or sociology course that offers multiple sections on different identities. Students select to take the intergroup dialogue course and are then placed into social identity topic sections based on their preference ranking of each identity topic.

As mentioned, the courses follow a binary model of identity to recognize and challenge the power binary in society. However, strong recognition of the multifaceted nature and continuum of identity lead facilitators to promote examination of the intersection of social identities (Cole, 2009; Dill & Zambrana, 2009) as well as to illuminate the relationships among different identities, structural power, and privilege. The pedagogy emphasizes learning about structural and institutional privilege, power, and challenging ideas such as meritocracy and post-feminism.

Peer facilitators of these intergroup dialogue courses take a one-semester training course emphasizing both content knowledge and group process with regard to discussions about privilege (Zúñiga et al., 2007), as well as the way in which identity privilege influences the co-facilitation experience (Maxwell, Chesler, & Nagda, 2011). Facilitators also take a one-semester practicum course concurrently with their intergroup dialogue to process their facilitation experiences.

Previous intergroup dialogue course topics have included race/ethnicity, gender, and socioeconomic status. Instructors introduced course topics on sexual orientation, religion, and the Arab–Jewish conflict to meet the needs and interests of additional identity populations. Reviewed below, curriculum, pedagogy, and outcomes for these course topics outline how these courses developed and their unique contributions to intergroup pedagogy.

Intergroup Dialogue Pedagogical Approaches

Intergroup dialogue integrates content related to learning about privilege with experiential activities to engage both cognitive and affective processes in learning (Nagda & Gurin, 2007). For example, a reading on the cycle of socialization, a theory that describes the socialization process around social identity, privilege, and oppression, aligns with a timeline activity that assists students in exploring their own socialization experiences (Harro, 2010). When students reach the last few weeks of the dialogue and focus on equalizing privilege imbalances, they participate in an intergroup collaboration project, in which they work across identities to engage in social justice actions (Zúñiga et al., 2007). They review what it means to be an ally and discuss actions that one can take to be an ally when the dialogue is over (Adams et al., 2007).

The sexual orientation dialogue courses follow a standard curriculum, where heterosexual students are identified as the privileged group, and lesbian, gay, and bisexual (LGB) students as the marginalized group. However, instructors acknowledge the non-binary and fluid nature of sexual orientation (Diamond, 2005), and a number of exercises and resources incorporated into the curriculum reflect this non-binary recognition. Exercises help students explore the range of sexual orientation identities and the varying degrees of power these different identities afford. For example, dialogue facilitators lead students in a sexual orientation privilege walk, an experiential activity that adapts McIntosh's (1988) list of white privileges designed to illuminate the privileges that a heterosexual identity offers. A privilege inventory helps students examine and analyze the differences among individual, institutional, and structural heterosexual power and privilege (Hardiman et al., 2007). A written activity developed by program faculty offers another opportunity to explore the non-binary and fluid nature of social identity as it relates to power and privilege. Readings and dialogue sessions allow exploration of heterosexism as a concept (Griffin, D'Errico, Harro, & Schiff, 2007). The action continuum exercise challenges heterosexual students to not only refrain from using terms such as "that's so gay," but also explore advocacy and prevention of injustice (Adams et al., 2007).

The Arab–Jewish dialogue curriculum adapts and uses a number of different exercises to examine privilege. An Ashkenazi privilege walk (Jewish Multiracial Network, 2009), adapted from a list of white privileges (McIntosh, 1988), highlights the privileges White Jewish students from Eastern European descent hold due to their racial identity in the United States, as well as privileges that Christian Arab students might hold related to their religion. In this way, students examine the intersection of their religious and racial identities.

Another exercise, called the "power map out," was developed collaboratively with faculty and students to help student participants in the dialogues analyze the different kinds of power and privilege that Jews and Arabs hold and the oppressions that they experience. The activity provides a handout listing examples of Zionist Jewish privilege, Jewish oppression, Arab privilege, and Arab oppression and prompts exploration of these concepts. Students are encouraged to consider power and privilege as contextual and to focus on power and oppression related to living in the United States, Israel, or Palestine. The adapted gallery walk (Adams & D'Errico, 2007) activity involves students locating and posting pictures on the wall to provide visual examples of current topics such as land resources and diaspora experiences. They then walk around and view these images, write down their reflections, and discuss them. This activity helps students to identify group power and privilege related to different social issues and political situations.

In religion dialogues, students tend to prefer interfaith experiences that explore commonalities and differences, neglecting power and social inequality. Here again, we adapted the privilege walk to highlight Christian privilege as well as the oppression experienced by atheists (Blumenfeld & Jaekel, 2012). Students also have three "hot topics" sessions in which they raise areas of conflict, such as abortion and sexual orientation, and they use the dialogic communication skills they developed to engage with one another around these issues.

During various courses in the past, when, for one class period, students divide into marginalized or privileged caucus groups, participants in the religion dialogues often opted to divide in the following four ways based on self-identification: (a) Christians and non-Christians, (b) one group of religiously observant "believers" and one group of agnostics and atheists, or (c) three groups representing Christians, religious non-Christians, and agnostics and atheists. The lack of a clear privileged/marginalized dialogue structure creates opportunities for students to see similarities both across and within religious groups. The caucus groups offer an opportunity for safety within a homogenous identity group that can produce important reflections to share with the other group in a fishbowl setting (Griffin et al., 2007). Each caucus group takes a turn having a discussion in the middle of the classroom ("the fish"), while the other members of the class listen silently ("the bowl").

Intergroup Dialogue Pedagogy: Overcoming Resistance to Acknowledging Privilege

As mentioned, faculty and staff train undergraduates to facilitate the dialogue courses. A number of key pedagogical approaches enhance learning about privilege in these three intergroup dialogue topics. These include facilitator examination of their own social identities and privilege so that they can model this for participants, an understanding of the unique content on privilege for the particular dialogue identity topic, the tightly structured nature of the curriculum, and the integration of content and process. We provide examples of facilitator and instructor goals and reflections below.

Raising Awareness of Heterosexual Privilege

The intergroup dialogue courses on sexual orientation seek to raise awareness about heterosexual privilege (Griffin et al., 2007). Students often overlook the numerous and hidden privileges related to heterosexual orientation, which include:

• over 1,100 federal benefits, rights, and protections afforded to married heterosexual couples (Human Rights Campaign, 2011);
• job protections (ACLU, 2009);
• a lower risk of being targeted by bullying and harassment as a youth (Harris Interactive & GLSEN, 2005); and
• the right to adopt, receive a partner's health insurance coverage, and have family visitation if a partner is in hospital (Allen, 1995).

Pedagogical learning goals include defining and understanding terminology around sexual orientation, recognizing diversity within LGB communities, understanding the complexities of coming out, and understanding the connections between sexual orientation and gender identity. Course materials also include transgender identity issues. Within all of these areas, dialogues highlight heterosexual privilege and challenge students to consider the way in which they can be allies to the LGB community.

Heterosexual students in these dialogues often avoid exposing their biases for fear of insulting LGB students (Dessel et al., in press) and therefore resist confronting their unearned privilege. Heterosexual students of color, in particular, need to be invited to consider their privileges related to their sexual orientation because of their inclination to focus on their marginalized identity experience. Dialogues also focus on ally work and encouraging members of a privileged group take action to balance social inequalities (Adams et al., 2007). This can take the form of interrupting heterosexist jokes or joining an organization to work together with LGB students to combat prejudice and discrimination.

Challenging Christian Hegemony

Christian privilege is one of the most pervasive yet unacknowledged contributors to oppression in the United States (Blumenfeld & Jaekel, 2012). Christian privilege in the education system, which manifests in institutional structures like the academic calendar, marginalizes students who practice religions other than Christianity as well those students who consider themselves non-religious (Clark, Vargas, Schlosser, & Alimo, 2002). Because Christian practices represent the dominant norm in U.S. society, Christian privilege remains invisible and thus is often one of the more difficult forms of oppression for students enrolled in dialogues to grasp (Case, McMullen, & Hentges, this volume). The intersection with race and Christianity further complicates this teaching, in that challenging Christian hegemony may mean challenging racial minority groups (Adams & Joshi, 2007). For example, facilitators report that Christian African American females, who experience both gendered and racialized oppression, sometimes find it difficult to acknowledge that they may benefit from religious privilege. Additionally, in the United States, where over 80% of adults claim a religious affiliation (Pew Forum on Religion & Public Life, 2008), the marginalization associated with atheism or agnosticism often surfaces in the religion dialogues as another form of oppression.

The structure of the religion dialogue courses is somewhat different than other dialogues because they have not been populated based on a binary with a privileged and marginalized social identity, but rather a mix of religious, atheist, and agnostic identities, based on student interest in interfaith dialogue experiences. Ideally, the dialogues comprise a balance of Christian and non-Christian participants, and the focus remains on Christian privilege. However, the intragroup religious identities among the Christians and non-Christians vary widely. This complexity led to collecting information in the course placement form on students' religious upbringing as well as current religious practice, to more accurately place them in the dialogue course. Further, instructors and facilitators examine their own religious identity to be aware of the way in which it impacts their own privilege and positionality. Exploration of religious identity remains taboo in academia (Ecklund, 2010). Intergroup dialogue pedagogy challenges that assumption and encourages facilitators to explore and share their religious privileges. Finally, our future courses will be more intentional about a more binary Christian privilege focus with readings and exercises.

Addressing the Arab–Israeli Conflict Productively

Heated debates over the Israeli–Palestinian conflict take place on many U.S. college campuses (Dessel & Ali, 2012). Teaching about this conflict presents challenges for faculty who include this highly contested issue in their curriculum (Gravois, 2004). The Arab–Jewish intergroup dialogue course focuses on the conflict in Palestine and Israel and the ways in which this conflict affects relationships between Jewish and Arab students on college campuses. Tension may be high in this dialogue, and Jewish students typically resist acknowledging their privileged status (Dessel & Ali, 2012). This course uses the standard curriculum that identifies marginalized and privileged identities based on societal privilege. However, the concept of privileged group status in an Arab–Jewish dialogue is complicated. In other intergroup dialogue courses where being Jewish was one of the identities of focus, Jewish students have been identified as both privileged and marginalized with shifting dominant and subordinate roles (Khuri, 2004). Jewish students in the United States may experience both oppression and privilege as a result of their Jewish identity, depending on religious affiliation and whether they represent a cultural minority in their local community. Arab students in the United States typically represent a targeted oppressed group due to Arab stereotypes in the media and increased anti-Arab sentiment since the World Trade Center attacks (Wingfield & Karaman, 2001). However, this also differs depending on whether they are Christian or Muslim, with Christian Arab people holding more privilege (Jaschik, 2005).

These dynamics require constant negotiation in the dialogues with regard to which groups are privileged or oppressed. The complexity of analyzing privilege in this dialogue starkly illuminates the intersectional and positional nature of privilege. Co-facilitators of the dialogue share their views with one another about the conflict so that they can understand and support one another. Jewish facilitators need to be willing to examine and acknowledge their privilege in relation to Arab students, in order to support Jewish participants in exploring these concepts in the dialogue. The highly structured curriculum provides the safety needed to negotiate strong emotions. All readings assigned reflect authors from both Arab and Jewish identities. The development, agreement, and frequent revisiting of group guidelines provide a structure that allows participants who may be resistant to examining privilege to explore these ideas. All these approaches offer students a safe, facilitated opportunity to examine the concept of privilege as it relates to this particular ethno-national conflict (Dessel & Ali, 2012).

Privileged Student Outcomes: What do They Learn?

Methods

This study received approval from the university's institutional review board. Data analyzed from the sexual orientation dialogues is from a sample of 46 final papers (2003–2007), and 8 post-interviews (2011) of heterosexual undergraduate students, and included 32 women and 22 men. Students reported race as White (40), Black (6), Latino (3), Asian (3), and not reported (2). Data from the religion dialogue courses included pre- and post-interviews and final papers collected from 56 students who participated in 6 dialogues (2009–2010). Religious identities included Jewish (19), Christian (11), agnostic (8), other (4), Catholic (4),

Muslim (3), atheist (3), Hindu (3), and not reported (1). Data from the Arab–Jewish dialogue courses is final course papers and qualitative interviews from Jewish (13) students collected in 2009 and 2010, 9 women and 4 men. Reported race/ethnicity was American, Israeli, Hong Kong national, and Iranian.

Trained undergraduate student researchers conducted the interviews, and for the sexual orientation and Arab–Jewish dialogue, interviewers were matched with interviewee by the salient topic identity in order to increase trust (e.g., Jewish students interviewed Jewish students). Interviews lasted from 20 to 60 minutes, and followed a protocol that asked about motivations and expectations for the course, safety and conflict in the dialogue, learning about ingroups, outgroups, power, privilege, oppression, communication skills, and any anticipated changes in behavior as a result of the course. For the religion dialogues, the pre-course interview asked about the students' religious background, particularly emphasizing contexts in which students have discussed their religious beliefs and attitudes. The post-course interview focused on what it was like to be a participant in the religion dialogue. Final paper assignments for all three topics followed the same format and asked students to reflect on their learning about social identity, group interaction and communication, challenges, rewards, and future implications.

Program faculty trained undergraduate and graduate student research teams who completed all final paper and interview coding. Teams used grounded theory and qualitative coding methods whereby pairs of students across social identities coded data using an iterative process, checking themes for agreement, and revising as needed to develop a codebook for each dialogue topic (Mays & Pope, 1995). All data was then analyzed using NVivo qualitative software (QSR NVivo, 2012). This participatory action research method offers students the opportunity to engage in learning about their own academic process and community, and contributes to the validation of the results (Bland & Atweh, 2007). Results from the analysis of these three intergroup dialogue courses illuminate heterosexual, Christian, and Jewish student learning about privilege.

Learning about Heterosexual Privilege

Analysis of heterosexual student final papers indicates significant learning for many students about their own numerous heterosexual privileges. This occurred more often for students without prior known interactions with LGB people, and was fostered by listening to the stories of other students, completing the readings, and engaging in their own self-reflection about their lives (Dessel et al., in press). One heterosexual male student illuminates this learning:

> I never realized the significance my sexual orientation played in my life until this class. There were many hardships and setbacks my fellow classmates went through because they were not part of the heterosexual orientation group. Before this class, I never stepped back and thought about how easy

I had it because I was part of the "mainstream" sexual group. I learned in this class to be more aware of the different social groups I am in.

Many students realized the invisibility of their many unearned heterosexual privileges, and they often attributed privileges to being in the "majority." One heterosexual woman noted "how lucky I am that I can display my affection for my boyfriend in public without fear." Many students expressed their discomfort with these realizations, and acknowledged that they took these privileges for granted. Students reported feeling a sense of guilt and defensiveness, or feeling responsible for societal injustice.

For heterosexual women who understood male privilege, the focus on intersection of identities led to new awareness, and was their "first step in becoming an LGB ally," and wanting to work for equality. A Latina woman saw the intersection of her privileged heterosexual identity with her marginalized racial identity as a "great advantage in helping to open up dialogue with those in the heterosexual group who did not have the same personal perspective." LGB students in intergroup dialogue courses indicate the way in which learning about the intersection of their White, male, or upper middle class identities with their sexual orientation helped them recognize previously unknown privileges (Dessel, Woodford, & Warren, 2011). This learning about intersectionality with regard to identity and privilege is a valuable outcome of these dialogues (Montgomery & Stewart, 2012).

Learning about Christian Privilege

Even though the dialogue curriculum intends to raise awareness of Christian privilege, analyses of interviews with students and their final papers indicates that few students explicitly mention their own or their classmates' Christian privilege. An Eastern Orthodox woman who "had never truly evaluated what it means to have or lack privilege" was an exception. She made sense of religious privilege by drawing an analogy from racial oppression:

> Once I heard the white privilege examples, it was quite easy to come up with a list of things that Christians are privilege [sic] to that others are not. This realization of the privilege I had in comparison to others made me uncomfortable.

The student experienced discomfort with this new awareness. However, readings that specifically address working for social justice helped her realize that she could channel her new awareness of privilege into concrete actions aimed at dismantling structural inequalities. In her final paper she reflected, "If I can successfully convince one person that people with privilege have to be the ones to act against the system, I will be able to call myself an ally." This student's transition from awareness to action illustrates the effectiveness of the dialogue model.

Perhaps related to the finding that students find it difficult to focus on religious privilege, they extrapolate from their experiences in the religion dialogue to gain awareness of the way in which social identity is intersectional and complex. For example, an Arab American wrote that he felt oppressed because of his Muslim identity after 9/11, but he also learned that:

> ... regardless whether or not I am cognitively aware of it, my target and agent identities go a long way in affecting my life on a daily basis. For example, by virtue of being male, I am automatically in the agent identity group that gives me privileges that I may not even be aware of.

Prior to his dialogue, this student was more aware of his oppression as a Muslim than his privilege as a man, which reflects the tendency to focus more on marginalized than privileged identities (Hardiman et al., 2007). Through the dialogue process, the student made sense of the way his different target and agent identities intersect in complex ways.

Learning about Jewish Privilege

Analysis of final papers and interviews indicate that some Jewish students resisted recognition of their privilege and power and expressed confusion about who held power and privilege in the Middle East, perhaps attributable to Jewish victimization in the Holocaust and Arab countries bordering the state of Israel. Students surfaced questions about whether a group can be both oppressed and oppress others, illuminating the intersectionality of privilege and oppression. Many Jewish students experienced new levels of awareness about their privilege related to their racial identity. The privilege walk contributed to this learning, as the majority of the Jewish students were White, and most students described the complexity of their intersectional identities in great detail. One student said:

> Though always subject to some discrimination, I am generally able to avoid negative stereotyping in my daily life as a Jewish American. Being Caucasian, I am able to blend into contemporary American society and even have the ability to ignore my Jewish heritage should I choose to do so. I am acutely aware, however, that my recent ancestors enjoyed no such similar luxury.

Jewish students also recognized their privilege to freely visit Israel, and their status as second- or third-generation Americans that provides them with benefits. However, they often cited their own group history of oppression and discrimination and the urgency for a safe Jewish homeland. Ultimately, Jewish students described becoming allies for Arab students in terms of interrupting bias and improving campus climate (Dessel & Ali, 2012).

Pedagogical Lessons Learned

A number of lessons learned emerged from our initial analysis of these intergroup dialogue courses and student learning about privilege. The first came in the form of the shifting nature of privilege. The degree to which these students experience privilege depends on complex identities, social and cultural context, and thus their social locations and positionality (Case, this volume). The tendency to focus on one's targeted identity may serve as an obstacle to recognizing privilege (such as seen in the religion and Arab–Jewish dialogues). A few heterosexual women in the sexual orientation dialogues shifted from focusing on their oppression due to sexism to appreciating their sexual orientation privilege and seeking out ways to be allies. A number of White Jewish students also shifted from their tendency to see themselves as historically discriminated against to recognizing their racial privilege. Related to this, intersectional identities interact to influence experiences of and awareness of privilege (Dill & Zambrana, 2009). Depending on the salience of different social identities for students, they may become more aware of the social privileges they are afforded. It is common for people to focus more on their oppressed identities than ones that give them power (Adams et al., 2007). Students in intergroup dialogue courses claim their privilege and develop perspective-taking and empathy. This combination of new learning promotes recognition of the ways they may become allies with and for others.

Second, while emotions become activated when awareness about privilege is raised (Leach, Iyer, & Pedersen, 2006), many Christian and Jewish students did not experience the same kind of negative emotions, such as guilt, that are associated with recognizing one's privilege (Adams et al., 2007; Cole et al., 2011). Resistance to acknowledging one's privilege, and, for Jewish students specifically, their group history of persecution, may account for this finding. We recommend that facilitators of these dialogues explore their own Christian or Jewish privilege to offer examples and models for their participants. We also emphasize the importance of explicitly identifying the privileged group and the focus on exploration of social identity-based power imbalances at the outset of the course.

Third, students in these dialogues learned about intersectionality through recognizing that they are oppressed based on some social identities and privileged based on others. In the religion dialogues, students' increased appreciation for intra-religious difference and inter-religious similarities as a result of participating in the religion dialogues may play a key role in helping students recognize lived experience as complex, multidimensional, and situational. The emphasis on Christian privilege also raises students' awareness that individuals with non-visible social identities may face systematic institutional forms of oppression.

This was an initial foray into data regarding learning about privilege for these understudied populations. Future longitudinal research should examine whether the learning documented here lasts beyond the course timeframe. Further curriculum work should continue to develop intergroup dialogue activities to analyze structural and institutional power and privilege, concepts much harder for students to grasp than individual privilege. The limited learning about Christian privilege in the religion dialogues points to the need for structuring those dialogues in a more binary fashion with regard to populating the dialogue.

For faculty at smaller campuses with less diverse student populations, many of these activities, readings, and methods can be adapted and implemented in more traditional classroom settings. Examples include attention to physical space in the classroom to promote dialogic interaction, such as circular seating, use of agreed-upon guidelines to create safety, sharing of personal narratives to promote empathy and perspective-taking, co-teaching across privileged identities when possible to represent the range of student identities, acknowledging the presence of power dynamics in the room, and use of exercises that help students negotiate strong emotions around privilege and oppression.

Intergroup dialogue pedagogy is interdisciplinary and offers a tested teaching method that can lead to new learning about privilege that sparks commitment to social action. Students are challenged to genuinely inquire about each other's experiences and reflect on unearned advantages in order to share power more equally. This pedagogy offers a unique opportunity for students to be both teachers and learners about social identity privilege, thereby taking responsibility for their own education. Educators who utilize intergroup dialogue methods promote the growth and learning of all their students.

References

ACLU. (2009). Employment Non-Discrimination Act. Retrieved May 22, 2011, from www.aclu.org/hiv-aids_lgbt-rights/employment-non-discrimination-act

Adams, M., Bell, L.A., & Griffin, P. (Eds.). (2007). *Teaching for diversity and social justice* (2nd ed.). New York, NY: Routledge.

Adams, M., & D'Errico, K. H. (2007). Antisemitism and anti-Jewish oppression curriculum design. In M. Adams, L.A. Bell, & P. Griffin (Eds.), *Teaching for diversity and social justice* (2nd ed., pp. 285–308). New York, NY: Routledge.

Adams, M., & Joshi, K. (2007). Religious oppression curriculum design. In M. Adams, L.A. Bell, & P. Griffin (Eds.), *Teaching for diversity and social justice* (2nd ed., pp. 255–284). New York, NY: Routledge.

Allen, K. (1995). Opening the classroom closet: Sexual orientation and self-disclosure. *Family Relations, 44*(2), 136–141. doi:10.2307/584799

Allport, G.W. (1954). *The nature of prejudice.* Cambridge, MA: Addison-Wesley.

Bell, L., Love, B., & Roberts, R. (2007). Racism and white privilege curriculum design. In M. Adams, L.A. Bell, & P. Griffin (Eds.), *Teaching for diversity and social justice* (2nd ed., pp. 123–145). New York, NY: Routledge.

Bland, D., & Atweh, B. (2007). Students as researchers: Engaging students' voices in PAR. *Educational Action Research, 15*(3), 337–349. doi:10.1080/09650790701514259

Blumenfeld, W. J., & Jaekel, K. (2012). Exploring levels of Christian privilege awareness among preservice teachers. *Journal of Social Issues, 68*(1), 128–144. doi:10.1111/j.1540-4560.2011.01740.x

Case, K. A. (this volume). Beyond diversity and whiteness: Developing a transformative and intersectional model of privilege studies pedagogy. In K. A. Case (Ed.), *Deconstructing privilege: Teaching and learning as allies in the classroom* (pp. 1–14). New York, NY: Routledge.

Case, K. A., & Cole, E. R. (this volume). Deconstructing privilege when students resist: The journey back into the community of engaged learners. In K. A. Case (Ed.), *Deconstructing privilege: Teaching and learning as allies in the classroom* (pp. 34–48). New York, NY: Routledge.

Case, K. A., Iuzzini, J., & Hopkins, M. (2012). Systems of privilege: Intersections, awareness, and applications. *Journal of Social Issues, 68*(1), 1–10. doi:10.1111/j.1540-4560.2011.01732.x

Case, K. A., & Lewis, M. (2012). Teaching intersectional LGBT psychology: Reflections from historically Black and Hispanic serving universities. *Psychology and Sexuality, 3*(3), 1–17. doi:10.1080/19419899.2012.700030

Case, K. A., Miller, A., & Jackson, S. B. (2012). "We talk about race too much in this class!" Complicating the essentialized woman through intersectional pedagogy. In S. Pliner & C. Banks (Eds.) *Teaching, learning, and intersecting identities in higher education* (pp. 32–48). New York, NY: Peter Lang.

Clark, C., Vargas, M. B., Schlosser, L., & Alimo, C. (2002). It's not just "secret Santa" in December: Addressing educational and workplace climate issues linked to Christian privilege. *Multicultural Education, 10*(2), 52–57.

Cole, E. R. (2009). Intersectionality and research in psychology. *American Psychologist, 64*(3), 170–180. doi:10.1037/a0014564

Cole, E. R., Case, K. A., Rios, D., & Curtin, N. (2011). Understanding what students bring to the classroom: Moderators of the effects of diversity courses on student attitudes. *Cultural Diversity and Ethnic Minority Psychology, 17*(4), 397–405. doi:10.1037/a0025433

Dessel, A., & Ali, N. (2012). Arab/Jewish intergroup dialogue courses: Building communication skills, relationships and social justice. *Small Group Research, 43*(5), 559–590. doi:10.1177/1046496412453773.

Dessel, A., Woodford, M., Routenberg, R., & Breijak, D. (in press). Heterosexual students' experiences in sexual orientation intergroup dialogue courses. *Journal of Homosexuality*.

Dessel, A., Woodford, M., & Warren, N. (2011). Intergroup dialogue courses on sexual orientation: Lesbian, gay and bisexual student experiences and outcomes. *Journal of Homosexuality, 58*(8), 1132–1150. doi:10.1080/00918369.2011.598420

Diamond, L. (2005). A new view of lesbian subtypes: Stable versus fluid identity trajectories over an 8-year period. *Psychology of Women Quarterly, 29*(2), 119–128. doi:10.1111/j.1471-6402.2005.00174.x

Dill, B. T., & Zambrana, R. E. (2009). Critical thinking about inequality: An emerging lens. In B. T. Dill & R. E. Zambrana (Eds.), *Emerging intersections: Race, class, and gender in theory, policy, and practice* (pp. 1–21). New Brunswick, NJ: Rutgers University Press.

Ecklund, E. (2010). *Science vs. religion: What scientists really think*. New York, NY: Oxford University Press.

Ferber, A. L., & Herrera, A. O. (this volume). Teaching privilege through an intersectional lens. In K. A. Case (Ed.), *Deconstructing privilege: Teaching and learning as allies in the classroom* (pp. 83–101). New York, NY: Routledge.

Goodman, D. J. (2001). *Promoting diversity and social justice: Educating people from privileged groups*. Thousand Oaks, CA: Sage.

Gravois, J. (2004). A history course forces students to look at both sides of the Israeli–Palestinian conflict. *The Chronicle of Higher Education, 51*(13), A10.

Griffin, P., D'Errico, K. H., Harro, B., & Schiff, T. (2007). Heterosexism curriculum design. In M. Adams, L. A. Bell, & P. Griffin (Eds.), *Teaching for diversity and social justice* (2nd ed., pp. 195–218). New York, NY: Routledge.

Hardiman, R., Jackson, B. W., & Griffin, P. (2007). Conceptual foundations for social justice courses. In M. Adams, L. A. Bell, & P. Griffin (Eds.), *Teaching for diversity and social justice* (2nd ed., pp. 35–66). New York, NY: Routledge.

Harris Interactive, & GLSEN. (2005). *From teasing to torment: School climate in America, a survey of students and teachers.* New York, NY: GLSEN.

Harro, B. (2010). The cycle of socialization. In M. Adams, W. Blumenfeld, R. Castañeda, H. W. Hackman, M. Peters, & X. Zúñiga (Eds.), *Readings for diversity and social justice* (2nd ed., pp. 16–21). New York, NY: Routledge.

Human Rights Campaign. (2011). An overview of federal rights and protections granted to married couples. Retrieved from www.hrc.org/resources/entry/an-overview-of-federal-rights-and-protections-granted-to-married-couples

Jaschik, S. (2005). Different kinds of diversity. *Inside Higher Ed*, August 22, 2005. Retrieved from www.insidehighered.com/news/2005/08/22/counseling

Jewish Multiracial Network. (2009). Ashkenazi privilege checklist. Retrieved from http://www.jewishmultiracialnetwork.org/resources/educational/

Khuri, M. L. (2004). Facilitating Arab-Jewish intergroup dialogue in the college setting. *Race, Ethnicity, and Education, 7*(3), 229–250. doi:10.1080/1361332042000257056

Kivlighan, D., & Arseneau, J. (2009). A typology of critical incidents in intergroup dialogue groups. *Group Dynamics: Theory, Research, and Practice, 13*(2), 89–102. doi:10.1037/a0014757

Leach, C. W., Iyer, A., & Pedersen, A. (2006). Anger and guilt about ingroup advantage explain the willingness for political action. *Personality & Social Psychology Bulletin, 32*(9), 1232–1245. doi:10.1177/0146167206289729

Maxwell, K. E., Chesler, M., & Nagda, B. A. (2011). Identity matters: Facilitators' struggles and empowered use of social identities in intergroup dialogue. In K. E. Maxwell, B. A. Nagda, & M. C. Thompson (Eds.), *Facilitating intergroup dialogues: Bridging differences, catalyzing change* (pp. 163–178). Sterling, VA: Stylus.

Maxwell, K. E., Fisher, R. B., Thompson, M. C., & Behling, C. (2011). Training peer facilitators as social justice educators: Integrating cognitive and affective learning. In K. E. Maxwell, B. A. Nagda, & M. C. Thompson (Eds.), *Facilitating intergroup dialogues: Bridging differences, catalyzing change.* (pp. 41–54). Sterling, VA: Stylus.

Maxwell, K. E., Nagda, B. A., & Thompson, M. C. (Eds.). (2011). *Facilitating intergroup dialogues: Bridging differences, catalyzing change.* Sterling, VA: Stylus.

Mays, N., & Pope, C. (1995). Qualitative research: Rigour and qualitative research. *British Medical Journal, 311*, 109–112. doi:10.1136/bmj.311.6997.109

McIntosh, P. (1988). *White privilege and male privilege: A personal account of coming to see correspondences through work in women's studies* (Working Paper No. 189). Wellesley, MA: Wellesley Centers for Women.

Miller, J., & Donner, S. (2000). More than just talk: The use of racial dialogues to combat racism. *Social Work with Groups, 23*(1), 31–53. doi:10.1300/J009v23n01_03

Montgomery, S. A., & Stewart, A. J. (2012). Privileged allies in lesbian and gay rights activism: Gender, generation, and resistance to heteronormativity. *Journal of Social Issues, 68*(1), 162–177. doi:10.1111/j.1540–4560.2012.01742.x

Nagda, B., & Gurin, P. (2007). Intergroup dialogue: A critical-dialogic approach to learning about difference, inequality, and social justice. *New Directions for Teaching and Learning, 111*, 35–45. doi:10.1002/tl.284

Nagda, B. A., Gurin, P., Sorensen, N., & Zúñiga, X. (2009). Evaluating intergroup dialogue: Engaging diversity for personal and social responsibility. *Diversity & Democracy, 12*(1), 4–6.

Nagda, B. A., & Maxwell, K. E. (2011). Deepening the layers of understanding and connection: A critical-dialogic approach to facilitating intergroup dialogues. In K. E. Maxwell, B. A. Nagda, & M. C. Thompson (Eds.), *Facilitating intergroup dialogues: Bridging differences, catalyzing change* (pp. 1–22). Sterling, VA: Stylus.

Pew Forum on Religious & Public Life. (2008). *U.S. religious landscape survey*. Retrieved from http://religions.pewforum.org/pdf/report-religious-landscape-study-full.pdf

QSR NVivo (Version 9) (2012). [Computer software]. Victoria, Australia: QSR International Pty Ltd.

Rozas, L. W. (2007). Engaging in our diverse social work student body: A multilevel theoretical process model. *Journal of Social Work Education, 43*(1), 5–30. doi:10.5175/JSWE.2007.200400467

Saguy, T., Pratto, F., Dovidio, J., & Nadler, A. (2008) Talking about power: Group power and the desired content of intergroup interactions. In S. Demoulin, J.-P. Leyens, & J. Dovidio (Eds.), *Intergroup misunderstandings: Impact of divergent social realities* (pp. 213–232). New York, NY: Taylor & Francis.

Stewart, T. L., Latu, I. M., Branscombe, N. R., Phillips, N. L., & Denney, H. T. (2012). White privilege awareness and efficacy to reduce racial inequality improve White Americans' attitudes toward African Americans. *Journal of Social Issues, 68*(1), 11–27. doi:10.1111/j.1540-4560.2012.01733.x

Wingfield, M., & Karaman, B. (2001). Arab stereotypes and American educators. In E. Lee, D. Menkart, & M. Okazawa-Rey (Eds.), *Beyond heroes and holidays: A practical guide to K-12 anti-racist, multicultural education, and staff development* (pp. 132–136). Washington, D.C.: Network of Educators on the Americas.

Zúñiga, X., Nagda, B. A., Chesler, M., & Cytron-Walker, A. (2007). Intergroup dialogue in higher education: Meaningful learning about social justice. *ASHE Higher Education Report, (32)*4, 1–128. doi:10.1002/aehe.3204

PART III

Privilege in the Classroom: Strategies and Applications

10

ARE WE QUEER YET?

Addressing Heterosexual and Gender-Conforming Privilege

Markie L. C. Blumer, Mary S. Green,
Nicole L. Thomte, and Parris M. Green

Members of many contemporary societies continue to live in a world that privileges heterosexuality and gender conformity. Heterosexual privilege includes unearned benefits afforded to those with a heterosexual orientation and defines the sexual orientation norm (Griffin, D'Errico, Harro, & Schiff, 2007). Gender-conforming privilege "refers to unearned benefits awarded to those whose internal gender identity, perceived gender, and/or expressed gender matches cultural gender expectations for their [assigned] biological sex" (Case, Kanenberg, Erich, & Tittsworth, 2012, p. 147). Dominant groups maintain power through the mechanism of hegemony. Hegemony persuades subordinate groups that the privileges of the ruling group are natural (Gramsci, 1971). A "mythical norm" (Lorde, 1984) results and generates the bulk of intentional and unintentional anti-gay and anti-trans practices that many lesbian, gay, bisexual, and transgender (LGBT) individuals, couples, and families experience.

Members of the LGBT population experience more psychological distress, acts leading to distress, and structural challenges when compared to their dominant sexual and gender orientation counterparts (Cochran & Mays, 2009; Connolly, 2004). Psychological distress involves lack of societal and familial acceptance (Blumer & Green, 2012); elevated risk for mental health and substance abuse (Cochran & Mays, 2009); difficulty identifying viable role models for individual, couple, and family development (Connolly, 2004); and a lack of role models for sexual and gender identity development for individuals, couples, and families (Blumer & Green, 2012). Some acts lead to distress and include non-support for couple and family relationships (Blumer & Murphy, 2011), management of one's visibility as an "out" individual, couple, and family (Blumer & Green, 2012; Green & Blumer, 2013; Green & Mitchell, 2008) and bullying and violence

(Robinson & Howard-Hamilton, 2000). The LGBT population also faces structural challenges such as:

- barriers to marriage, civil union, and domestic partnership recognition;
- discrimination in the workplace, health care benefits, legal rights, and housing abilities;
- hate crimes; and
- rights around parenting and adoption (Human Rights Campaign, 2010).

The effects of dominant group privileges are not limited to those members of societies who identify as LGBT. Indeed, members of the dominant majority (i.e., members of heterosexual couples and different-sex headed families) also experience the effects of inequality, although to a lesser degree and in ways that often go unrecognized. The invisibility of society's standards of "normal" becomes rooted in privileges that maintain the status quo with regard to sexuality and gender presentation (Montgomery & Stewart, 2012). This allows for the legitimization of inequality for everyone. Dominant sexual and gender orientation group privileges ultimately lead to costs for both privileged members of society as well as non-privileged members (Wise & Case, this volume) in terms of the policing of sexuality and gender. The following examples (Blumenfeld, 1992) demonstrate the impact of sexual and gender-conforming normativity and privilege on dominant group members:

- limitations on individuality because of the perceived need to act according to sexuality and gender norms, as well as role expectations;
- difficulty being supported and in supporting one's children, grandchildren, parents, extended family members, friends, etc., who identify as LGBT as an ally;
- uncertainty in working with colleagues, peers, supervisors, educators, etc., who identify as LGBT.

Some dominant group individuals experience consciousness-raising as to what are often everyday problems for many people who identify as LGBT through experiences like those listed above. In other words, the reality of the invisibility of privilege among the privileged and the unique perspective of the marginalized minority become more visible to the majority.

Addressing Heterosexual and Gender-Conforming Privileges in the Classroom

The influence of dominant sexual and gender orientation privileges applies to all members of society. We as educators are not immune from the influence of dominant cultural assumptions and socialization processes. We think in privileged ways no matter the academic level (i.e., grades K–12, higher education; Case, this volume; Puchner & Klein, 2011). As discussed by other authors, heteronormativity remains alive and well in the classroom and is perpetrated by students, educators, administrators, and the system itself (Case, McMullen, & Hentges, this volume; Castro & Sujak, 2012; McIntosh, 2007; Toomey, McGuire, & Russell, 2012). Students who observe or are on the receiving end of heteronormative assumptions, heterosexual privileging, and intentional and unintentional anti-gay behaviors want teachers to speak up (Castro & Sujak, 2012; Young, 2011). Educators, however, often lack the awareness to recognize these issues or the necessary tools for responding to these events (Zack, Mannheim, & Alfano, 2010). Educators may also face institutional barriers in leading interventions.

The term "ally" refers to a member of a dominant group who advocates for an oppressed population (Washington & Evans, 1991). Educators are uniquely situated to focus on normative discourse that perpetuates privilege and disrupts the often unintended hidden curriculum present in academic institutions (Castro & Sujak, 2012; McIntosh, 2007). Coming out as an ally challenges the educator and others to monitor privileged conversation across the curriculum and, thereby, begin to institute systemic change (Furrow, 2012; McIntosh, 2007). This systemic change can be implemented early and even begin in middle school (Puchner & Klein, 2011). Educators support and create additional allies when they become an active ally in the classroom as students answer the call to engage in conversations about privilege (Castro & Sujak, 2012).

When educators and students recognize the effects of anti-gay and anti-trans practices on everyone in society, it becomes possible to expose dominant group privileges (McIntosh, 1988). Educator responsibility includes unpacking, or deconstructing and analyzing, their own invisible knapsack, personal and professional biases, and belief systems before assisting others in unpacking theirs (Payne & Smith, 2010; Sherwin & Jennings, 2006). Educators position themselves to help students become more aware of privileges when they explored their own assumptions (Lechuga, Clerc, & Howell, 2009).

Activities aimed at fostering awareness, education, and skills around diversity are the interrelated parts that make up effective diversity training (Kim, Cartwright, Asay, & D'Andrea, 2003). The activities in this chapter provide instructors with ideas for teaching about diversity around sexual and gender orientation in ways that attend to dominant group privileges in the context of a single class and support a model of privilege studies pedagogy as outlined by Case (this volume) in her introduction to this collection. Researchers demonstrated that attending to privileges in higher education increases awareness (Case et al., 2012; Case & Stewart, 2010; Rios, Stewart, & Winter, 2010). Therefore, even modest interventions make a difference in the lives of both majority and minority students. We cannot state this with more certainty until further systemic testing occurs. Based on student feedback, however, we (Markie and Mary Sue) agree with Case (this volume) that after co-construction of knowledge, the majority of students report increased awareness of dominant group privileges. The minimal research available supports this assertion.

Henquinet, Phibbs, and Skoglund (2000) measured the pre-post effect of a volunteer ally program at Metropolitan State University. The program aimed to decrease homophobia and heterosexism, while increasing ally behaviors in faculty, staff, students, administrators, community members, and colleagues from other universities (Henquinet et al., 2000). The ally program workshops consisted of activities such as role plays of teaching and advising situations, playing "Queer Jeopardy," engaging in question and answer with student and community panel members who identify as LGBT, and creating a "personal action plan for becoming an ally" (Henquinet et al., 2000, p. 24). The programmers reported that, after programming, there are increases in supportive behaviors of faculty allies. The supportive behaviors contributed to a more positive learning environment for all students and the visible fight against homophobia and heterosexism overall (Henquinet et al., 2000).

The reduction of anti-gay and anti-trans bigotry practices and an increase in LGBT affirming practices and discourse remain the overarching goals of addressing heterosexual and gender-conforming privileges through classroom activities. We conceptualize the framework for presenting the activities as one of providing opportunities for dialogue (Payne & Smith, 2010). We find it imperative to work collaboratively with students to decide on ground rules (i.e., voluntary self-disclosure, minimization of interruptions, "no shame, no blame" in discussions; Foreman & Quinlan, 2008) well before introduction of the activities because instructor–student dialogue impacts a large part of the learning experience. We find that revisiting the rules before actual engagement in each activity increases classroom community adherence to discussion guidelines and reiterates the importance of safety in the classroom environment. We list the specific learning goals of the activities below, and others can adopt or modify them for use within their courses as needed:

- increase awareness of heterosexual and gender-conforming privileges in oneself and others through recognition and acknowledgement of such privileges;
- gain knowledge of LGBT oppressive behaviors often rooted in dominant group privileges and of LGBT ally behaviors aimed at ending LGBT oppression; and
- practice dominant sexual and gender orientation group privileges recognition, awareness, and LGBT affirming skills.

Pedagogical Activities around Addressing Heterosexual and Gender-Conforming Privileges

Rooted in the classroom, each of the following activities ties to the learning goals. The learning goals reportedly decrease homophobia and heterosexism (Foreman & Quinlan, 2008; Henquinet et al., 2000).

Activity: Heterosexual and Gender-Conforming Privilege Walk

Learning Goals

The primary learning goal of any privilege walk is to help students become more aware and understanding of the nature of privileges in oneself and others (Foss & Carpenter, 2002; Marchman, 2002).

Pedagogical Rationale

Privilege walks are a relatively common tool used in many classrooms and trainings to help students understand privileges related to race, class, ethnicity, religion, etc. (Cannon, Wiggins, Poulsen, & Estrada, 2012; Deaton, 2006; Garcia, 2009; Marchman, 2002; Sassi & Thomas, 2008; Walls et al., 2009). The privilege walks developed from McIntosh's 1988 essay, which inspired new approaches to teaching privilege (Foss & Carpenter, 2002; Queers United, 2008).

It is difficult to trace the actual origins of the privilege walk exercise beyond Peggy McIntosh (1988). Foss and Carpenter (2002) wrote of their experience in challenging students of privilege and based their classroom activities on McIntosh's work. We noticed that the privilege walk is most accessible to instructors and students by electronic means, such as through Google, Yahoo, etc. The privilege walk consists of 28 statements and includes questions about race, ethnicity, socioeconomic status, and sexual orientation. I (Mary Sue) include more questions about heterosexual and gender-conforming privileges. For many questions, I simply added sexual and gender orientation to the original questions (e.g., "If you were ever denied employment because of your race, ethnicity, gender, or *sexual or gender orientation*, take one step back."). I also added 12 questions modified from the "heterosexual privilege checklist" produced by Queers United (2008).

- If you are able to work with preschool- through to high school–aged children without fear of losing your job any day because you are assumed to corrupt children, take one step forward.
- If you have ever had strangers ask you what your "real name" [birth name] is and then call you by that name after informing them, take one step back.
- If you have ever tried to change you appearance, mannerisms, or behavior to avoid others judging you, take one step back.
- If you have always had the right to get married to someone that aligns with your own sexual/affectional orientation, take one step forward.
- If paid leave from employment is a guaranteed right when grieving the death of your partner/lover, take one step forward.
- If your partner died and you would automatically be entitled to inheritance under probate laws, take one step forward.

- If you were ever discouraged from academia or jobs because of gender, or sexual orientation, take one step back.
- If you have ever been referred to through the use of an incorrect pronoun after correcting the person, take a step back.
- If you have immediate access to your loved ones in cases of accident or emergency, because health professionals will allow you to see your loved ones without protest, take one step forward.
- If you are able to kiss, hug, or be affectionate with your romantic partner in public without threat or punishment, take one step forward.
- If a pink triangle has special personal significance for your identity, take one step back.
- If you have always been able to obtain a driver's license, passport, or any other identification card because your assigned sex, gender, and name are all compatible, take one step forward.

Instructor Role

For my classroom purposes, I (Mary Sue) include multiple forms of diversity in the activity (e.g., race, class). I do this so I do not accidently out someone to the class who has chosen to keep their sexual or gender orientation private. The instructor includes only heterosexual and gender-conforming questions if that is the focus of the exercise.

My teaching focus is at the master's and doctoral levels, and the class size consists of between 15 and 20 students. Less than 7% of the students at the university are male. I find it important to preface this activity with earlier lectures about privilege, including male privilege. I keep in mind that those with privilege are often the last to recognize their privilege (McIntosh, 1988). The ethnic and racial breakdown of the university is approximately 52% White, 21% African American, 17% Latino, 7% Asian, 1% Native American, and 2% other. I do not know the sexual orientation and gender identity of students. I find it important to maintain awareness that those with less privilege may become extremely uncomfortable and experience emotional reaction to the exercise (McDade, 2004). In my experience, the emotional reaction often results in tears. Anger just as likely occurs (Deeb-Sossa & Kane, 2007; McDade, 2004). For this reason, I include preparatory work so students become accustomed to exploring their experiences, sharing with others, and experiencing a non-judgmental stance from the instructor and classmates. Attending to privilege should be a common occurrence in the classroom and part of a living curriculum (Allen, 1995; Sassi & Thomas, 2008).

Activity Instructions

The modified privilege walk requires movement that enhances the experiential aspect of the activity (Dewey, 1938; Kolb & Kolb, 2005). Therefore, the instructor may need creativity to find an area large enough. I often take my class outside or into a hallway. The students start out in a straight line standing shoulder to shoulder. I prefer that participants hold hands so they experience the letting go of each other when their different degrees of privilege become too great. The instructor asks students to refrain from talking during the walk. The students can opt out of participating in the walk at any time during the activity. Students can also choose not to take a step even if their experience indicates they should. This is common and often shared during the follow-up discussion, along with their rationale. This provides further material for discussion. The instructor makes statements, and the students respond to each statement by either taking a step forward or a step backward. One student's comment exemplifies the importance of making this a physical experience when she stated, "When I participated in the activity last semester, we did not actually line up after, so doing the activity this time was much more powerful for me by seeing it visually."

After the walk, students are encouraged to note the location of classmates in relation to each other. The instructor's comfort with silence is important as it allows students time to engage in introspection about their positions. The instructor begins by asking students what they are thinking and feeling. This teachable moment provides the instructor with an opportunity to explore the various perspectives (Allen, 1995). I (Mary Sue) ask students what surprised them and monitor the intensity of the conversation. At times, students become very intense, and I (Mary Sue) decrease the tension through reframing. For example, I found it important to stop majority students from trying to move themselves into a marginalized position (i.e., White living in Latino neighborhood) as they attempt to relate that to the experience of an oppressed population while ignoring their current privilege (i.e., White, heterosexual).

Follow-Up Assignments

Upon returning to the classroom, the students complete a brief reflection questionnaire that asks if they experienced a similar activity in the past, their thoughts and feelings with explanations, what surprised them, and whether or not their placement would differ if the exercise included questions about disability or religion. Instructors may choose to receive student reports through personal journals, an individual blog reviewed only by the instructor, or a course blog open to everyone in the class (Walls et al., 2009). A personal journal allows the student to reflect on their experience privately. An individual blog reviewed by the instructor allows the instructor to challenge a student's impulse to provide justifications or reasons for their privilege and expands the teachable moment. With a course blog, the respectful conversation continues and multiple perspectives are heard and acknowledged.

Student Wows!

The modified privilege walk is often an emotional exercise because it includes many different privileges and related issues. As noted, I (Mary Sue) also include privileges of race, ethnicity, and financial resources. Students report empathy for students with less privilege. Many students report feeling "guilty" or "uncomfortable" with their privileged position. One student stated that she had a "mixed feeling of privilege and shame for being fortunate to have such privilege." A student on the more privileged side reported that she believed that discrimination was a perception and that [African American] people needed to change their perception. In response, an African American student wrote, "I was upset by the comment that 'discrimination is a perception' that came from the more privileged side." Although this comment was about race, the same situation can occur in regard to sexual or gender orientation.

Activity: Oppression and LGBT Ally Behaviors

Learning Goals

The learning goals of this activity are to (a) help students gain knowledge of oppressive behaviors often rooted in dominant group privileges and (b) increase student understanding of ally behaviors aimed at curtailing LGBT oppression.

Pedagogical Rationale

Privilege is pervasive and often overlooked. Heterosexual and gender-conforming privileges are two of the more insidious forms of privilege. Privilege provides benefits to some and leads to discrimination of those with less privilege. Ignoring the harmful impacts of discrimination on LGBT persons leads to greater harm (Blumer & Murphy, 2011). Classroom activities aimed at fostering understanding of dominant sexual and gender orientation privilege are essential given that effective diversity training includes fostering awareness, education, and skills (Kim et al., 2003). This activity focuses on increasing student knowledge of heterosexual and gender-conforming privileges, avenues for minimizing oppression that is rooted in these privileges, and increasing ally behaviors.

Instructor Role

I (Markie) find it helpful to revisit the ground rules that we established at the beginning of the term to ensure that the dialogue around the activity is productive and the environment feels safe for students to share. I use written follow-up assignments to assess students' feelings of safety and the degree to which the activity met student learning outcomes. I teach graduate courses of approximately 12 to 25 students of diverse (e.g., racial, ethnic, religious, sexual and gender orientation, etc.) backgrounds. I conduct the activity in classes where the focus is on diversity in families, and students are those majoring in education, counseling, psychology, family studies, and family therapy.

Activity Instructions

I (Markie) prompt students to reflect on the privileges commonly held via membership in groups of varied backgrounds and their oppressive effects, as well as the need for allies to stand up for marginalized groups in order to combat oppressive forces. Next, I read the following speech made by the German, anti-Nazi theologian Martin Niemöller (1946):

> In Germany they came first for the Communists, and I didn't speak up because I wasn't a Communist. Then they came for the Jews, and I didn't speak up because I wasn't a Jew. Then they came for the trade unionists, and I didn't speak up because I wasn't a trade unionist. Then they came for the Catholics, and I didn't speak up because I was a Protestant. Then they came for me, and by that time no one was left to speak up.
>
> (pp. 13–16)

Then I facilitate a class discussion and ask each student to answer the questions listed below. In a class of less than 20 students, students sit in a circle. For a larger class, students divide into small groups of five. I then bring the small groups back together for a large group discussion. I use questions that focus the conversation on self-reflection around privilege:

- If you do nothing about the injustices against persons who identify as LGBT (or religious, ethnic, economic minority, etc.), then how do you see others as helping you in the injustices you might face?
- How have you experienced membership in non-privileged groups or when you have not been of privileged identity/ies (e.g., dominant race or ethnicity–minority race or ethnicity, male-identified–female-identified, economically advantaged–economically disadvantaged, etc.)? How do these non-privileged experiences enhance your understanding of non-privileged experiences of persons who identify as LGBT?
- What was it like for you when people have stood up on your behalf as a person whose identity/ies or group membership/s is lesser or non-privileged?
- Even if you may disagree personally with the lives of those persons who identify as LGBT, how does your understanding of membership in non-privileged groups affect your views of LGBT-identifying persons from a social justice standpoint?

Follow-Up Assignments

The follow-up assignments I (Markie) use are aimed at assessing the degree to which the students attained the learning goals, to assess each student's feelings of safety, as well as provide an opportunity to extend the learning beyond the classroom. For this activity, I provide reflection prompts that the students respond to in writing and submit before our next class meeting.

I prefer to use reflection prompts such as:

- Briefly comment on your experience of safety in the classroom during the in-class activity.
- What are some of the consequences of privileges like heterosexual and gender-conforming privileges?
- What is the role privileges like heterosexual and gender-conforming privileges play in oppression and prevention of oppression?
- How important is it to become aware of one's privileges and how they can be harmful towards minority individuals?
- How important it is to be an ally to minority persons to prevent or put an end to oppression?

Student Wows!

In my (Markie's) experience, students express curiosity about experiences associated with certain identities or membership in various groups. As a student said after the completion of this activity, "I now wonder how others in my life like my family and friends feel about sexuality, gender, and same-sex partners. And what they do about how they feel." After completing this activity, it is not uncommon for students to want to do more to stand up for marginalized groups.

Activity: "Why Aren't You Queer Like Everybody Else?" Heterosexual and Gender-Conforming Privileges Role Play

Learning Goals

The learning goals of the role play are to (a) practice awareness and recognition of heterosexual and gender-conforming privileges in oneself and others and (b) practice skills aimed at increasing behaviors that are LGBT affirmative. The activity helps students gain insight into the effects of oppressive and discriminatory privileges and related frames of reference on individuals, couples, and families who identify as sexual and gender orientation minorities. More specifically, the activity helps students become less oppressive and discriminatory in their dialogue about and with people who identify as LGBT.

Pedagogical Rationale

Individuals may be aware of and understand dominant group privileges and their effect on LGBT people, yet remain unsure of what to do with that awareness and knowledge (Russell, 2011). In other words, informed people may feel hopeless, helpless, powerless, immobile, or lacking the necessary skills to address such oppression (Russell, 2011). Thus, instructors give students an opportunity to transform their awareness and knowledge into skills via practice. As stated earlier, effective diversity training involves fostering awareness, education, and skills (Kim et al., 2003). Put simply, what good does awareness and knowledge do if one cannot put into actions for the better? The role play primarily focuses on providing students with a place to begin recognizing dominant group privileges in themselves and others and to practice commenting on these privileges and related oppressions in the hopes of minimizing oppression and increasing ally behaviors.

Instructor Role

Before beginning this activity, we (Markie and Mary Sue) like to review the ground rules created earlier to make sure the environment feels safe to students. We also reiterate the voluntary nature of participating. We note that some of the questions in the role play may seem absurd or humorous and explain that humor does not diminish the effects of intentional or unintentional anti-gay or anti-trans questions. When available, we utilize a teachable moment to discuss the use of humor to hide discomfort or injury caused by the statements of others. In this activity, students take a stance often in direct opposition to their own and societal reality. Students adopt a lens that centers homosexuality and gender nonconformity as the norm. This lens also marginalizes heterosexuality and gender conformity as "other."

We obtain feedback on this activity through anonymous course evaluations in undergraduate and graduate courses with students from diverse (e.g., racial, ethnic, religious, sexual and gender orientation) backgrounds. This activity includes students enrolled in psychology, human services, family studies, and sociology programs. Class size varies from 12 students in graduate-level courses to 140 students in undergraduate courses.

Activity Instructions

This activity is a role play based on "homocentric role play" (Blumer & Green, 2011) that, in turn, is based on the "heterosexual questionnaire" (Rochlin, 1972/2003). The instructor separates the students into groups, with 3 to 5 students per group. Smaller groups for role plays are less intimidating than a performance-type role play in front of an entire class. In each group, one student plays the role of the interviewer asking uninformed questions through homocentric and gender diversity lenses. A homocentric lens means that the interviewer takes the stance that the "mythical norms" of society are ones of homosexuality and gender diversity. One student adopts the part of being a new dominant sexual and gender orientation group, or two students play the part of being a new dominant group couple. Any remaining students act as respectful observers of the role play.

Next, the student interviewer asks the interviewees a series of questions commonly asked by the current dominant privileged group of LGBT individuals, partners, and families, only in reverse. This means that, instead of a heterosexual and gender-conforming person of privilege asking questions of someone who identifies as LGBT, a homosexual, gender diverse privileged person asks the questions of the less privileged heterosexual and gender-conforming individuals (Blumer & Green, 2011; Rochlin, 1972/2003). We use the following questions for the role play:

- What do you think caused your heterosexuality?
- What do you think caused you to be gender-conforming (i.e., identify as "male"/"masculine" or "female"/"feminine")?
- When and how did you decide you were a heterosexual?
- When and how did you decide you were gender-conforming?
- Is it possible that your heterosexuality is just a phase that you may grow out of?
- Is it possible that your gender-conforming is just a phase that you may grow out of?
- If you have never had sex with a person of the same sex, is it possible that all you need is a "good gay lover"?
- Do your parents know that you are gender-conforming? Do your friends or roommate(s) know? How did they react?
- Do your parents know that you are straight? Do your friends or roommate(s) know? How did they react?
- There seem to be very few happy heterosexuals. Techniques have been developed that might enable you to change if you really want. Have you considered trying conversion therapy?
- There seem to be very few happy people who are gender-conforming. Techniques have been developed that might enable you to be more gender diverse if you really want. Have you considered trying conversion therapy?
- Would you want your child to be heterosexual, knowing the problems that they would face?
- Would you want your child to be gender-conforming, knowing the problems that they would face?

After completing the role play, each group processes the experience of this activity by respectfully answering and discussing the following questions:

- Describe what it was like to be "forced" to ask, answer, or listen to these kinds of questions.
- As a participant interviewer, interviewee, or observer in this role play, what was it like hearing those with heterosexual and gender-conforming privileges being marginalized?
- What are some of the emotional reactions (e.g., anger, frustration, confusion, etc.) that you experienced during this role play? What about some of your

intellectual (e.g., thoughts, beliefs, etc.) and physical reactions (e.g., heart racing, accelerated breathing, stomach nausea, etc.)?

- What do you think it is like for people who identify as sexual and gender orientation minorities to be asked these kinds of questions, only in reverse (i.e., by persons who typically identify as heterosexual and gender-conforming and hold heterosexual and gender-conforming privileges)?
- If you do not identify as heterosexual or gender-conforming, explain what it was like for you to experience this role play activity as a participant interviewer, interviewee, or observer?
- How are these kinds of questions oppressive? How are these kinds of questions, when asked in reverse, oppressive towards persons who identify as LGBT?
- What are some ideas you have for how people can dialogue about sexual and gender orientation in a way that is affirming rather than oppressive?

Follow-Up Assignments

We (Markie and Mary Sue) use follow-up assignments aimed at assessing the degree to which the students attained the learning goals and felt safe, as well as providing an opportunity to extend the learning beyond the classroom. We use reflection prompts and ask students to complete the assignment individually before the next class period. I (Mary) often provide time in class for this follow-up activity so that their thoughts and feelings are fresh. Instructors know their students best and may adjust the reflection prompts based on the class demographics and dynamics. We prefer to choose from the prompts below.

- Briefly comment on your experience of safety in the classroom during the in-class activity.
- How has this role play activity helped inform your awareness and recognition of heterosexual and gender-conforming privileges in yourself and others?
- How did the activity enhance your understanding of the role that heterosexual and gender-conforming privileges play in oppression?
- What did you learn about yourself and your peers in terms of heterosexual and gender-conforming privileges, oppression, and affirmation skills through participating in this role play activity?
- What are some of the ideas that you and your peers came up with for how people can dialogue about sexual and gender orientation in ways that are affirmative?

Student Wows!

We (Markie and Mary Sue) obtain feedback on this activity through anonymous course evaluations in undergraduate and graduate courses with students from diverse (e.g., racial, ethnic, religious, sexual and gender orientation) backgrounds.

Students are enrolled in psychology, human services, family studies, and sociology programs. Class size varies from 12 students in graduate-level courses to 140 students in undergraduate courses.

This activity can be challenging for both dominant and non-dominant students. I (Markie) observed several commonalities across classrooms academic levels when completing this activity. Students who identify with a dominant group had a harder time understanding the role play during the exercise and sometimes even after completion. Sexual and gender orientation minority students often report difficulty answering the questions in a genuine and authentic manner when interviewed as member of the hypothetical dominant homosexual or gender non-conforming group. I (Mary Sue) hear student comments about the "fakey" questions and the belief that no one would ever ask such questions of the LGBT population. For example, a student said, "I cannot believe that someone would ask if being gay—or, in this role play, straight—is a phase!" Our observations mean that the discussion that takes place after the activity is essential in order to help with student comprehension. It is a very powerful experience when a student who is a member of the dominant group gains an understanding of the role play and shares it with the class. One student stated:

> I found the … role play in which the tables were turned as being gay or lesbian was considered the norm extremely enlightening. I've … become less tolerant when my family members make remarks indicating that this group of people is somehow sub-human.
>
> (heterosexual female student)

Student comments support the research findings that attending to diversity in even one class raises awareness (Murphy, Parks, & Lonsdale, 2006).

The discussion also gives sexual and gender minority students the opportunity to identify themselves in a way that is authentic if they so choose. As one student wrote in an anonymous evaluation, "What … surprised me [was] how comfortable I was talking about my sexual orientation and how comfortable my classmates were listening" (lesbian student). Student comfort in sharing their sexual or gender identity with the larger class indicates that, overall, students are becoming more LGBT affirmative.

Beyond Addressing Heterosexual and Gender-Conforming Privileges in the Classroom: Continuing the Conversation

We believe that the presented activities are helpful in addressing heterosexual and gender-conforming privileges in the context of the classroom. However, these activities merely serve as a starting point for educators and students in terms of attending to these privileges. Thus, we encourage others to consider additional opportunities and ways to discuss and address dominant sexual and gender orientation privileges across multiple contexts.

We present students with stories or case studies that include persons identifying as LGBT individuals, couples, and families and encourage discussion about privileges. We explore the intersecting in the lives of sexual and gender orientation minority persons. We discuss ways to act in a more affirming manner. Alternatively, we encourage students to develop their own scenarios to stimulate dialogue about ways to minimize oppression and maximize LGBT affirming behaviors. We position ourselves as allies and continue to address dominant group privileges outside of classroom activities through modeling LGBT affirmative language and behaviors.

This chapter provides tools to incorporate into classroom curriculums to assist other educators to begin incorporating privilege studies pedagogy into the curriculum (Case, this volume). These tools aim primarily at creating space for students as a precursor to increasing awareness and knowledge of heterosexual and gender-conforming privileges and facilitating dialogue about the effects that societal-condoned privilege has on both marginalized and dominant group members. These tools act as visibility glasses that give students the power to gain informed acuity for recognizing the invisibility of privilege among those that are privileged and to visibly act in ways that are affirming on behalf of those that experience oppression as a result of these privileges.

References

Allen, K. (1995). Opening the classroom closet: Sexual orientation and self-disclosure. *Family Relations, 44*(2), 136–141. doi:10.2307/584799

Blumenfeld, W. J. (Ed.) (1992). *Homophobia: How we all pay the price.* Boston, MA: Beacon Press.

Blumer, M. L. C., & Green, M. S. (2011, March 4). *Homocentric role play* [Video podcast]. Retrieved August 16, 2012, from www.youtube.com/watch?v=V3VH_okVJqw

Blumer, M. L. C., & Green, M. S. (2012, January). *The role of same-sex couple development in clinical practice.* Nationally Broadcast Professional Continuing Education Workshop, American Association of Marriage and Family Therapy, Alexandria, VA. Available at www.aamft.org

Blumer, M. L. C., & Murphy, M. J. (2011). Alaskan gay males' couple experience of societal non-support: Coping through families of choice and therapeutic means. *Contemporary Family Therapy: An International Journal, 33*(3), 273–290. doi:10.1007/s10591-011-9147-5

Cannon, E., Wiggins, M., Poulsen, S., & Estrada, D. (2012). Addressing heterosexist privilege during orientation: One program's experience. *Journal of LGBT Issues in Counseling, 6*(1), 3–17. doi:10.1080/15538605.2011.598225

Case, K. A. (this volume). Beyond diversity and whiteness: Developing a transformative and intersectional model of privilege studies pedagogy. In K. A. Case (Ed.), *Deconstructing privilege: Teaching and learning as allies in the classroom* (pp. 1–14). New York: Routledge.

Case, K. A., Kanenberg, H., Erich, S. A., & Tittsworth, J. (2012). Transgender inclusion in university nondiscrimination statements: Challenging gender-conforming privilege through student activism. *Journal of Social Issues, 68*(1), 145–161. doi:10.1111/j.1540-4560.2011.01741.x

Case, K. A., McMullen, M., & Hentges, B. (this volume). Teaching the taboo: Walking the tightrope of Christian privilege. In K. A. Case (Ed.), *Deconstructing privilege: Teaching and learning as allies in the classroom* (pp. 188–206). New York, NY: Routledge.

Case, K. A., & Stewart, B. (2010). Changes in diversity course student prejudice and attitudes toward heterosexual privilege and gay marriage. *Teaching of Psychology, 37*(3), 172–177. doi:10.1080/00986283.2010.488555

Castro, I. E., & Sujak, M. C. (2012). "Why can't we learn about this?" Sexual minority students navigate the official and hidden curricular spaces of high school. *Education and Urban Society.* doi:10.1177/0013124512458117

Cochran, S. D., & Mays, V. M. (2009). Burden of psychiatric morbidity among lesbian, gay, and bisexual individuals in the California quality of life survey. *Journal of Abnormal Psychology, 118*(3), 647–658. doi:10.1037/a0016501

Connolly, C. M. (2004). Clinical issues with same-sex couples: A review of the literature. In J. J. Bigner & J. L. Wetchler (Eds.), *Relationship therapy with same-sex couples* (pp. 3–12). New York, NY: Haworth Press.

Deaton, K. (2006). Understanding racial identity development through intergroup dialogue. *Campus Activities Programming, 39*(3), 44–48.

Deeb-Sossa, N., & Kane, H. (2007). "It's the word of God": Students' resistance to questioning and overcoming heterosexism. *Feminist Teacher, 17*(2), 151–169.

Dewey, J. (1938). *Education and experience.* New York, NY: Simon and Schuster.

Foreman, M., & Quinlan, M. (2008). Increasing social work students' awareness of heterosexism and homophobia: A partnership between a community gay health project and a school of social work. *Social Work Education, 27*(2), 152–158. doi:10.1080/02615470701709485

Furrow, H. (2012). LGBT Students in the college composition classroom. *Journal of Ethnographic & Qualitative Research, 6*(3), 145–159.

Foss, A., & Carpenter, M. (2002). Peeling the onion: Teaching critical literacy with students of privilege. *Language Arts, 79*(5), 393–403.

Garcia, J. M. (2009). Privileges with a price: Heterosexism debunked. *Campus Activities Programming, 41*(6), A9–A11.

Gramsci, A. (1971). *Selections from the prison notebooks.* Q. Hoare & G. Nowell-Smith (Trans. & Eds.). New York, NY: International Publishers.

Green, M. S., & Blumer, M. L. C. (2013). (In)visibility in lesbian and gay families: Managing the family closet. *Family Therapy Magazine, 12*, 28–29.

Green, R. J., & Mitchell, V. (2008). Gay and lesbian couples in therapy: Minority stress, relational ambiguity, and families of choice. In A. Gurman (Ed.), *Clinical handbook of couple therapy* (4th ed., pp. 662–680). New York, NY: Guilford Press.

Griffin, P., D'Errico, K. H., Harro, B., & Schiff, T. (2007). Heterosexism curriculum design. In M. Adams, L. A. Bell, & P. Griffin. (Eds.), *Teaching for diversity and social justice: A sourcebook* (2nd ed., pp. 195–218). New York, NY: Routledge.

Henquinet, J., Phibbs, A., & Skoglund, B. (2000). Supporting our gay, lesbian, bisexual, and transgender students. *About Campus, 5*(5), 24–26. doi:10.1002/abc.55

Human Rights Campaign. (2010). Equality from state to state 2010: A review of state legislation affecting the lesbian, gay, bisexual, transgender community and a look ahead to 2011. Retrieved December 10, 2011, from www.hrc.org

Kim, B. S. K., Cartwright, B. Y., Asay, P. A., & D'Andrea, M. J. (2003). A revision of the Multicultural Awareness, Knowledge, and Skills Survey—Counselor Edition. *Measurement and Evaluation in Counseling and Development, 36*(3), 161–180.

Kolb, A.Y., & Kolb, D.A. (2005). Learning styles and learning spaces: Enhancing experiential learning in higher education. *Academy of Management Learning & Education, 4*(2), 193–212. doi:10.5465/AMLE.2005.17268566.

Lechuga, V. M., Clerc, L. N., & Howell, A. K. (2009). Power, privilege, and learning: Facilitating encountered situations to promote social justice. *Journal of College Student Development, 50*(2), 229–244. doi:10.1353/csd.0.0064

Lorde, A. (1984). *Sister outsider: Essays and speeches*. Trumansburg, NY: Crossing Press.

Marchman, B. K. (2002). Teaching about homophobia in high school civics course. *Theory & Research in Social Education, 30*(2), 302–305. doi:10.1080/00933104.2002.10473197

McDade, T. (2004). For resident assistants: A race for inequality. *Chronicle of Higher Education, 50*(48), B5.

McIntosh, P. (1988). *White privilege and male privilege: A personal account of coming to see correspondences through work in women's studies* (Working Paper No. 189). Wellesley, MA: Wellesley Center for Women.

McIntosh, L. (2007). Does anyone have a band-aid? Anti-homophobia discourses and pedagogical impossibilities. *Educational Studies, 41*(1), 33–43. doi:10.1080/00131940701308874

Montgomery, S. A., & Stewart, A. J. (2012). Privileged allies in lesbian and gay rights activism: gender, generation and resistance to heteronormativity. *Journal of Social Issues, 68*(1), 162–177. doi:10.1111/j.1540–4560.2012.01742.x

Murphy, M. J., Park, J., & Lonsdale, N. J. (2006). Marriage and family therapy students' change in multicultural counseling competencies after a diversity course. *Contemporary Family Therapy: An International Journal, 28*(3), 303–311. doi:10.1007/s10591–006–9009–8

Niemöller, M. (1946). A sermon entitled "Über die deutsche Schuld, Not und Hoffnung" ["Once again, the German guilt, suffering and hope"]. (Trans. R. Spodheim) New York, NY: Philosophical Library.

Payne, E., & Smith, M. (2010). Reduction of stigma in schools: An evaluation of the first three years. *Issues in Teacher Education, 19*(2), 11–36. doi:10.1016.j-stueduc.2010.08.001

Puchner, L., & Klein, N. A. (2011). The right time and place? Middle school language arts teachers talk about not talking about sexual orientation. *Equity & Excellence in Education, 44*(2), 233–248. doi:10.1080/10554584.2011.563182

Queers United. (2008, October 12). *The heterosexual privilege checklist* [Web log post]. Retrieved from http://queersunited.blogspot.com/2008/10/heterosexual-privilege-checklist.html

Rios, D., Stewart, A. J., & Winter, D. G. (2010). "Thinking she could be the next President": Why identifying with the curriculum matters. *Psychology of Women Quarterly 34*(3), 328–338. doi:10.1111/j.6402.2010.01578.x

Robinson, T. L., & Howard-Hamilton, M. F. (2000). Converging sexual orientation. In T. Robinson (Ed.), *The convergence of race, ethnicity, and gender: Multiple identities in counseling* (pp. 128–136). Upper Saddle River, NJ: Merrill/Prentice Hall.

Rochlin, M. (1972/2003). Heterosexual questionnaire. In M. S. Kimmel & A. L. Ferber (Eds.), *Privilege: A reader* (pp. 75–76). Cambridge, MA: Westview Press.

Russell, G. M. (2011). Motives of heterosexual allies in collective action for equality. *Journal of Social Issues, 67*(2), 376–393. doi:10.1111/j.1540–4560.2011.01703.x

Sassi, K., & Thomas, E. E. (2008). Walking the talk: Examining privilege and race in a ninth-grade classroom. *English Journal, 97*(6), 25–31.

Sherwin, G., & Jennings, T. (2006). Feared, forgotten, or forbidden: Sexual orientation topics in secondary teacher preparation programs in the USA. *Teaching Education, 17*(3), 207–223. doi:10.1080/10476210600849664

Toomey, R. B., McGuire, J. K., & Russell, S. T. (2012). Heteronormativity, school climates, and perceived safety for gender nonconforming peers. *Journal of Adolescence, 35*(1), 187–196. doi:10.1016/j.adolescence.2011.03.001

Walls, E. N., Griffin, R., Arnold-Renicker, H., Burson, M., Johnston, C., Moorman, N., Nelsen, J., & Schutte, E. C. (2009). Mapping graduate school social work student learning journeys about heterosexual privilege. *Journal of Social Work Education, 45*(2), 289–307. doi:10.5175/JSWE.2009.200800004

Washington, R. L., & Evans, N. J. (1991). Becoming an ally. In N. J. Evans & V. A. Wall (Eds.), *Beyond tolerance: Gays, lesbians, and bisexuals on campus* (pp. 195–204). Alexandria, VA: American College Personnel Association.

Wise, T., & Case, K. A. (this volume). Pedagogy for the privileged: Addressing inequality and injustice without shame or blame. In K. A. Case (Ed.), *Deconstructing privilege: Teaching and learning as allies in the classroom* (pp. 17–33). New York, NY: Routledge.

Young, A. B. (2011). LGBT students want educators to speak up for them. *Phi Delta Kappan 93*(2), 35–37.

Zack, J., Mannheim, A., & Alfano, M. (2010). "I didn't know what to say": Four archetypal responses to homophobic rhetoric in the classroom. *The High School Journal 93*(3), 98–110. doi:10.1353/hsj.0.0047

11

CLASS ACTION

Using Experiential Learning to Raise Awareness of Social Class Privilege

Wendy R. Williams and Kala J. Melchiori

Economic inequality in the United States continues to grow. Since the late 1990s, the gap between the "haves" and the "have nots" has widened steadily, and income inequality has reached its highest peak since the Great Depression (U.S. Census Bureau, 2012). Despite these disparities, scrutiny of social class privilege occurs much less often than critical examinations of other categories of privilege, such as gender, race, ethnicity, or sexuality (American Psychological Association (APA), 2008). Although researchers call for increased attention to social class and economic inequality (e.g., Lott & Bullock, 2007; Williams, 2009), specific pedagogical strategies for examining social class privilege within college classrooms remain rare.

We propose that faculty can successfully teach social class privilege by utilizing experiential learning within a critical, feminist pedagogical framework. Because experiential learning is the process by which knowledge comes from reflection on personal experiences (Kolb, 1984), assignments that allow students to critically examine the unearned power that exists because one belongs (or is perceived to belong) to a middle or higher socioeconomic group will foster awareness of social class privilege. We believe faculty can not only reach their teaching and learning goals by teaching social class privilege using experiential learning, but that with these pedagogical tools they can also work toward the amelioration of the systems that create and maintain privilege.

What is Social Class Privilege?

Researchers define social class in a variety of ways, but the two most common characterizations are either in demographic terms (i.e., as one's financial wealth, education, or occupation) or as one's subjective experience (i.e., one's values, beliefs and behaviors; see APA, 2007). Yet these definitions lack an emphasis on power, despite the fact that in most societies social class exists within a structure that confers power to those at the top while blocking access for those at the bottom (APA, 2007). Thus, we define *social class* as the organization of people based on a combination of their wealth, values, and social capital wherein those with the most economic resources hold incrementally more power than those with less economic resources (APA, 2008; Lott & Bullock, 2007). We define *social class privilege* as the unearned power that exists because one belongs (or is perceived to belong) to a middle or higher social class group in a system that confers advantage to this status specifically (Liu, Pickett, & Ivey, 2007; Sanders & Mahalingam, 2012).

Which Pedagogies Work Best for Teaching Social Class Privilege?

Faculty can use a number of pedagogical frameworks to examine social class privilege. Although no "right" way to teach social class privilege exists, we find that the most useful pedagogies include feminist or critical frameworks (e.g., Case, Kanenberg, Erich, & Tittsworth, 2012; Weis & Fine, 2012). In general, feminist and critical frameworks examine the attitudes, traditions, behaviors, and institutions that systematically reinforce power and privilege, and they encourage individuals to examine themselves, their social situations, and existing hierarchies (e.g., Collins, 1989; Freire, 1970; hooks, 2000). When used as teaching pedagogies, these frameworks foster collaboration, self-reflection, empowerment, and collective action (e.g., Enns & Forrest, 2005). Thus, faculty should adopt whichever specific frame within the critical, feminist literature that best fits their educational goals.

Personally, I (Wendy) find that "standpoint theory" (Harding, 1986) works well as a frame in my course on the Psychology of Poverty and Social Class. I begin from the position that by ignoring one's standpoint, one ignores the subjectivity of knowledge (Harding, 2004). To illustrate this, I discuss Harding's (1997) example of a stick floating in the middle of a large body of water. At first, the stick may appear long and bent, but, if you walk around the body of water, thus changing your perspective, the stick may appear straighter or shorter than it had only a moment before. No "correct" perspective exists, and each interpretation of the shape of the stick reflects one's standpoint. Thus, every standpoint in the classroom, whether a specific role (e.g., teacher, student) or position within the larger social class structure (e.g., low income, middle class), offers a valid perspective for interpreting social class, and the presence of those perspectives leads to a more nuanced view of social class privilege. Although a student who expresses a privileged perspective (e.g., "poor people are just lazy") might find validation by the use of this framework, when they hear alternative perspectives voiced by other participants (e.g., "tax breaks for the super-rich cost us millions each year"), it becomes hard for those same students to believe that their perspective is the only perspective, or even the "correct" one. When these instances arise, I remind students that just as our knowledge about the "true" shape of the stick depends on the number of perspectives we consider, our knowledge about social class privilege and the way it shapes our class-consciousness depends upon the perspectives of people from all social strata. Thus, I find using critical and feminist frameworks (such as standpoint theory) allows students to examine the concept of "truth" and the ways in which "truth" fluctuates according to our position within society (Markowitz, 2005).

What are Learning Goals for Teaching Social Class Privilege?

When teaching social class privilege, faculty may use a variety of learning goals including those that focus on content, skills, and values. Table 11.1 provides an example that can aid pedagogical planning around social class privilege.

I (Wendy) find that I can elucidate the core ideas of my pedagogy through the expression of my course goals and outcomes (e.g., identification of structural barriers, recognizing others' standpoints, critical reflection, taking action), and so I include a chart like Table 11.1 within my syllabus. Equally, I (Kala) find that this format gives me, as a student, valuable guidance when reflecting on my academic

TABLE 11.1

	Learning Goal	*Students Will:*	*Assignment Related to Goal*
Content	Provide information on the way in which systems of privilege create and maintain social class inequalities	Identify structural barriers that prevent mobility at various life stages and explain the way in which these structures reify privilege for individuals within different social strata	Response papers, classroom discussion of readings, and the final exam
Skills	Encourage the application of course content to the "real world" by examining social class privilege in everyday experiences	Use critical reflection on experiential learning to express the way in which psychological research on social class privilege and standpoint theory can be applied to daily life	Experiential learning critical reflections essays, in-class discussions, and the final exam
Values	Foster social change for low-income people by challenging social class privilege	Demonstrate increased social sensitivity and empathy for low-income individuals by taking action with them or on their behalf to confront systems that foster and maintain social class privilege	Performance in service-learning hours and final service-learning project

and service experiences, and helps me make my written assignments more thoughtful. By articulating for students (a) clear learning goals, (b) the ways in which learning gets evaluated by the instructor, and (c) which specific assignments achieve these goals, students can identify the links between the theory, pedagogy, and assignments.

How Do I Put this Pedagogy into Action?

To examine social class privilege, professors can help students recognize where they and others stand within these systems. When students understand the impact of privilege on a personal level (i.e., who possesses power and why), they then appreciate the need for fighting against systemic oppression. In particular, challenging social class privilege requires disputing the commonly held belief of meritocracy, where the allocation of resources results from hard work and perseverance rather than depending on one's birth within the social class structure (Liu et al., 2007). Because privilege is often invisible to those who possess privilege (McIntosh, 1988), faculty need to utilize assignments that illuminate the way in which the system creates and maintains unearned benefits for those with higher social class standing. Although faculty can effectively teach social class privilege in a number of ways, we find that experiential learning with structured reflection most effectively elicits an awareness of, and a willingness to challenge, social class privilege.

Experiential Learning

Faculty can put critical and feminist pedagogies into practice by using experiential learning as a tool for helping students understand social class privilege. Drawing on the work of John Dewey, Kurt Lewin, and Jean Piaget, Kolb (1984) defines experiential learning as the process by which knowledge is generated as a direct result of reflection on personal experiences. Research consistently finds that experiential learning improves students' understanding of material as well as other personal outcomes (see Kolb & Kolb, 2012, for an extensive, three-volume bibliography of experiential learning research). Activities that foster experiential learning allow students to think critically about "truth" and the way it relates to their own and others' experiences. Readings, papers, class activities, and service-learning provide excellent platforms for experiential learning about social class privilege (Kolb & Kolb, 2012).

Readings and Reflections

We find that readings on critical and feminist analyses of privilege give students the language to deconstruct their own and others' personal experiences. The experiential learning comes not from the reading itself, but from the reflection on the reading. With reflection, students cannot receive the information passively, but rather must consider it carefully and thoughtfully.

We believe faculty can effectively teach social class privilege using class discussion to aid students' reflection on readings. For example, in McIntosh's (1988) widely taught article, she argues that privilege is an "invisible knapsack" that allows the privileged to live in a very different world than those without privilege. When I (Wendy) assign McIntosh's (1988) article, I ask students to consider their standpoint as they read (e.g., What do you think is the author's most important point? What critique do you have of the author's argument? What questions remain for you after reading this article?). Then, I encourage students to share their thoughts during class discussion. In this way, I can both determine students' ability to grasp the author's ideas, and I can foster the exchange of perspectives. Students, in turn, see the way in which their original perspective reflects their own standpoint, but also that others express different standpoints which they must consider during discussion.

Moreover, because McIntosh's (1988) article addresses white, male, and heterosexual privilege, students use the insight gained from discussing these forms of privilege to unpack social class privilege during our discussion. In particular, I (Wendy) ask students to create a list of "class privileges" as part of the discussion, and we compare our list to similar lists inspired by McIntosh's (1988) work (e.g., Liu et al., 2007). I find that, as a result of peer input, students report that the experience raises their awareness of privilege to a new level (even for those who already understand privilege). For example, when I (Kala) participated in this activity in Wendy's classroom, the experience helped me understand not only my classmates' background, but also helped to situate my own class background within the social setting of a college classroom. I was better able to understand both my privileges and disadvantages in relation to my fellow students.

Finally, the article provides me (Wendy) with an opportunity to push students to identify the ways in which race, gender, and social class privilege intersect (Collins, 1989; Crenshaw, 1989). Research supports that experiential learning enhances students' understanding of the daily impact of social class as it intersects with other social identities like race, ethnicity, and gender (Espino & Lee, 2011), and I find that this type of sustained reflection on readings during class discussion leads students to consider their intersectionality. Through the process of reading and reflecting on the assigned articles, students grapple with social class privilege as well as intersection with other standpoints.

Paper Assignments

By writing about, and reflecting on, their own personal experiences, students can engage in experiential learning about social class privilege. Writing provides an avenue for students to learn about the numerous ways social class shaped their instructor's and peers' past, present, and future. It also provides powerful, personal evidence for the students to draw on when they critically write about their own social class privilege. For example, I (Wendy) ask students to read my "social class autobiography" prior to class (see the Appendix at the end of this chapter). In class, we then discuss my personal narrative of moving through social class boundaries, and we connect it to the idea of personal standpoint and social class privilege. Students then come to the next class ready to share their own "social class autobiography." By writing a narrative that gives examples of class privilege or deprivation in their own life, students demonstrate their critical reflection on their own experiences with social class. In discussing each student's narrative, students make connections between personal experiences and academic theories. Finally, at the end of the course, I ask students to revise their narratives, including any new insights gained about their own social class privilege. In this way, students learn from others' experience of social class privilege and take sustained time to reflect on their own privilege (or lack thereof). I find that I gain a greater sense of my students' social class backgrounds through this kind of assignment. I also find that writing assignments like this allow students to share their diverse experiences with privilege (or deprivation) in a non-threatening way. For instance, I find that shy, private, or extremely privileged or deprived students will not necessarily share personal stories spontaneously in a class discussion, but that they more frequently share their experiences if they write about them first.

As an illustration of the effectiveness of using reflection on writing, after reading Wendy's social class encounters (see Appendix), I (Kala) remembered my own experience with lunchroom social class politics. One of my friends in high school ate breakfast every day in the school cafeteria, and one day she invited me to join her and talk before class. In my high school, the students who ate breakfast at school were stigmatized as "poor" and pitied because they relied on the school for an additional meal. Although I ate breakfast with my friend, I tried my best to "lay low" so that my other friends would not see me. Reading Wendy's experience in the cafeteria prompted me to remember this similar example from my own life. Through the "social class autobiography" exercise, I made an important connection between the internalization of dominant social class narratives, stigma, and the concealability of social class. It prompted me to examine why I engaged in the same problematic behavior as those with greater social class privilege. I realized I internalized the implicit message that being low income is a negative trait. Thus I was motivated both to conceal my status as a working-class student and to judge those who did not conceal their low-income status. Through reflection, I could see both my former standpoint and the way in which the course changed my perspective.

Activities

The report of APA's Task Force (2008) concerning "resources for the inclusion of social class in psychology curricula" provides one of the few sources of materials for teaching social class privilege. Although faculty can use this report as a helpful resource, the text itself does not describe ways to include these ideas within a critical, feminist pedagogical framework of privilege. Because the report describes in detail a number of activities that can raise awareness of social class privilege (e.g., classroom exercises, fiction, film, television, music, and websites), the following section will detail an additional online resource created after the report to illustrate the way in which activities (like those in the APA Task Force report) can foster awareness of social class privilege.

An online activity called "Spent" provides a glimpse into what millions of low-income people experience every month (http://playspent.org/). The game asks you to imagine that you are a recently unemployed single parent with only $1,000 in savings. You then make a series of choices to determine if you can survive until the end of the month without running out of money or experiencing a major personal crisis (e.g., losing your job, your car, your health, or your principles). This virtual reality forces students to wrestle with their privilege by challenging their implicit beliefs and assumptions about the choices that low-income people make. When I use this activity, I find that, although students can intellectually understand poverty, and some experience it themselves, the process of making difficult choices (e.g., Do I give money to my child for her school trip or put gas in my car?) allows for a new level of understanding of the issue of class privilege. For example, students comment on the fact that, even though it was a computer simulation, they struggled with their choices. Moreover, having to place themselves in someone else's shoes provides students with an opportunity to reflect on their standpoint before, during, and after the simulation. Students report that playing this "game" makes a stronger impact on them than just theoretically discussing social class privilege or standpoint theory. In this way, students use reflection on new experiences to make connections with theoretical concepts (see also www.classism.org/resources for additional sources of activities).

Service Learning

Researchers define service learning as a subtype of experiential learning that increases students' academic understanding and personal growth by having them engage in a community project that benefits both the student and the community (Eyler & Giles, 1999; Furco, 1996). More specifically, in discipline-based service learning, students work at a community placement relevant to course content over the span of the semester (Heffernan, 2001). In addition to well-planned placements, research finds that structured reflection makes discipline-reflective service learning successful (Conway, Amel, & Gerwien, 2009; Hatcher & Bringle, 1997). Through structured assignments (e.g., readings, papers, projects), students reflect on the ways their experiences in the community compare and contrast to content in their discipline. Thus, service learning provides an opportunity for students to engage in experiential learning outside of the campus community.

In order to effectively illuminate social class privilege, faculty should carefully consider which placements best meet both course goals and community needs (Stoecker, Tyron, & Hilgendorf, 2009). I (Wendy) find social service agencies that provide shelter, clothing, and food ideal for studying social class privilege, but that students can only make necessary connections with course content when they work together with staff and clients (i.e., hear their standpoints). For example, effective assignments may include taking meals to senior citizens, playing with children at a low-income daycare center, or helping women receiving public assistance craft personal résumés (see also Dunlap, Scoggin, Green, & Davi, 2007; Tallant, 2011). Each of these service-learning environments provides opportunities for students to interact with low-income people and confront their beliefs about social class and privilege. At the same time, these placements benefit the community by assisting agencies in meeting their existing social justice goals (Leiderman, Furco, Zapf, & Goss, 2003). Faculty must converse openly with community partners to establish that students' work differs from other volunteer work (i.e., students need assignments that meet their learning goals) and to determine whether students can provide the type of assistance the agency needs (i.e., students' assignments accomplish needed tasks; Stoecker et al., 2009).

As with other experiential learning, faculty can enhance student understanding by requiring reflection on the service-learning component (Conway et al., 2009; Hatcher & Bringle, 1997), so faculty should plan to devote several class meetings (i.e., before the service starts, while in progress, and after completion) to reflection on social class privilege within students' placements. For example, without clear guidance from faculty, students may label their work as "charity." Students may think they are serving people who are unable to help themselves, rather than conceptualizing their service learning as working with a community organization to bring about social change. To prevent this outcome, community partners and their constituents should be treated as co-educators and equal stakeholders (Eby, 1998; Stoecker et al., 2009). Faculty should include community partners in the creation of the service-learning assignments so that the work benefits the community (Leiderman et al., 2003). This type of collaboration makes the distinction between working for and working with the organization clear to students. I (Wendy) reinforce the view of community partners as co-educators when I ask them to guest lecture and provide input on student final grades (e.g., the amount of credit students deserve for their work in the community). Finally, conceptualizing community partners as co-educators provides an opportunity to add important additional "standpoints" to the course.

Additionally, structured reflection allows faculty to deal with the potential problem of students developing individualistic explanations for structural problems (e.g., explaining poverty as laziness rather than a lack of well-paying jobs) or unintended reinforcement of stereotypes while at their service placements (Eby, 1998). Reflection allows faculty to raise students' awareness of their own biases and encourage students to ensure that their work in the community ameliorates disadvantage rather than upholds privilege. For example, in my (Wendy's) experience, students often feel trepidation about working in the community, particularly with low-income populations. To examine their biases and assumptions, I ask students to write about their expectations for the service learning at the start of the semester (e.g., What do you want to gain from service learning? What do you expect from your placement? What questions or fears do you have about going to your site or engaging in service learning?). After they go to their placement, I ask students to record whether their site looks like what they expected and the ways that their placement either met or fell short of their expectations. Finally, at the end of the semester, I ask them to consider their previous answers by comparing and contrasting what they wrote to what they experienced. Students frequently report that repeatedly considering their assumptions adds layers of insight to their understanding of social class privilege. Repeated reflection allows students to examine the ways in which their own standpoint changed over time. Furthermore, this process makes it difficult for students to hold onto individualistic explanations because they use standpoint theory to broaden their understanding of the causes and consequences of social class privilege.

When I (Kala) was in Wendy's class, I was placed at a daycare facility in which all of the children's families were below the poverty line, and the majority (90%) of the children were African American. Therefore, many of my experiences highlighted my social class and white privilege. In one instance, I put a child in "time out" for exhibiting "bad" behavior, but I was reprimanded by the daycare staff, most of whom were also low income and African American, who said it was not my place to discipline the students. In my reflections on this event in class, I processed through my initial shock and offense at having been reprimanded to gain an understanding of the staff's rationale. I was an outsider because of my social class and ethnicity, as well as my volunteer (i.e., temporary) status. I realized that what I perceived as "bad" behavior and "appropriate" punishment (i.e., a "time out") may not coincide with the cultural norms of the daycare center. Finally, I realized that discipline should come from a regular staff member who shared the student's race and social class, rather than from a White (relatively wealthy and educated) stranger. I doubt I would have examined the multiple layers of privilege embedded in my reaction to this instance if not for the input of other students in the course.

Thus, through a variety of experiential learning techniques, students better understand social class privilege because they connect their subjective experience and standpoint, before, during, and after the experience, with the course information by reflecting on the connections between these pieces. Therefore, in terms of course objectives, experiential learning with structured reflection can facilitate a deeper and multifaceted understanding of social class privilege. It allows students to examine their own and others' positions, to interrogate the "truth," and to deconstruct the factors that lead to the creation and reification of privilege.

What are the Challenges of Teaching Social Class Privilege?

Multiple challenges come with the pedagogical approaches described above. To aid faculty interested in using experiential activities, the following section describes challenges and provides suggestions for overcoming each. We find the four most common challenges include lack of faculty time, insufficient institutional support, student resistance, and unintended negative consequences to communities and disadvantaged students.

First, incorporating experiential learning into one's teaching takes significant time. Although no shortcut to lessen the work involved exists, faculty can use the opportunities created through their innovative teaching techniques to demonstrate tenure requirements. For example, I (Wendy) developed a relationship with a domestic violence shelter because of my service-learning course. As a result of that partnership, I collected data for them and, with their approval, presented my findings at a conference. I also joined their board of directors. I then documented all this work as part of my teaching, research, and service tenure requirements.

Second, because experiential learning often involves additional costs (i.e., increased faculty time, transportation of students, expenses associated with projects), faculty need financial support. Yet even institutions that provide some funding rarely provide enough support to offset all costs. Because administrators often lack awareness of the positive outcomes achieved through experiential learning techniques, faculty can argue effectively in support of experiential learning by demonstrating that research supports the effectiveness of these techniques (Kolb & Kolb, 2012). For example, a dean may be able to find money to support a service-learning project if the faculty articulates the benefits of this experience to the students and the community. A number of resources (both curricular and financial) exist that can aid faculty in demonstrating the effectiveness of service learning, including the websites for the National Service-Learning Clearinghouse (www.servicelearning.org), Campus Compact (www.campuscompact.org), and the *Michigan Journal of Community Service Learning* (www.umich.edu/~mjcsl).

Third, faculty may encounter resistance from students who see experiential learning as "extra work" or who deny that they possess unearned privilege (Case & Cole, this volume). If students see that the experiential learning is integral to their understanding of social class privilege, faculty can overcome resistance to experiential learning as "extra work." As discussed above, placing experiential learning in the course objectives and connecting it explicitly to learning goals in the syllabus, as well as in specific assignments through the semester, make the importance of experiential learning to the course content clear to students (Howard, 2001).

As far as recognizing privilege, students may accept that inequality exists but resist acknowledging personal privilege and, in rare cases, even engage in hostile backlash against the curricula (Case & Cole, this volume; Espino & Lee, 2011; Gotell & Crow, 2005; Tatum, 1992). Privileged individuals may feel guilt after being introduced to the concept, leading to denial of social class privilege to assuage their feelings of responsibility for inequality (Abrams & Gibson, 2007; Gillespie, Ashbaugh, & DeFiore, 2002; Wise & Case, this volume). Although many students use the information they learn through experiential learning to challenge their existing worldviews, some choose instead to reinforce their meritocratic belief system and deny their own privilege (Dunlap et al., 2007; Espino & Lee, 2011). Even when students sign up for optional courses that explicitly aim to raise awareness of social class privilege, they still find it difficult to engage in discourse on the topic (Sanders & Mahalingam, 2012). Faculty can reach these students, however, by supporting their ability to create social change and to develop a sense of efficacy regarding their ability to combat inequality and shape social policy (McIntosh, 2012). For example, I ask students to create a final project of their choice in which they take action with, or on behalf, of low-income people. I find that this activity enables students to see that using one's privilege to advocate for social justice does not come at a real cost to the privileged, but instead encourages students to use their unearned advantages for social good instead of perpetuating inequality.

Additionally, by monitoring students' resistance over time, faculty may find that, although students resist at first, the process of hearing their peers' social class experiences challenges students' denial of social class privilege. I (Wendy) can usually overcome student resistance and backlash by refocusing those students on our standpoint theory framework. When I validate their standpoint, but challenge them to try to put aside those beliefs and take on another's perspective, students usually let go of their resistance.

Finally, although we believe that experiential learning benefits students and communities, potential negative impacts exist. For example, in a survey of community colleges using service learning, although 61% of schools assess student outcomes, less than 35% of institutions survey community partners and only 4% ask community members about their reactions to the service-learning partnership (Prentice, Robinson, & McPhee, 2003). Often, then, faculty treat community agencies and community members as supplemental sources of information, rather than as full partners in the learning experience. Research finds that, if instructors regularly listen to and communicate with community partners to determine problems, they can overcome these issues (Stoecker et al., 2009). Moreover, by engaging in the reflection activities described above while students work at their community placements, faculty can help ensure students' work will positively affect communities.

Because less privileged students often already understand their disadvantage, raising awareness of social class privilege can result in the unintended consequence of discouraging already disadvantaged students. Although discussions focused on what each group experiences remain an important piece for those with privilege, these conversations can provide an important lesson for those without privilege. Because understanding social class privilege necessitates a discussion of the way in which those with power stack the deck against low-income people, economically disadvantaged students may disengage from the class content (using denial as a psychological defense mechanism) or may become depressed because they feel powerless (Higginbotham, 1996). In this situation, feminist and critical pedagogies become particularly helpful. Encouraging disadvantaged students to take action against existing unfair hierarchies helps them work through the feelings of powerlessness raised by calling attention to their lack of privilege (Stoudt, Fox, & Fine, 2012). Although faculty cannot tell these students that hard work will be their salvation, they can show them that challenging these hierarchies is the only way to make the system fair. In my (Wendy's) work with low-income students, I find that even economically disadvantaged students recognize that they possess some social class privilege (e.g., their educational attainment) through reflection activities and that this often blunts the otherwise discouraging information about social class privilege.

What are the Rewards of Teaching Social Class Privilege?

Teaching social class privilege through experiential learning can radically transform the relationships between instructors, students, and communities (Buch & Harden, 2011; Espino & Lee, 2011; Seider, Rabinowicz, & Gillmor, 2010; Tallant, 2011). Instructors exploring social class privilege through experiential learning can find satisfaction in seeing their students gain a deeper understanding of material and in creating a generation of students who engage with their communities. Instructors also can gain meaningful connections with community partners, and even enhance their own commitment to service and activism by teaching about privilege through experiential techniques.

Students in experiential learning classrooms gain an enriched, active learning experience. In fact, students in service-learning courses report that their "real world" experiences enhance their "textbook learning." For example, the following comments from my (Wendy's) students illustrate this enriched experience:

> It is a lot of work, but it will be unlike any class they have ever taken. The class is the most hands on they will get, but that factor makes the class more interactive and satisfying than most other classes.
>
> (Black, middle-class female)

> Being at my placement made me aware of my income privilege growing up. [This privilege] makes people notice there are those who need help and it can also produce a guilty feeling. Guilt for being privileged can help someone actually take action.
>
> (White, low-income male)

> I believe that my placement has made me aware that I have had access to experiences and education that has made me more aware and understanding

of issues than others who have not had the same opportunities or undergone the same circumstances.

(White, low-income female)

If someone I knew were going to take a service-learning course I would tell them to take it. The class will change them in ways they may not expect. I would tell them that they will learn things through service learning that they could never learn in the classroom. You are giving back to the community and they are also giving to you.

(White, working-class female)

There were some things I didn't truly agree with or understand during lecture that I saw going on at my service-learning placement. Once I saw these things going on I finally realized what the lecture notes meant.

(White, middle-class female)

When comparing these comments to the course objectives, students clearly recognize structural barriers and that some individuals experience privilege within the hierarchy. They understand that their learning was enhanced through the experiential learning, and they can see the connections between course content and the "real world." Finally, they demonstrate their increased social sensitivity by recognizing their ability to affect change.

Community agencies primarily benefit through the attainment of volunteer help, but they can also gain partners willing to develop solutions to local problems (Leiderman et al., 2003). Furthermore, students who participate in service learning often serve as role models for participants in community programs, especially when they work with children and adolescents as part of their placement. For instance, over the course of two service-learning courses, I (Kala) had the chance to listen to and provide support for children 8–10 years of age staying with their mothers in a domestic violence shelter and to interact with children 3–5 years of age at a low-income daycare facility. Finally, because service-learning experiences can inspire students to volunteer in the community in the future, community organizations can "home grow" their future support (Levesque-Bristol, Knapp, & Fischer, 2010). In my (Wendy's) experience, a number of students placed in community settings either completed more hours at the placement than required (as Kala did), returned later to work as volunteers or paid staff, or both. I find that students also make donations of both supplies and money to these organizations after finishing their placements.

Experiential Learning: Teaching Social Class Privilege and Supporting Social Justice

Experiential learning, and especially service learning, encourages a worldview where oneself and one's community are the sources of knowledge. Through experiential learning, students share responsibility for learning, and they apply their gained knowledge in partnership with their community and one another. An educational model based on connection and support with the community offers profound opportunities for learning. Specifically, courses that use experiential learning as a way to enhance education about social class privilege educate students about the importance of working for social justice. In addition, service-learning courses create university faculty in tune with their communities, and community organizations receive much needed support for their social justice work. Thus, teaching social class privilege through experiential learning techniques can lead to greater understanding, empathy, respect and dialogue about relevant social issues for instructors, students, the community, and our society as a whole.

References

Abrams, L. S., & Gibson, P. (2007). Teaching notes: Reframing multicultural education—teaching white privilege in the social work curriculum. *Journal of Social Work Education*, *43*(1), 147–160. doi:10.5175/JSWE.2007.200500529

American Psychological Association, Task Force on Socioeconomic Status. (2007). *Report of the APA task force on socioeconomic status*. Retrieved from www.apa.org/pi/ses/resources/publications/task-force-2006.pdf

American Psychological Association, Task Force on Resources for the Inclusion of Social Class in Psychology Curricula. (2008). *Using curriculum materials on social class to enhance and enrich teaching in psychology*. Retrieved from www.apa.org/pi/ses/resources/publications/social-class-curricula.pdf

Buch, K., & Harden, S. (2011). The impact of a service-learning project on student awareness of homelessness, civic attitudes, and stereotypes toward the homeless. *Journal of Higher Education Outreach and Engagement*, *15*(3), 45–61.

Case, K. A., & Cole, E. R. (this volume). Deconstructing privilege when students resist: The journey back into the community of engaged learners. In K. A. Case (Ed.), *Deconstructing privilege: Teaching and learning as allies in the classroom* (pp. 34–48). New York, NY: Routledge.

Case, K. A., Kanenberg, H., Erich, S., & Tittsworth, J. (2012). Transgender inclusion in university nondiscrimination statements: Challenging gender-conforming privilege through student activism. *Journal of Social Issues*, *68*(1), 145–161. doi:10.1111/j.1540–4560.2011.01741.x

Collins, P. H. (1989). The social construction of Black feminist thought. *Signs*, *14*(4), 745–773. doi:10.1086/494543

Conway, J. M., Amel, E. L., & Gerwein, D. P. (2009). Teaching and learning in the social context: A meta-analysis of service learning's effects on academic, personal, social, and citizenship outcomes. *Teaching of Psychology*, *36*(4), 233–245. doi:10.1080/00986280903172969

Crenshaw, K. (1989). Demarginalizing the intersection of race and sex: A Black feminist critique of anti-discrimination doctrine, feminist theory, and anti-racist politics. *University of Chicago Legal Forum*, *1989*, 139–167.

Dunlap, M., Scoggin, J., Green, P., & Davi, A. (2007). White students' experiences of privilege and socioeconomic disparities: Toward a theoretical model. *Michigan Journal of Community Service Learning*, *13*(2), 19–30.

Eby, J. W. (1998). Why service-learning is bad. Retrieved from www.messiah.edu/external_programs/agape/servicelearning/articles/wrongsvc.pdf

Enns, C. Z., & Forrest, L. M. (2005). Toward defining and integrating multicultural and feminist pedagogies. In C. Z. Enns & A. L. Sinacore (Eds.), *Teaching and social justice: Integrating multicultural and feminist theories in the classroom* (pp. 3–23). Washington, D.C.: American Psychological Association.

Espino, M. M., & Lee, J. J. (2011). Understanding resistance: Reflections on race and privilege through service-learning. *Equity & Excellence in Education, 44*(2), 136–152. doi:10.1080/10665684.2011.558424

Eyler, J., & Giles, D. E. (1999). *Where's the learning in service-learning?* San Francisco, CA: Jossey-Bass.

Freire, P. (1970). *Pedagogy of the oppressed.* New York, NY: Seabury Press.

Furco, A. (1996). Service-learning: A balanced approach to experiential education. In B. Taylor (Ed.), *Expanding boundaries: Service and learning* (pp. 2–6). Washington, D.C.: Corporation for National Service.

Gillespie, D., Ashbaugh, L., & DeFiore, J. (2002). White women teaching White women about white privilege, race cognizance, and social action: Toward a pedagogical pragmatics. *Race Ethnicity and Education, 5*(3), 237–253. doi:10.1080/1361332022000004841

Gotell, L., & Crow, B. (2005). Antifeminism and the classroom. In E. L. Kennedy & A. Beins (Eds.), *Women's studies for the future* (pp. 287–303). New Brunswick, NJ: Rutgers University Press.

Harding, S. (1986). *The science question in feminism.* Ithaca, NY: Cornell University Press.

Harding, S. (1997). Comment on Heckman's "Truth and method: Feminist standpoint theory revisited": Whose standpoint needs the regimes of truth and reality? *Signs, 22*(2), 382–391. doi:10.1086/495163

Harding, S. (2004). A socially relevant philosophy of science? Resources from standpoint theory's controversiality. *Hypatia, 19*(1), 25–47. doi:10.1111/j.1527–2001.2004.tb01267.x

Hatcher, J. A., & Bringle, R. G. (1997). Reflections: Bridging the gap between service and learning. *Journal of College Teaching, 45*(4), 153–158. doi:10.1080/87567559709596221

Heffernan, K. (2001). *Fundamentals of service-learning course construction.* Boston, MA: Campus Compact.

Higginbotham, E. (1996). Getting all students to listen: Analyzing and coping with student resistance. *American Behavioral Scientist, 40*(2), 203–211. doi:0.1177/0002764296040002011

hooks, b. (2000). *Where we stand: Class matters.* New York, NY: Routledge.

Howard, J. (2001). Principles of good practice for service-learning pedagogy. In J. Howard (Ed.), *Service-learning course design workbook* (pp. 16–19). Ann Arbor, MI: OCSL Press.

Kolb, D. A. (1984). *Experiential learning: Experience as the source of learning and development.* Englewood Cliffs, NJ: Prentice Hall.

Kolb, A., & Kolb, D. A. (2012). *Experiential learning theory bibliography* (Vols. 1–3). Retrieved from http://learningfromexperience.com/research/

Leiderman, S., Furco, A., Zapf, J., & Goss, M. (2003) *Building partnerships with college campuses: Community perspectives.* Washington, D.C.: Council of Independent Colleges.

Levesque-Bristol, C., Knapp, T. D., & Fisher, B. J. (2010). The effectiveness of service-learning: It's not always what you think. *Journal of Experiential Education, 33*(3), 208–224. doi:10.5193/JEE33.3.208

Liu, W. M., Pickett, T., & Ivey, A. E. (2007). White middle-class privilege: Social class bias and implications for training and practice. *Journal of Multicultural Counseling and Development, 35*(4), 194–206. doi:10.1002/j.2161–1912.2007.tb00060.x

Lott, B., & Bullock, H. E. (2007). *Psychology and economic injustice: Personal, professional, and political intersections.* Washington, D.C.: American Psychological Association.

Markowitz, L. (2005). Unmasking moral dichotomies: Can feminist pedagogy overcome student resistance? *Gender and Education, 17*(1), 39–55. doi:10.1080/0954025042000301294

McIntosh, P. (1988). *White privilege and male privilege: A personal account of coming to see correspondences through work in women's studies* (Working Paper No. 189). Wellesley, MA: Wellesley Centers for Women.

McIntosh, P. (2012). Reflections and future directions for privilege studies. *Journal of Social Issues, 68*(1), 194–206. doi:10.1111/j.1540–4560.2011.01744.x

Prentice, M., Robinson, G., & McPhee, S. (2003). *Service learning in community colleges: 200 national survey results.* Retrieved from www.aacc.nche.edu/Resources/aaccprograms/horizons/Documents/2003_survey_rb.pdf

Sanders, M. R., & Mahalingam, R. (2012). Under the radar: The role of invisible discourse in understanding class-based privilege. *Journal of Social Issues, 68*(1), 112–127. doi:10.1111/j.1540–4560.2011.01739.x

Seider, S. C., Rabinowicz, S. A., & Gillmor, S. C. (2011). Changing American college students' conceptions of poverty through community service learning. *Analyses of Social Issues and Public Policy, 11*(1), 105–126. doi:10.1111/j.1530–2415.2010.01224.x

Stoecker, R., Tyron, E. A., & Hilgendorf, A. (2009). *The unheard voices: Community organizations and service learning.* Philadelphia, PA: Temple University Press.

Stoudt, B. G., Fox, M., & Fine, M. (2012). Contesting privilege with critical participatory action research. *Journal of Social Issues, 68*(1), 178–193. doi:10.1111/j.1540–4560.2011.01743.x

Tallant, A. (2011). Rock on! Band together to fight hunger: Results from a food insecurity awareness project. *International Journal for the Scholarship of Teaching and Learning, 5*(2), 1–12.

Tatum, B. D. (1992). Talking about race, learning about racism: The application of racial identity development theory in the classroom. *Harvard Educational Review, 62*(1), 1–24.

U.S. Census Bureau. (2012). *Income, poverty, and health insurance coverage in the United States: 2011.* Retrieved from www.census.gov/prod/2012pubs/p60–243.pdf

Weis, L., & Fine, M. (2012). Critical bifocality and circuits of privilege: Expanding critical ethnographic theory and design. *Harvard Review, 82*(2), 173–201.

Williams, W. R. (2009). Struggling with poverty: Implications for theory and policy of increasing research on social class-based stigma. *Analyses of Social Issues and Public Policy, 9*(1), 37–56. doi:10.1111/j.1530–2415.2009.01184.x

Wise, T., & Case, K. A. (this volume). Pedagogy for the privileged: Addressing inequality and injustice without shame or blame. In K. A. Case (Ed.), *Deconstructing privilege: Teaching and learning as allies in the classroom* (pp. 17–33). New York, NY: Routledge.

Appendix

Wendy's Social Class Autobiography: "No Yellow Tickets for Me"

I never remember being denied anything that I wanted as a child—Barbies, Cabbage Patch dolls, Easy-bake ovens—I had it all. Birthdays and Christmases were happy and lavish. We lived in suburban Virginia in a four-bedroom, two-bath, three-story colonial-style house with a large yard. My father commuted everyday into Washington, D.C., to work for the government while my mother stayed home to care for me and my two siblings.

My father had an affair, and my parents separated when I was in the fifth grade. Although the outside of our home had not changed, every time I walked into the house I was aware of what was missing. Empty spaces where furniture used to be were both a tangible reminder of the fact that my father had left and that we couldn't afford to replace the lost furniture. Moreover, my mother wasn't there as much either because she had to get a job to help support us. Not only did I grieve that my family would no longer be whole, but I became painfully aware of my loss of freedom as well since I was now the primary after-school babysitter for my younger handicapped sister. Two years after my father left, my mother remarried and we moved to Knoxville, Tennessee. Although our new house was significantly smaller than our house in Virginia, we were still in a middle-class neighborhood and I attended a well-regarded public high school. But our slide down the economic ladder was only stalled, not stopped.

When I was a sophomore, my stepfather lost his job and could not find work. This time our decline was swift. Before my mom and step-father filed for bankruptcy, they took what capital they had and bought a small piece of land in the country, just outside the Great Smokey Mountains National Park. They plotted the design of the house on graph paper, and my step-father and a friend built the house. I now had to share a bedroom with my younger sister.

That summer, instead of hanging out with my friends, my time was spent working on the house. I hammered nails, stapled insulation, and laid pipe for our waterline, but I didn't do it willingly. Much of the time, I was angry and sullen. I raged against what was happening to me. It wasn't fair. This isn't who I was. My parents scolded me for my attitude, and I yelled back with my anger at them for not protecting me. I didn't understand how they could let this happen.

As soon as the house was up to code, we moved in. Although the house was technically deemed "livable," nothing was finished; there was only unpainted drywall on the walls and sub-flooring on the floors. It remained that way until well after I left for college two years later.

Once we started having economic troubles and I stopped getting an allowance, I worked at a series of small, after-school jobs to buy the things I wanted. I cleaned offices, babysat, and worked at a fast-food restaurant. I was no longer the same social class as my friends, but many never knew. Although we now lived in a different county that was more than an hour away from my middle-class high school, I lobbied my parents to allow me to commute there (illegally) every day for class. I used any excuse to get out of having friends come over to visit my new house. I was desperately afraid they wouldn't like me anymore if they saw how we were living. In addition, I spent a large chunk of my paychecks on clothing, favoring items that could be easily recognized as the "popular" labels of the time.

I religiously shopped sales and travelled to the local outlet mall looking for name-brand clothing at cheaper prices. When I bought expensive clothing, I hid the bags from my parents and made sure they didn't see the clothes when I did my laundry. I was devastated one day when I wore my new (expensive) cream sweater and a boy bumped into me with his cheese nachos, staining the front of the sweater with orange goo. I was late to my next class because I stayed so long in the bathroom alternately scrubbing the sweater to clean it and wiping the tears from my face because I knew it was ruined. I was working incredibly hard to keep up appearances; however, the year my family filed for bankruptcy, my mother completed the paperwork for the free/reduced school lunch program. When my mother told me we qualified for the program, I yelled at her, "Are you kidding me? Why did you do that?" She was perplexed. "But Wendy, now you won't have to spend your money on lunch. You can use it for other things. This will help us." I couldn't believe she was so naïve; she was undoing all my hard work. I was adamant, "No it won't because I am NOT using it." What my mom didn't know was that all I could think about was my elementary school friend, Tiffani. Every day at lunch, Tiffani had to give the lunch lady a yellow ticket. We all knew what that meant. Tiffani's family was "poor." I had no intention of finding out what I needed to do to actually receive the reduced lunch benefit. I wanted nothing to do with any markers that would signal my new, lower status. I bought my lunch with the cash that was left from my paychecks.

In the cafeteria, there was the standard hot lunch line on one side, but there was also an a la carte stand in a separate open space in the middle of the cafeteria. The a la carte stand sold mini-pizzas, French fries, nachos, candy bars and other junk food, but they only accepted cash. Because the food prices were higher at the a la carte stand, it was an unspoken truth that the hot lunch line was for the low-income kids. As a result, for months I made a beeline for the a la carte stand to conspicuously pay for my lunch. One day, though, I wanted a baked potato, and those were only available by going through the hot lunch line. I carefully counted out the change I needed ($1.25) and got into line to pay for my potato. When I got to the front of the line, the woman working the register told me what I owed. *Thirty-five cents.* She never skipped a beat nor did her expression give away a flicker of recognition, but this was clearly a reduced rate. How did she know? My body went cold. My face flushed. I heard a rushing sound in my ears. I thought I might faint. Surely, I must have heard her wrong. I asked her to repeat herself. She did. The amount had not changed and neither did her expression. I hurriedly handed her the money and rushed out of the line. I could only hope that no one else had heard.

I returned to the table where my friends were, but I couldn't eat. How could this woman who had never met me and who didn't know anything about me know my most intimate secret, the one secret that I had worked so hard to hide from everyone? In a school of 2,600 students, how could she possibly have associated my name on a piece of paper for the reduced lunch program with the girl standing in front of her? And, more importantly, if my charade hadn't fooled her, had it fooled anyone else? I was panicked, ashamed, and scared. During this time, I saw many of the changes that occurred as structural things that were happening to me, but I did not think that these events reflected anything about me personally. For the first time since our economic downward slide began, someone had looked at me and seen the truth.

I was convinced it was a mistake, but it took me months to work up the courage to go back and try again. I dressed carefully that day, making sure I was obviously wearing my most expensive outfit and that my hair and makeup were flawless. I attempted to be breezy and unconcerned, but I was panicked inside. As I inched closer to the register with my potato, my heart beat wildly. By the time I got to the front of the line, I was convinced I would hear the "right" amount from her. She couldn't possibly look at me and think that I was "poor." I was sure it wasn't going to happen again. But it did. *Thirty-five cents.* I never went back through the hot food line again.

Two years later, I graduated and left for college. I attended a small, wealthy, liberal arts college where I continued to hide my social class just as carefully as I did in high school. I told only a few trusted friends about my family's situation, and it wasn't until my senior year that I felt comfortable enough to invite my college roommate to visit my family. I continued to work small jobs to buy my clothing and to pay for the things I wanted. I did everything I could to pretend that I was just like everyone else. I avoided doing anything that would betray my social class.

I think one of the privileges of being middle class is that I don't remember thinking about money until we didn't have it. Yet it wasn't until I entered graduate school and I took a class on "stigma and prejudice" that I started to critically examine my experiences crossing back and forth between social classes. I began to think a lot about my experiences in the cafeteria and what it taught me about the stigma of poverty: how poverty can be visible, invisible, or become visible over the course of an interaction. I've thought about how certain signs are used as markers of social class, and how one's identity can be tied to those signs. I've pondered the psychological and social consequences of poverty for children, as well as the messages that are taught to them about the relationship between education, hard work, and the American Dream.

And I've thought about the lunch lady herself. I never learned how she did it. I suspect that she looked up the yearbook pictures of all the kids who qualified for the free/reduced lunch program and memorized their faces, but I'll never be sure. At the time, I wanted nothing to do with her. Now I wish I could talk to her—to ask her how she did it, to ask her why she did it, but most of all to thank her for her kindness.

12

TEACHING THE TABOO

Walking the Tightrope of Christian Privilege

Kim A. Case, Mike McMullen, and Beth Hentges

A sociology class retreats into silence after a student emphatically states that "all Muslims are terrorists!" A psychology student pulls out her Bible and begins reading Leviticus to the panel of lesbian and trans-women that are visiting class to discuss issues of sexuality and gender identity. As she informs them of their destined afterlife in hell, the tension in the classroom is palpable. These behaviors actually occurred in courses that challenged student assumptions about social identity, outgroup homogeneity, and privilege. Both stories paint a picture that becomes quite difficult to envision if the Muslim, lesbian, and transgender targets were replaced with Christians. Imagine a student declaring to the entire class that all Christians are terrorists or reading passages from the Qur'an that condemn all Christians to hell. As allies in the classroom, instructors carry the responsibility for effectively navigating such moments to maximize student learning. However, educators often feel ill-equipped to skillfully navigate the terrain to promote academic dialogue for deeper learning. In these moments, Christian privilege expands beyond course content to dominate classroom interactions and potentially disengage learners. The pedagogical challenges unique to teaching and learning about religious privilege call for effective strategies for these teachable moments to support student learning.

Defining Christian Privilege

If current trends continue, by 2050 Americans of European descent will comprise less than 50% of the U.S. population (Farley & Haaga, 2005; Hobbs, 2002). Patterns of immigration became relevant for religion as new immigrants arrived with a variety of religions in tow. In the last four decades, the number of Islamic mosques, Buddhist and Hindu temples, and other religious centers has increased significantly.

In addition to these public outlets, home shrines commonly exist in many Buddhist, Shinto, Hindu, and Latin American Catholic homes (Ebaugh, 2000; Eck, 2001; Warner, 1998; Wuthnow, 2005). Given the evolving religious landscape, an increasing number of instructors incorporate religious privilege into course curriculum.

Drawing from McIntosh's (1988) definition of white privilege, Blumenfeld and Jaekel (2012) defined Christian privilege as an "invisible, unearned, and largely unacknowledged array of benefits given to Christians, with which they often unconsciously walk through life" (p. 128). These advantages are systemic across social institutions, bestow dominant group membership on Christians, and restrict atheist and agnostic individuals, as well as members of non-Christian faiths, to subordinate status (Blumenfeld & Jaekel, 2012). In reference to the invisibility of privilege, Schlosser (2003) refers to this lack of awareness as resulting from the collective "nonconscious ideology" (p. 47) that constructs Christian values and customs as the cultural norm in the United States. The centering of Christian practices, holidays, and beliefs (Fried, 2007) perpetuates systematic Christonormativity (Ferber, 2012) that provides benefits to members of the privileged group. Given the institutionalization of religious privilege at the societal level, Clark, Vargas, Schlosser, and Alimo (2002) recognized that all Christians benefit from privilege simply by being members of the dominant group that defines the norms. Privileged social identity—in this case, based on religion—results from social forces at the institutional level that allow dominant group members to avoid acknowledgement and even basic awareness of their unearned benefits (Case, Iuzzini, & Hopkins, 2012).

Do students recognize the dominance of Christian symbols/privilege in our society via Christmas vacation, references to Noah's ark in advertising, allusions to the garden of Eden in literature classes, or the ubiquity of the cross in architecture? As noted by privilege scholars, privileged group members are unlikely to recognize the unearned advantages that permeate the oxygen they breathe and the very fabric of society (Blumenfeld & Jaekel, 2012; Schlosser, 2003; Wildman, 1995). In these and other ways described by Schlosser (2003), Christian identity awards members with privileges commonly invisible to the privileged. Based on the McIntosh (1988) model, Schlosser (2003) developed a list of Christian privileges to illustrate the daily advantages associated with membership in the dominant religious group. The list highlights Christonormative benefits such as access to radio stations that play Christian music, work and school schedules that honor Christian holidays and weekly days of worship, broad access to foods that do not violate Christian dietary restrictions, and cultural endorsement of Christianity through ceremonies and displays of Christmas trees and Easter decorations via public schools, local government, and retail stores.

When tackling complex issues of identity, religion, and unearned benefits in the classroom, teaching about this privilege presents a daunting task, given religion's importance in many students' lives and the strong social taboo against discussing religion. Although promoting students' critical analysis of religious privilege within courses focusing on religious topics provides some introduction to the concept, Christian privilege is also quite relevant for a long list of courses with a variety of disciplines, such as social sciences, business, education, humanities, and interdisciplinary studies (e.g., women's studies, ethnic studies, environmental studies). As Case's (this volume) privilege studies pedagogical model argues, infusing privilege content across the curriculum in an interdisciplinary fashion will strengthen student learning. Therefore, a movement toward teaching and learning about Christian privilege across the curriculum would serve to raise awareness and increase critical thinking among students.

Instructors Walking the Tightrope as Allies in the Classroom

Approaching the concept of Christian religious privilege in the classroom means addressing a taboo and overwhelmingly sensitive topic with students. Although learning about any form of privilege presents unique pedagogical challenges, Christian privilege presents one of the most volatile forms of privilege when introduced into academic discussion (Ferber, 2012). In response to her efforts to deconstruct Christian privilege, Ferber (2012) found that responses to her blog on Huffington Post minimized discrimination against non-Christians, trivialized religious privilege benefits, and attempted to naturalize Christian customs as simply part of secular culture. Despite these challenges, Schlosser (2003) calls for breaking the sacred taboo and making the reality of Christian privilege visible. One aspect of the current culture that supports the taboo nature of these discussions is the pervasive idea that any critique of how religion operates in U.S. society constitutes a personal attack on all Christians. For example, Christian students may perceive discussions of religious oppression as a direct attack on their own religious values and identity. When conducting an academic discussion of Christian influence on national, state, and local policies (e.g., requiring Texas textbooks to label both creationism and evolution as equally valid theories), Christian-identified students may claim the very discussion verbally attacks or even religiously oppresses them. Such accusations of Christian victimization reframe academic deconstructions of privilege and return the dominant group to the center, reestablishing a "Christocentric" learning environment. In fact, claims of Christian victimization not only operate to prevent open dialogue and diminish the chances of student engagement and learning, but also discourage instructors from broaching this sensitive issue.

The topic of Christian privilege often arises in the classroom via a curriculum that appears unrelated on the surface. In other words, many students view non-religious topics through the lens of their individual religious beliefs. Specific religious frameworks may be applied to such diverse academic topics as the origins of life, social systems, moral behavior, gender roles, parental discipline, and sexual orientation. Thus, even when the course title is not explicitly religiously focused, students' religious beliefs often either directly or indirectly affect learning in the classroom. Due to the dominant status of Christianity in the United States, students may view their Christian beliefs and values as a set of universally shared assumptions, rather than personal. Making students aware of the diversity of religious beliefs, that their personal values are not shared by all, and that academic discussions must occur in a respectful atmosphere that supports multiple viewpoints is essential across the curriculum. This approach not only enhances learning within the classroom, but also aids student development of greater awareness of religious diversity, privilege, and the socially constructed "Christian culture" in the United States.

What does it mean for faculty to engage in pedagogy that brings an extremely sensitive subject to light? For faculty motivated to develop their own identities as pedagogical allies, moving forward may be challenging due to very real risks associated with curricular inclusion of religious privilege. Given the importance of student evaluations, merit reviews, and promotion and tenure reviews, avoidance of including Christian privilege in the curriculum may appear to be the only viable solution. In the context of potentially tense and socially taboo classroom discussions, administrative support, or lack thereof, becomes vitally important in terms of pedagogical decisions. Severe student resistance and "deeply emotional discussions" (Watt, 2009, p. 66) may occur when Christian privilege is on the table for discussion. Student resistance may result in reduced student evaluations of the instructor and the course or even official student complaints. All of these responses potentially impact the administrators' perceptions of an individual instructor. Within some programs and universities, complaints from Christian students against an instructor may result in very real negative consequences. Our reflections below explore strategies for effectively explaining the pedagogical value of including Christian privilege in the curriculum and for addressing accusations of Christian victimization with students and also peer faculty and administrators serving in evaluative roles.

Local Context and Instructor Identity

The local context, in terms of political and institutional culture, also influences an instructor's ability to balance on the tightrope when teaching about Christian privilege and practice as an ally in the classroom. Cultural customs, belief systems, and long-held traditions tied to local context affect the classroom climate and may aid or hinder discussions of privilege. Our particular context, the state of Texas, includes a history of legislative and governor integration of Christian religious values into government policy. However, many of these examples extend beyond Texas as Christonormativity reveals itself in broader policies, the workplace, laws, the education system, and media (Cole, Avery, Dodson, & Goodman, 2012; Ferber, 2012). In 2011, Governor Rick Perry organized a national Christian prayer event hosted by the American Family Association, an activist organization for traditional

Christian values. The previous governor, George W. Bush, declared June 10, 2000, as "Jesus Day." The Texas state legislature frequently converts evangelical Christian principles into law; for example, restricting access to abortion and attempting to create obstacles for university lesbian, gay, bisexual, and transgender (LGBT) resource centers. Prayer before public high school football games and graduation ceremonies, as well as at state university graduations, is quite common and expected. Local high schools frequently illegally prevent the formation of LGBT student organizations due to religious objections by teachers, administrators, or parents. All of these contextual components collide with university values for promoting understanding of diversity among students. Although not all local contexts reflect the culture in Texas, instructor reflection on the religious culture of the local area, where many of their students grew up, may aid pedagogical preparation for possible reactions to learning about religious privilege.

As allies within these local political and institutional contexts, instructors also bring their own social locations into the classroom. Ally perspectives based on an intersecting matrix of privilege and oppressed social identities provide a particular pedagogical lens for teaching about privilege, and they may also affect student learning (Williams & Melchiori, this volume). When Christian privilege becomes the focus of the learning environment, student assumptions about instructor identity and belief systems abound and may help or harm learning. For example, one faculty colleague, who considers herself an ally in the classroom, regularly includes sexual orientation and gender identity development in her required psychology course. Although she identifies as a Protestant Christian, students repeatedly label her as atheist. Another ally instructor purposely avoids any reference to her own personal religious identity, values, and beliefs, but students consistently assume an atheist identity, reflecting dichotomous thinking that separates the act of questioning Christian privilege from Christian identity. In other words, students appear to divide an instructor's engagement in academic deconstruction of privilege and Christian group membership into mutually exclusive categories. In this environment, any critique of the religious status quo is interpreted as anti-Christian. Students assume a Christian instructor would never require them to analyze and critique religious privilege while assuming any instructor that does require this work must be atheist or at least non-Christian. These assumptions of instructor "non-Christian" identity may also serve to discredit the academic merit of the instructor as well as the concept of and classroom discussions of Christian privilege. In other words, if a student frames instructor identity as somehow outside of accepted Christonormativity, then discounting the curriculum and the learning goals and avoidance of examination of religious privilege become easier. Provided that one's religious or non-religious identity will likely impact student learning, disclosing instructor social location and coming out as a "non-believer" or as Christian in the classroom has potential benefits and disadvantages that must be weighed carefully. For example, if an atheist, agnostic, or Buddhist faculty member shares this identity with a student or the entire class, the information may result in discrediting the instructor's expertise and hindering learning, even for some non-Christian students. On the other hand, open instructor identification as Christian while leading discussion of such privileges may result in less resistance among Christian students and greater understanding of the concept. However, these responses are not always predictable based on student religious identity.

Whether members of the dominant religious group or not, instructors striving to be allies in the classroom aim to create a learning environment where non-Christian students feel included rather than marginalized, where Christian students can critically reflect on their own privilege, and where students can begin to construct their own ally identities. As an ally to marginalized students, I (Kim) view one of my pedagogical roles as being a mentor to Christian students. Using my own dominant group roles in the spheres of race and sexuality, I try to model reflection on personal privilege for religiously privileged students. On the other hand, as an ally to atheists and religious and spiritual students that do not identify as Christian, I serve as a mediator and facilitator during difficult dialogues around religious oppression and privilege. By including religious privilege in the course curriculum, assignments, and discussions, instructors serve as allies and bridge the communication gaps between the privileged and marginalized.

Approaches for Balancing on the Tightrope

Critical pedagogy values the creation of learning environments that encourage students to think critically about their own position in society (Chaisson, 2004). Critical pedagogy facilitates students not only questioning their own prejudices and privileges, but also challenging the social systems with which they interact. At the same time, it provides reflective spaces for becoming agents of change themselves (Bonilla-Silva, 1997; Quillian, 2006). As the previous sections highlighted, religious privilege, specifically Christocentrism, is an important but somewhat forgotten part of larger privilege issues. Despite the taboo nature of this topic, we argue that Christian privilege or religious privilege in general should be addressed in the context of larger critical pedagogical concerns. Likewise, because of the taboo nature of these issues, we argue that addressing them must be done with sensitivity through sound approaches.

The problems that arise when teaching courses that address prejudice and privilege issues are numerous and have been the central focus of many discussions about pedagogical approaches (Case & Cole, this volume; Wahl, Perez, Deegan, Sanchez, & Applegate, 2000). These courses often require instructors to explore so-called "uncomfortable" subjects. When these subjects are not approached with sound pedagogy, the courses can actually illicit a negative impact on students' understanding of these issues (Jakubowski, 2001). Over the last decade, a host of pedagogical models have been elaborated to ease students' sensitivity to these subjects and heighten their understanding of privilege and discrimination.

Whether these models include reducing ethnocentrism and prejudice through, for example, instructor-led field observations and service-learning projects (Hondagneu-Sotelo & Raskoff, 1994; Marulio, 1998; Puffer, 1994) or the use of popular music in the classroom (Martinez, 1994), the central focus of these approaches has been to better connect students to course content and critical pedagogical concerns. These approaches often ask students to take the role of the other (Smith, 1992) through oral histories (Poll, 1995) or the use of intensive interview data, which focus on personal explorations and experiences with issues of race or privilege, versus traditional texts (Davidson, 1987). The consensus across these studies is that by making these issues more personal, students understand the course content better and take strides toward reducing their own prejudicial or privileged attitudes and beliefs. Although these studies make invaluable contributions to our pedagogical approaches, few have explored the specific problems associated with teaching and learning about Christian privilege.

There are several practical approaches for preparing students to learn about Christian privilege and religious diversity. We focus below on several key pedagogical goals, including:

- creating a comfortable classroom environment and learning community;
- establishing boundaries for academic discussion; and
- focusing on pedagogical preparation for myths and potential resistance.

In addition, we describe assignments used to promote critical thinking and analysis about religious privilege and diversity.

Creating a Comfortable Learning Environment

In courses addressing taboo or sensitive topics, taking time to develop a community and foster a comfortable classroom for maximum learning can yield positive results (Case, 2011; Case, Bartsch, McEnery, Hall, Hermann, & Foster, 2008; Case, Miller, & Jackson, 2012; Henslee, Burgess, & Buskist, 2006; Platt, this volume). By promoting an atmosphere of trust and respect, the instructor enhances comfort in the classroom and learners become "more likely to modify positions, re-examine their own assumptions, and remain open to learning about the consequences of decisions made from a privileged perspective on those who are not members of the privileged group" (Fried, 2007, p. 4). While there are unique challenges to creating a safe place for learning about Christian privilege, faculty efforts to co-create a positive learning environment in collaboration with students as co-intentional learners (Freire, 1970) will lay important groundwork for sensitive conversations. Creating a comfortable classroom environment also better prepares students for possible uncomfortable dialogue moments and supports student learning that may result if they examine their initial discomfort rather than retreating from it.

According to Kegan's (1982) model of learner development, students enter the course in the "confirmation" stage. During this initial stage, the pedagogical approach of the instructor affects the comfort level and whether the group can begin to develop into a community of co-learners. Active listening, promotion of participation, inviting multiple viewpoints, and soliciting elaboration by asking questions help to create a comfortable classroom environment that promotes a safe space for the learning process. Instructors often implement pedagogical approaches on the first day designed to create a comfortable space while fostering student interaction and community building (DiClementi & Handelsman, 2005; Henslee et al., 2006; Perlman & McCann, 1999). Case (2011) described an approach for the first day of class that serves the pedagogical goal of creating a classroom community of learners within a course that covers sensitive topics and presents concepts that may result in student resistance to learning. The exercise, referred to as the classroom interview or reciprocal interview (Case, 2011; Case et al., 2008), provides students the opportunity to interview the instructor after the instructor interviews the students in a small group format. The activity provides an avenue for students to express their fears, assumptions, and concerns about the course content from the very first day. Following the interview, students recognize common ground with their peers in terms of background, concerns, and learning needs while also benefiting from the instructor responses to those common fears and assumptions (Case, 2011). Discussions of taboo topics including the matrix of privilege and oppression, religious diversity, and Christian privilege become more accessible as students feel connected to a community of learners in a comfortable environment.

By taking the time to build a community of learners and carefully planning the timing of taboo conversations, instructors better prepare students for difficult dialogues and discomfort that may occur when discussing religious privilege. Depending on the learning goals for the overall course topic, introducing this topic early in the course versus later in the term presents advantages and disadvantages. Holding the topic until midterm or even later during the course schedule provides time to establish class rapport while analyzing less controversial topics before introducing the concept of Christian privilege. However, if the course emphasizes systems of oppression and privilege (diversity courses) or religious diversity in the United States and around the world (religion-focused courses), introducing the concept earlier in the course will allow for continued and potentially deeper critical analysis over the life of the course. In my (Kim's) Psychology of Gender, Race, and Sexuality graduate-level course, Christian privilege becomes an essential part of the conversation during the first third of the semester. Given the course focus on intersectionality of privileged and marginalized identities and the matrix of oppression (Collins, 1990), I require students to analyze multiple forms of privilege, social locations, and the impact of those identities on lived experiences early in the course schedule. Students analyze and integrate their learning about not only discrimination and oppression but also privilege during the first phase of the course, in order to prepare for a major "intersections of identity" public education project that requires months of preparation (for detailed course and project descriptions, see Case & Lewis, 2012, and Case, Miller, et al., 2012). When planning the pedagogical timing in courses that may appear unrelated to the topic, such as education, business, and courses not dealing directly with diversity or religion, introducing Christian privilege after the midterm will allow rapport building and potentially reduce student resistance and defensiveness. Given the sensitivity of such conversations, introducing community ground rules for discussion may minimize resistance and increase student engagement and academic dialogue.

Even when deferring the topic of Christian privilege until later in the semester, the instructor can set the stage by emphasizing distinctions between academic inquiry and personal beliefs or feelings. As students identify and explore their personal beliefs, they better understand the influence of their own beliefs, including religious beliefs, on interactions with others (Grillo, 2005). Instructors might approach these distinctions from a general level, as well as with less sensitive belief systems, before tackling religion. For instance, on the first day of my Child Psychology course, I (Beth) ask students to explore their personal views on whether parents should allow their children to sleep in the same bed. The students discuss the different views represented in the class, which are then analyzed compared to global sleeping practices. This facilitates student distinctions between global "truths" and personal beliefs. This topic lacks social taboo and student sensitivity. Therefore, students rarely resist this discussion since it does not seem particularly sensitive to them, although many express definite intense views on the subject. These kinds of discussions help set the stage for later discussion of religious views as personal belief systems, not absolute "truths."

Establishing Boundaries for Academic Discussion

Creating Ground Rules for Effective Dialogue

In order to support efforts to promote a comfortable classroom environment, instructors often build a strong learning community through co-creation of ground rules for student exchanges (Dessel, Massé, & Walker, this volume). Whether introduced by the instructor or created through collective brainstorming, classroom ground rules for dialogue provide a foundational space for discussion (Fried, 2007; Yankelovich, 1999). The sensitive nature of discussing religion, and especially Christian privilege, within a classroom setting calls for careful attention to establishing discussion guidelines that emphasize respect, openness, and listening skills. For many students, religion occupies a core location in terms of personal identity, values, politics, and morality. Christian students, as well as students from a variety of religious backgrounds, may view their religion as truth, rather than beliefs or value systems open to analysis. Therefore, discussions of religious privilege lend themselves to misunderstanding and may be experienced as personal attacks. Avoiding any personal attacks or judgments of classmates or any religion as a whole is an essential ground rule in this context. When I (Mike) facilitate creation of discussion ground rules, we discuss the importance of never engaging in personal attacks. Although debating and questioning ideas may occur, questioning personal faith commitments of other students or the beliefs of non-religious students would serve to negate the safe classroom environment needed for enhanced learning.

Fried (2007) described additional essential components of facilitating an effective conversation on religious privilege based on Yankelovich's (1999) more general cooperative dialogue model. Fried recommended explicitly identifying assumptions and making socially constructed meanings visible. This process allows the group to examine common ground while also recognizing privileged positions and creating a space for critique of systems that maintain privilege and oppression (Dessel et al., this volume). Students examine their individual assumptions and the group engages in academic analysis of the consequences of such assumptions resulting from privileged and marginalized positions. As the collective creation of ground rules takes place, the instructor might suggest and open discussion of ground rules that will support critical analysis of assumptions and encourage deconstructions that help make privilege visible.

Once the group agrees on safe ground rules for dialogue, I (Mike) request that all members of the learning community contribute to monitoring the discourse and to reminding their peers and me of these collective agreements when necessary. In fact, creating a ground rules poster and handouts that are present for each and every class meeting will keep the agreements fresh and available in students' minds during discussions. These policies not only contribute to creating a comfortable learning environment and a safe space for discussion, but also contribute to establishing boundaries for academic discussion. The presence of clear, consistent, and community-generated ground rules will aid in establishing boundaries that distinguish academic approaches to religion and privilege from religious debates that evaluate the merits and truths of each religion.

Establishing Academic Boundaries

Distinguishing between personal belief and academic knowledge and analysis can support the instructors' efforts to establish boundaries, without necessarily challenging students' deeply held religious beliefs. If the course is a science or social science, the instructor can refer frequently to research-based evidence. In my (Beth's) Psychological Thinking course, I frequently stress the difference between knowledge and belief. In a course devoted to teaching critical thinking and critical analysis skills along with technical and scientific writing, the ability to distinguish data-based fact from opinion or viewpoint is an essential learning goal. Students learn that knowledge relies on things that may be objectively established, such as "Does being raised by homosexual parents affect children negatively?" This is presented in contrast to beliefs such as "Homosexual behavior is immoral/moral." As instructors establish these boundaries and facilitate moving students toward such learning goals, it is important to acknowledge the importance of personal beliefs, while emphasizing that they are not "facts" and may not be shared by all. By separating morals and truth associated with religious texts and belief systems from facts and data, faculty can introduce academic approaches to religion within a social science context, or, more broadly, an academic context. In my (Mike's) Sociology of Religion courses, I explicitly outline learning goals that ask students to analyze the dialectic relationship between religious text and religious behavior, between religious authority and social custom, and between religious ritual and the maintenance of social order. As I spell out each learning goal for the students, I emphasize and lead discussion about the academic nature of these goals and introduce models, such as Berger's (1967) functional approach, for keeping the focus on critical analysis within that context.

To fully elaborate on these academic boundaries as the class co-creates a comfortable learning environment, I (Mike) emphasize that discussions will not debate the merits or truth claims of the Bible, Qur'an, Dhammapada, Bhagavad Gita, Kitáb-i-Aqdas, Torah, or any other religious scripture. Particular truth claims of a specific theology may be debated within appropriate institutionalized setting (in one's home, mosque, church, synagogue, or temple). However, the course encourages analysis of the impact of religious beliefs on individual and collective behavior, political beliefs and actions, career choices, efforts to help the poor, or personal choices about adhering to religious obligations. In other words, we will take the truth claims of religion as a given, and then investigate what people who believe in them actually do about them. In these pedagogical contexts, I am frequently confronted with the issue of how to balance helping students understand a social scientific perspective on religion, and thereby take a more "objective" analysis of religious phenomenon in society, versus recognizing that many students have deeply held religious convictions that should be respected and supported. I try to do this by stating up front that what we are doing in this space is to look at religion sociologically and scientifically, and not engage in "Bible-study" discussion about Biblical truth. Rather, instead of assessing the "truth" of the Bible (or any other religious text), we will endeavor to analyze and understand the social consequences for those who do believe in Biblical or religious truth. In other words, we will study the consequences of beliefs in terms of voting, attitudes about abortion and school prayer, child-rearing practices, or views of Middle Eastern peace.

One pedagogical approach that supports this academic context distinction comes from what sociologist Berger (1967) calls "substantive" versus "functional" definitions of religion. Drawing on the classical sociological thinker Emile Durkheim, Berger separates the substantive aspects of religion, such as faith and dogma, from the functional approach that considers how religion functions in society. In the classroom context, once we move the discussion from a substantive definition of religion (one in which we compare "truth claims" between Christian denominations, or between faith traditions) to a discussion about how all religions function in a similar sociological way, students become less defensive about deeply held beliefs and less likely to feel the academic discussion represents a criticism of their faith. Berger (1967) argues that taking a functional view of religion for analytic purposes does not preclude also accepting the ultimate truth claims of a substantive definition of religion. In other words, one can be a believer (or non-believer) and still analyze religion from a functional or social scientific perspective. Thus the pedagogical value of focusing on functional religious definitions is that it frees students to learn through comparisons of belief systems and rituals and how they function in society as a whole or within a sub-group (for example, orthodox Jews or Shi'ite Muslims in the United States). The functional definition also allows the instructor to facilitate deconstruction of the relative pervasiveness of Christian symbols (crosses in architecture, décor and jewelry, arks and references to floods of "Biblical proportion," hands on Bibles in the courtroom, Good Samaritan laws, Adam and Eve references in popular culture, references to "Genesis" as the beginning of some event, workplace closing on Christian holidays, names of cities like St. Louis, Los Angeles, San Antonio, St. Paul) without eliciting a defensive reaction from students. Given that students use the functional approach to engage in academic discussion of sociological observation, perceptions of classroom discussions as religious attack or critique of personal faith are minimized.

Pedagogical Preparation for Myths and Resistance

For faculty working to create comfortable and safe classrooms with established academic boundaries, addressing student assumptions about the course and curriculum early on often helps dispel myths that present obstacles to learning. Discussing common student expectations and misconceptions of the course at the beginning of the semester can help prevent misunderstandings and minimize student resistance. As mentioned in our discussion above about establishing boundaries, many students enter religion courses with only a faith-based view of religion that prevents them from applying functional analyses of how religion operates in conjunction with social systems. Therefore, students often need faculty guidance to deconstruct the assumption that academic analysis of religious privilege equals an attack on Christianity or individual student beliefs and values. Advanced planning for these common assumptions allows for pedagogical preparation to address and correct myths before they interfere with learning via passive or active student resistance. In some cases, students simply expect certain topics will not be broached within a course based on their schema for that course. For example, in my (Beth's) Child Psychology course, students expect topics such as genetics, early childhood physical and intellectual development, and perhaps social development. Each semester without fail, students express surprise when they discover the curriculum will cover religious identity development, LGBT family structures, and sexual orientation development phases. In order to better prepare them, I spend time in the first few weeks of the course explicitly outlining the topics we will cover and why they are essential aspects of an academic understanding of childhood development. Another myth I (Kim) encounter involves the "sage on the stage" view of faculty. My Psychology of Women and Introduction to Women's Studies courses both address various forms of privilege and oppression, including Christian privilege. During the first phase of the course, while we are working to co-create ground rules, establish trust and respect, and build a learning community, I ask students to question traditional views of faculty as telling them what to think rather than asking them to conduct critical analysis themselves. Through these deconstructions of the traditional classroom schema, I challenge them to engage in a learning model that requires them to question, evaluate, analyze, synthesize, and integrate. Later in the course, I specifically avoid "telling" students that Christians are privileged as the dominant group in the United States. Instead, I conduct a class activity that requires them to define "power" and then identify privileged groups based on a variety of dimensions (religion, sex, sexuality, class, race, and more). As they co-create knowledge for synthesis and integration, they deepen their understanding of privilege and its impact on lived experiences. Planned discussions and activities to dispel student myths about course content and production of knowledge may prevent some misunderstandings that negatively impact learning. However, additional advanced preparation is needed for possible episodes of overt student resistance or inappropriate class disruptions.

When severe class disruptions occur, previous planning allows for a calm response from the instructor. In the middle of the third class meeting, a White male student climbed up on top of his desk and proclaimed, "You must believe in Jesus or you will go to hell!" A White female student pulled out her personal Bible and began reading Leviticus scripture out loud to the class, then told the panel of lesbian and trans-women guest speakers they are going to hell. A student writing a paper about the psychological research on sexual orientation cited the Bible as an academic source to support her view that homosexuality is an abomination. During class discussion of discrimination faced by Muslim Americans, a Christian student referred to "our lord and savior" as if all classmates and the instructor shared the same faith, beliefs, and values. Each of these student displays served to illustrate ways that Christian privilege enters the classroom not only as a topic for analysis, but also embodied and present in the behaviors of students. In these moments, faculty members are often caught off guard without a plan for ceasing the teachable moment. Without a pre-conceived plan of pedagogical action, the potential shock of the moment can decrease the likelihood of effectiveness in terms of the instructor response.

On the class day when a student preached from on top of his desk, I (Mike) had just introduced the statistics that illustrate increasing religious diversity within the U.S. population. Although this unexpected behavior surprised me, I immediately announced a 10-minute break, even though we had only been in class for a few minutes. This provided the opportunity to speak privately with the student and explain the distinction between academic discussion of religion and proselytizing. The student chose to leave with his belongings and never returned to class. In order to provide a space for processing this class disruption, I asked students to share their reactions to the incident following the break. In response to the student comment claiming "our lord and savior" as a collective assumption, one instructor responded by asking, "Who are you talking about?" This question required the student to consider that others may not understand or endorse the same deity and reflect on her own privileged assumptions.

During a debate on violence in the media in my (Beth's) Psychological Thinking course, a student offered a critique of television images of Muslim terrorists as problematic. Another student misunderstood and proceeded to endorse stereotypes of Muslims as terrorists. The other students corrected the misguided statement, pointing out that not all Muslims were terrorists and that the student sitting next to her was Muslim. As the instructor, I chose to drop my plan for that class session, discontinued the debate, and led the class in a discussion of media perpetuation of stereotypes. The class also explored the impact of assumptions of shared dominant identity (e.g., "There are no Muslims here.") on making marginalized populations invisible. Given that this event occurred near the end of the term and the class benefited from good rapport among classmates, this learning opportunity resulted in an academic discussion of stereotypes. In this teachable moment, instructor ally behavior intervened to guide discussion and directly address stereotypes.

In all of these examples, we found that remaining calm, overtly addressing the controversy, and using classroom tension as an opportunity for learning helps highlight religious diversity as well as Christocentrism and privilege in U.S. culture and social systems.

Experiential Learning about Christian Privilege

Having students experience this functional diversity of religious belief and ritual is another way of helping them understand the invisibility of their unexplored Christian assumptions and privileges. One assignment I (Mike) designed involves student visits to one or more religious services of a group outside their own belief system (with an option of writing a different paper if religious concerns prevent participation). Lifelong Catholics may choose to attend a Protestant church to complete the project, for example. However, I encourage students to stretch their intellectual and emotional growth by attending a Mormon ward house, Muslim community center, or Metropolitan Community Church (LGBT-affirming community). During the religious service, the assignment calls for student observation of people, rituals, leadership, symbolism, service structure and components, significance of music and food, as well as personal interactions among attendees. Each semester, 10–15 students label this assignment as one of their most profound and meaningful educational experiences. Through the power of experiential learning and interfaith interaction, students develop a more complex interpretation of religious diversity and Christian privilege within a safe learning context primed for academic analysis. This type of applied functional understanding of religion helps students understand their own religious worldview as one of many and aids their analysis of privileged assumptions about religious homogeneity versus religious diversity.

Pedagogical Implications

Although privilege based on race gets the greatest amount of attention within privilege studies (Case, this volume), Ferber (2012) and Ferber and Herrera (this volume) argue for unraveling the entire tapestry of privilege, including Christian privilege, within the complex and interwoven matrix of oppression. Given the increasing religious diversity in the United States, and projections of even more diversity in the coming decades, pedagogical strategies for teaching and learning about Christian privilege should not be overlooked or neglected. Instructors addressing social inequalities, stratification, multiculturalism, and diversity have a responsibility to infuse opportunities for reflecting and learning about Christian privilege across the curriculum. In fact, we argue that students need a particular form of instructional guidance when learning about Christian privilege. When learning about religious privilege, students may exhibit higher rates of concrete and literal thinking that stands in the way of reflective and abstract critical thinking that instructors hope to facilitate. Religious privilege is undoubtedly the forgotten topic of privilege and central to students' socially constructed worldview, but plays a key role in students' understanding of societal-level issues of stratification and inequality.

As Fried (2007) explains, learning about Christian privilege involves long-term commitment to making privilege visible:

> The outcome of this effort will not be a product. It will be an ongoing process of inquiry, reflection, and dialogue that supports the evolution of authentic relationships that are strong enough to acknowledge and manage conflict without being destroyed . . . The problem of unraveling privilege and standing for justice will never be solved, but it must be engaged.
>
> (p. 6)

In order to promote this ongoing process of learning about religious diversity and privilege, instructors across a variety of disciplines must incorporate these topics into the curriculum and act as allies. Religion-focused courses, such as world religions and sociology of religion, offer obvious locations for these essential dialogues. In addition, courses with an emphasis on multiculturalism, diversity, or social inequalities provide another space for academic discussions of Christian privilege. However, as Case (this volume) argues, the academy also offers some unexpected courses where learning about Christian privilege might occur. Development-focused courses, such as child psychology, or professional program courses in nursing, counseling, social work, or even clinical psychology are possible avenues for learning about religious privilege and diversity. In fact, students in medical and mental health professions need training that enhances their personal reflection and understanding of their own social location, which may include religious privilege, and appropriate professional boundaries when working with clients from a variety of religious backgrounds. For example, business faculty teaching courses addressing appropriate professionalism in communication, inclusive workplace culture, and international business relations may include Christian privilege and awareness of religious diversity in course materials and discussion. Education faculty training pre-service elementary and secondary teachers as well as school district administrators have the unique opportunity to facilitate critical discussions about Christian privilege and thereby raise future educators' awareness of inclusive K–12 classroom practices that will support students of all religious and non-religious backgrounds.

Calling for the field of privilege studies to embrace intersections of identity and avoid guilt-inducing pedagogical approaches, Peggy McIntosh (2012) argues that "teaching about privilege should enable people to recognize the systems and raise their curiosity about their own experiences of them" (p. 202). One of the most invisible aspects of oppression, academic discourse around Christian religious privilege provides avenues for learning about pervasive unearned advantage, increasing religious diversity, and invisible religious culture that permeates social institutions. Comfortable and safe classroom spaces allow assumptions to be unmasked and inform critical discussions. With academic analysis of Christian privilege across the curriculum, students will learn not only about mosques, synagogues, and temples, but also about the Muslims, Jews, atheists, Hindus, and Buddhists sitting next to them in class.

References

Berger, P. L. (1967). *The sacred canopy: Elements of a sociological theory of religion.* New York, NY: Doubleday.

Blumenfeld, W. J., & Jaekel, K. (2012). Exploring levels of Christian privilege awareness among preservice teachers. *Journal of Social Issues, 68*(1), 128–144. doi:10.1111/j.1540–4560.2011.01740.x

Bonilla-Silva, E. (1997). Rethinking racism: Toward a structural interpretation. *American Sociological Review, 62*(3), 465–480. doi:10.2307/2657316

Case, K. A. (2011). The class interview: Student engagement in courses covering sensitive topics. *Psychology of Learning and Teaching, 10*, 52–56. doi:10.2304/plat.2011.10.1.52

Case, K. A. (this volume). Beyond diversity and whiteness: Developing a transformative and intersectional model of privilege studies pedagogy. In K. A. Case (Ed.), *Deconstructing privilege: Teaching and learning as allies in the classroom* (pp. 1–14). New York, NY: Routledge.

Case, K. A., Bartsch, R., McEnery, L., Hall, S. P., Hermann, A., & Foster, D. (2008). Establishing a comfortable classroom from day one: Student perceptions of the reciprocal interview. *College Teaching, 56*(4), 210–214. doi:10.3200/CTCH.56.4.210–214

Case, K. A., & Cole, E. R. (this volume). Deconstructing privilege when students resist: The journey back into the community of engaged learners. In K. A. Case (Ed.), *Deconstructing privilege: Teaching and learning as allies in the classroom* (pp. 34–48). New York, NY: Routledge.

Case, K. A., Iuzzini, J., & Hopkins, M. (2012). Systems of privilege: Intersections, awareness, and applications. *Journal of Social Issues, 68*(1), 1–10. doi:10.1111/j.1540–4560.2011.01732.x

Case, K. A., & Lewis, M. (2012). Teaching intersectional LGBT psychology: Reflections from historically Black and Hispanic serving universities. *Psychology and Sexuality, 3*(3), 1–17. doi:10.1080/19419899.2012.700030

Case, K. A., Miller, A., & Jackson, S. B. (2012). "We talk about race too much in this class!" Complicating the essentialized woman through intersectional pedagogy. In S. Pliner & C. Banks (Eds.), *Teaching, learning, and intersecting identities in higher education* (pp. 32–48). New York, NY: Peter Lang.

Chaisson, R. L. (2004). A crack in the door: Critical race theory in practice at a predominantly white institution. *Teaching Sociology, 32*(4), 345–357. doi:10.1177/0092055X0403200401

Clark, C., Vargas, M. B., Schlosser, L., & Alimo, C. (2002). It's not just "secret Santa" in December: Addressing educational and workplace climate issues linked to Christian privilege. *Multicultural Education, 10*(2), 52–57.

Cole, E. R., Avery, L. R., Dodson, C., & Goodman, K. D. (2012). Against nature: How arguments about the naturalness of marriage privilege heterosexuality. *Journal of Social Issues, 68*(1), 46–62. doi:10.1111/j.1540–4560.2012.01735.x

Collins, P. H. (1990). *Black feminist thought: Knowledge, consciousness, and the politics of empowerment.* New York, NY: Routledge.

Davidson, C. (1987). Ethnic jokes: An introduction to race and nationality. *Teaching Sociology, 15*(3), 296–302. doi:10.2307/1318345

Dessel, A. B., Massé, J. C., & Walker, L. T. (this volume). Intergroup dialogue pedagogy: Teaching about intersectional and under-examined privilege in heterosexual, Christian, and Jewish identities. In K. A. Case (Ed.), *Deconstructing privilege: Teaching and learning as allies in the classroom* (pp. 132–148). New York, NY: Routledge.

DiClementi, J. D., & Handelsman, M. M. (2005). Empowering students: Class-generated course rules. *Teaching of Psychology, 32*(1), 18–21. doi:10.1207/s15328023top3201_4

Ebaugh, H. R. (2000). *Religion and the new immigrants: Continuities and adaptation in immigrant congregations.* Walnut Creek, CA: AltaMira Press.

Eck, D. L. (2001). *A new religious America: How a "Christian country" has now become the world's most religiously diverse nation.* San Francisco, CA: Harper San Francisco.

Farley, R., & Haaga, J. (Eds.). (2005). *The American people: Census 2000.* New York, NY: Sage.

Ferber, A. L. (2012). The culture of privilege: Color-blindness, postfeminism, and Christonormativity. *Journal of Social Issues, 68*(1), 63–77. doi:10.1111/j.1540–4560.2011.01736.x

Ferber, A. L., & Herrera, A. O. (this volume). Teaching privilege through an intersectional lens. In K. A. Case (Ed.), *Deconstructing privilege: Teaching and learning as allies in the classroom* (pp. 83–101). New York, NY: Routledge.

Freire, P. (1970). *Pedagogy of the oppressed*. New York, NY: Continuum.

Fried, J. (2007). Thinking skillfully and respecting difference: Understanding religious privilege on campus. *Journal of College and Character, 9*(1), 1–7. doi:10.2202/1940-1639.1103

Grillo, L. M. (2005). Diversity is an action verb. *Diverse: Issues in Higher Education, 22*(21), 45.

Henslee, A. M., Burgess, D. R., & Buskist, W. (2006). Student preferences for first day of class activities. *Teaching of Psychology, 33*, 189–191. doi:10.1207/s15328023top3303_7

Hobbs, F. (2002). *Demographic trends in the 20th century*. Washington, D.C.: U.S. Census Bureau.

Hondagneu-Sotelo, P., & Raskoff, S. (1994). Community service-learning promises and problems. *Teaching Sociology, 22*(3), 248–254. doi:10.2307/1319139

Jakubowski, L. M. (2001). Teaching uncomfortable topics: An action-oriented strategy for addressing racism and related forms of difference. *Teaching Sociology, 29*(1) 62–79. doi:10.2307/1318783

Kegan, R. (1982). *The evolving self: Problem and process in human development*. Cambridge, MA: Harvard University Press.

Martinez, T. A. (1994). Popular music in the classroom: Teaching race, class, and gender with popular culture. *Teaching Sociology, 22*(3), 260–265. doi:10.2307/1319141

Marulio, S. (1998). Bringing home diversity: A service-learning approach to teaching race and ethnic relations. *Teaching Sociology, 26*(4), 259–275. doi:10.2307/1318767

McIntosh, P. (1988). *White privilege and male privilege: A personal account of coming to see correspondences through work in women's studies* (Working Paper No. 189). Wellesley, MA: Wellesley Centers for Women.

McIntosh, P. (2012). Reflections and future directions for privilege studies. *Journal of Social Issues, 68*(1), 194–206. doi:10.1111/j.1540-4560.2011.01744.x

Perlman, B., & McCann, L. I. (1999). Student perspectives on the first day of class. *Teaching of Psychology, 26*(4), 277–279. doi:10.1207/S15328023TOP260408

Platt, L. F. (this volume). Blazing the trail: Teaching the privileged about privilege. In K. A. Case (Ed.), *Deconstructing privilege: Teaching and learning as allies in the classroom* (pp. 207–222). New York, NY: Routledge.

Poll, C. (1995). More than reading books: Using oral histories in courses in race and ethnic relations. *Teaching Sociology, 23*(2), 145–149. doi:10.2307/1319344

Puffer, P. (1994). Reducing ethnocentrism: A cross-cultural experience for sociology classes. *Teaching Sociology, 22*(1), 40–46. doi:10.2307/1318609

Quillian, L. (2006). New approaches to understanding racial prejudice and discrimination. *Annual Review of Sociology, 32*(1), 299–328. doi:10.1146/annurev.soc.32.061604.123132

Schlosser, L. Z. (2003). Christian privilege: Breaking a sacred taboo. *Journal of Multicultural Counseling and Development, 31*(1), 44–51. doi:10.1002/j.2161-1912.2003.tb00530.x

Smith, W. L. (1992). Reflections on race: The debate continues. *Teaching Sociology, 20*(3), 254–257.

Wahl, A.-M., Perez, E. T., Deegan, M. J., Sanchez, T. W., & Applegate, C. (2000). The controversial classroom: Institutional resources and pedagogical strategies for a race relations course. *Teaching Sociology, 28*(4), 316–332. doi:10.2307/1318582

Warner, R. S. (1998). *Gatherings in diaspora: Religious communities and the new immigration*. Philadelphia, PA: Temple University Press.

Watt, S. K. (2009). Facilitating difficult dialogues at the intersections of religious privilege. *New Directions for Student Services, 2009*(125), 65–73. doi:10.1002/ss.309

Wildman, S. M. (1995). Privilege in the workplace: The missing element in antidiscrimination law. *Texas Journal of Women and the Law, 4*, 171–189.

Williams, W. R., & Melchiori, K. J. (this volume). Class action: Using experiential learning to raise awareness of social class privilege. In K. A. Case (Ed.), *Deconstructing privilege: Teaching and learning as allies in the classroom* (pp. 169–187). New York, NY: Routledge.

Wuthnow, R. (2005). *America and the challenges of religious diversity*. Princeton, NJ: Princeton University Press.

Yankelovich, D. (1999). *The magic of dialogue: Transforming conflict into cooperation*. New York, NY: Simon and Schuster. doi:10.1002/ss.309

13

BLAZING THE TRAIL

Teaching the Privileged about Privilege

Lisa F. Platt

Teaching students about privilege in any setting can be a difficult endeavor, but teaching these topics to undergraduate students who represent mostly privileged social identities (i.e., White, heterosexual, affluent socioeconomic status) presents unique challenges. These identities describe the typical student population enrolled in small, selective, liberal arts colleges (Pryor, DeAngelo, Blake, Hurtado, & Tran, 2011). This type of academic setting, with highly privileged students, represents one of the most difficult arenas for teaching about privilege (Ahmed, 2008; Boatright-Horowitz & Soeung, 2009). These students usually come from homogeneous, affluent neighborhoods (Pryor et al., 2011). Most rarely experience any substantive experiences with individuals different from themselves. Most importantly, almost all remain unaware of the privileges they possess and blind to the benefits of various forms of privilege and the impact on non-privileged groups (McIntosh, 1988). Educators in this type of setting who embark on teaching about privilege often face strong emotional responses from students, including defensiveness and a lack of openness to exploring these types of concepts (Case & Cole, this volume; Cole, Case, Rios, & Curtin, 2011; Sue, Rivera, Capodilupo, Lin, & Torino, 2010; Wise & Case, this volume). Despite the challenges, teaching privileged students about the nature of privilege enables those with the most privilege to initiate change in the future. Given the nature of the ways privilege functions in society, these privileged students will likely hold positions of power in the future and could potentially serve as allies and advocates for change.

As an educator, I focus on three approaches for teaching privileged undergraduate students about the nature of privilege:

- make it personal;
- make it relevant; and
- manage emotional responses.

Each section below outlines teaching strategies meant to reach undergraduate students who possess multiple privileged social identities while minimizing negative emotional responses and increasing an open attitude toward understanding the role of privilege in their own lives. I present specific classroom activities with the following pedagogical goals:

(a) increase awareness and knowledge of privilege;
(b) increase empathy and compassion for those who do not possess privilege; and
(c) promote action for initiating societal change in the future.

While many of these activities presented below receive attention in pedagogical literature with goals of teaching about discrimination or other social justice topics, the learning goals emphasized here shift the focus to teaching about privilege specifically.

Make it Personal

The impact of privilege includes personal experience as well as sociocultural realities, even without awareness of these unearned advantages. McIntosh (1988) argues that lack of awareness of one's privilege exists as a result of privilege. This lack of awareness and invisibility of privilege highlights one of the most striking realities of the different cultural worlds oppressed and non-oppressed individuals occupy (Sue, 2010). Undergraduate students with privileged identities attending selective private universities often have almost no personal experience with oppression based on their social identities (Pryor et al., 2011). Therefore, the goal of "making privilege personal" for privileged students includes two essential aspects. First, students must explore their own social identities to better understand themselves and establish more empathy for others (Ancis & Szymanski, 2001). Second, students must hear personal stories of privilege and marginalization from others (Soble, Spanierman, & Liao, 2011). By guiding students' exploration of themselves and others, instructors increase awareness and empathy while reducing defensiveness.

Activity: "Who I Am"

One classroom activity that helps students explore their own social identities is entitled "Who I Am." This activity models a classroom exercise described by numerous authors (Bell, Washington, Weinstein, & Love, 1997; Case, 2012; Griffin, 1997; Howard, 2003), where students write an essay about all of their social identities (race/ethnicity, gender, sexual orientation, ability status, socioeconomic status, religion, age, etc.) and the ways those identities relate to privilege. Students write this essay early in the semester but only after an introduction to privilege topics such as lists daily white, heterosexual, or male privileges (McIntosh, 1988).

In the essays, students discuss the ways they possess or do not possess privileges across their social identities. The essay portion of the activity addresses the learning goal of increasing student knowledge and awareness of privilege, particularly in their personal lives. The instructions below illustrate an example prompt for the assignment:

> Define and describe as many aspects of your culture and multiple social identities as you feel comfortable disclosing. This may include (but is not limited to) your ethnicity, race, religion, gender identity, sexual orientation, age, socioeconomic status, and ability status. Within each of these, discuss how you may or may not possess the privileges discussed in class.

This assignment prompt encourages student engagement with privilege awareness in their personal lives and helps foster potentially new self-awareness.

Students then present to the class the parts of their essay they feel comfortable sharing. As part of the presentation, they bring to class one object as a representation of their cultural identities. One woman brought her handmade Jewish prayer shawl for the presentation. She explained that her sister made the shawl for her even though tradition allows only men to wear such garments. She also discussed balancing the male privilege she faces in her faith while still retaining her Jewish identity. For her, this "Who I Am" activity presented an opportunity to reflect more deeply on male privilege in her life. Hearing and sharing stories of privilege or oppression with their classmates serves not only to increase individual awareness of privilege, but also builds empathy for the experiences of those around them.

Student Reactions: "Privilege Impacts Me?"

Many students report they enjoy this activity because it helps to shape a sense of community in the classroom by hearing about the lives of their peers and provides an opportunity for students to learn more about the personal experiences of privilege from their classmates. Most students report the activity assists in making the classroom environment feel more comfortable to have productive difficult dialogues about privilege later in the course. Also, many students enjoy sharing about themselves and find it rewarding to discuss parts of their cultural identities while beginning to delve into their own complex combination of privileges and oppressions.

While the "Who I Am" activity receives positive reviews from students, the most common challenge involves engaging students who may be reluctant to share. Often students, particularly White students (Tatum, 1992), feel as though they have nothing "interesting" to discuss about their cultural identities and face difficulty recognizing the privileges they possess. This stems from the tendency of White American culture to see only race or culture as belonging to racial minority groups but not to themselves. In other words, being White becomes synonymous with being the "norm" (Case, 2012; Pratto & Stewart, 2012). These statements reflect the common belief that white culture does not exist and therefore does not come with benefits or privilege (Armstrong & Wildman, this volume; Wildman & Davis, 1997; Wise, 2005). Reinforcing and emphasizing that each individual has cultural experiences aids student learning (Kivel, Johnson, & Scraton, 2009). For example, students struggling with this assignment might be encouraged to consider possible ways their privilege would change if they belonged to a different social group based on race, gender, sexuality, social class, or religion. This assists students with tuning into their own previously invisible cultural experiences.

Instructor participation in the activity effectively models active engagement for students (Wise & Case, this volume). By modeling a straightforward, calm demeanor in discussing his or her own personal privileged or oppressed identities, the instructor builds a community of safety and trust in the classroom (Wise & Case, this volume). In choosing what to disclose as an instructor, one must balance being open and genuine with maintaining a professional demeanor (Griffin, 1997). Disclosing too many unnecessary personal details could make students uncomfortable and reduce the effectiveness of the activity. For example, when I lead this activity, I choose details of my life I am comfortable sharing such as my working-class background and white racial and ethnic identity. These details reflect my various privileged or oppressed identities, but without getting too personal and potentially losing effectiveness due to students viewing me as weak or trying to work out personal issues in classroom (Griffin, 1997). In deciding what details I disclose, I work to balance meeting the learning objectives, modeling taking risks in the classroom discussion, but at the same time not disclosing irrelevant and overly personal, emotional, or sensitive information. For example, while I discuss some of the challenges I face coming from a working-class background, such as living in two worlds as an academic, I do not share some of my more difficult childhood social class experiences.

"Privilege Impacts Others Too?"

In addition to focusing on students' own personal identities, the other aspect of "making privilege personal" involves giving students the opportunity to hear personal stories from other individuals who have experienced the adverse impact of privilege. Adding guest speakers, books, short stories, personal narratives, or appropriate videos helps personalize privilege and oppression. For example, I frequently use a compilation of narratives about privilege (Anderson & Middleton, 2011) to supplement assigned classroom readings. Providing students with personal stories achieves the goal of promoting the human, deeply personal nature of privilege and oppression. Hearing stories of situations that happen to real people makes the information more meaningful and more difficult to discount

(Niehuis, 2005; Soble et al., 2011). After reading these narratives, students participate in classroom discussions and write critical analysis essays to discuss their reactions and explore the personal nature of privilege.

Given that many privileged undergraduates have the advantage of never needing to be aware of privilege, the previously outlined learning goals of making privilege personal for students include (a) raising awareness of their own social identities and (b) building empathy for others. The classroom activities discussed above facilitate understanding of privilege both in themselves and others.

Make it Relevant

"Why does this matter for me?" Undergraduate students with little prior experience critically analyzing privilege topics commonly express this sentiment. One of the important ways to improve student engagement in class material of this nature is to make it relevant to their current lives and future goals (Wildman, 1996). By making the material relevant, instructors emphasize that privilege impacts relationships, career opportunities, and educational quality and remains alive in every interpersonal encounter throughout one's life (McIntosh, 1988). Making the material relevant to their present and future lives presents a challenge for teaching privileged undergraduate students.

Starting small with examples that apply to many students will help meet the challenge of making it relevant. When presented with the white privilege checklist (McIntosh, 1988), many White students gravitate toward the items related to purchasing makeup, bandages, crayons in one's own skin tone, and other simple aspects of privilege (Bohmer & Briggs, 1991; Pence & Fields, 1999). Pence and Fields (1999) discussed common reactions such as, "I never thought of that," and "That would be difficult to not be able to find makeup or hair products that work for me." Starting with smaller, less controversial privilege items often serves to reduce defensiveness and start classroom discussions that are less threatening. Also, by noticing the "small" ways privilege plays out in daily life, students begin the process of appreciating the "large" issues (Pendry, Driscoll, & Field, 2007; Wise & Case, this volume).

Making the material relevant can also be accomplished by connecting content to students' future careers and relationships. Most students, regardless of major, have career aspirations that involve working with people in some capacity, either in the corporate world or in social services professions (Pryor et al., 2011). Most future careers involve working successfully with others by building relationships with colleagues and the general public. For example, jobs in the corporate world require effective communication and relationships with other colleagues, managers, clients, and subordinates. For each of these relationships, privilege and culture play a role in the interpersonal dynamics. Students need skills and knowledge about the impact of privilege to improve their professional success in the future.

Activity: "What Would I Think?"

This classroom activity serves as a starting point for introducing the relevance of privilege topics. Before introducing this activity, I present some privilege topics such as the privilege checklists. This builds basic knowledge to utilize during the activity and later discussion. In the activity, students role play as a professional role therapist, a lawyer, or a manager of a business, for example. The role play scenario sets the scene for meeting a new client for the first time. At this point, students view a series of pictures of individuals representing various marginalized groups (a man who uses a wheelchair, various racial/ethnic groups, a lesbian woman, a transgendered man, etc.) along with the prompt, "This is your new client." With each picture, they privately write down their reactions to each person's presented image. Reflection questions include:

- How would you feel if this person were someone you had to work with?
- What thoughts would you have as you approached this person for the first time?
- How are your privileges/oppressions different or similar to the person?
- How would privilege impact your working relationship with this client?

After viewing and writing about all of the images, students discuss why they reacted the way they did and how their reactions might reflect privileged status. Initially, small group discussions promote more sharing, moving to the larger group where the instructor can highlight privilege as a major component of student reactions. The learning goals achieved in this activity include (a) increasing personal awareness and (b) building empathy for others around privilege issues by challenging students to think about their own interpersonal reactions and the lives of others through a privilege lens.

Many students find this activity powerful because they acknowledge the reality that their future professional lives will involve meeting a diverse range of people. Each of these new interpersonal encounters will be influenced by privilege. As students usually have a commitment to being successful in their future careers, this activity brings a new level of relevancy to privilege topics. For example, a student once commented after this activity:

> My father always told me to be careful around Black men because he said they are "usually in gangs." I know this isn't true, but I realized in this activity that I still felt some fear. I can only imagine what it would be like to be this client and have people fear him all of the time because I am privileged to not have those kinds of experiences.
>
> (White female psychology major)

As the above quote highlights, making privilege professionally and personally relevant allows for more in-depth reflection during the activity.

Activity: "Take a Walk in My Shoes"

This activity, designed by Snyder-Roche (2011), involves student participation in a guided imagery and experiential learning encounter with privilege and oppression. Students read a script preparing them for the activity that explains the procedure and discloses they may feel uncomfortable or anxious. Each student is assigned a social identity different from her or his own. For highly privileged students, the activity works best when they imagine marginalized identities. Students with marginalized identities receive either a different type of marginalized identity or a privileged identity. Students then experience a guided imagery activity in which they imagine their current lives based on the assigned social identity. For example, a White student assigned to a racial identity of Latino/a imagines life as a Latino/a individual. The script for the imagery may be modified for maximizing relevance to the audience. As they visualize settings from their lives such as going shopping, they imagine how others react to them, what it feels like in the environment, and any obstacles they face. Conducting the activity with only one identity provided to students allows introduction of a particular form or privilege, which can be valuable for an introductory student experience. Alternatively, providing an intersectional identity provides an opening for discussing the real-life complexities of multiple privileges or oppressions (Adams, Jones, & Tatum, 1997; Dill & Zambrana, 2009).

After the guided imagery, students discuss in small groups the impact of privilege on the imagined interactions. The following discussion prompts provide guidance for discussion:

- Discuss in your small group how privilege impacts the identity you were assigned.
- How is this similar or different from your real life?
- How did it feel to not possess certain privileges?
- In terms of privilege, discuss how your life would be different if you were permanently assigned this identity.

These example prompts promote the learning goals associated with this activity, which include (a) increasing personal awareness and (b) building empathy for others around privilege issues by simulating real-life experiences with privilege.

Student Reactions: Discomfort

For privileged students, this activity may be the first time many consider their lives without privilege. For example, after participating in this activity, one student commented:

> I hadn't ever considered how uncomfortable I would feel in my classes if I were African American. I think people would treat me different, and I

would feel very out of place being the only non-White student in the class. It is a privilege to not have to worry about that kind of thing.

(White female education major)

For this student, the white privilege of being comfortable in one's surroundings was something she never needed to consider until participating in this activity. The guided imagery increased her personal awareness as well as her empathy for others who do not possess the same privileges.

In making the material relevant for students, instructors must remain aware of the impact of the activities on students who may be in denial about their own personal biases. In answering honestly during the "What would I think?" activity, some students may experience shame, surprise, or guilt about harboring some internalized prejudice related to systemic privilege (Adams, 1997). Likewise, in the "Take a walk in my shoes" activity, students often face difficult emotions as they recognize the true lived experiences of privilege and oppression. Giving voice to these common reactions before and after the activity may aid in normalizing the emotions for students (Case & Cole, this volume). These unpleasant emotions present a learning opportunity that may be supported by reminding students that personal awareness of internalized biases can lead to more productive personal and professional relationships with diverse groups in the future (Bucher, 2004).

As many privileged undergraduate students initially experience difficulty seeing the relevance of learning about privilege topics, these classroom activities highlight the importance of such issues in future careers, relationships, and other interpersonal settings. This type of education benefits students as it prepares them for the diverse society they will face after college.

Manage Emotional Responses

Student Emotional Responses

"This white privilege checklist is stupid. These things don't really happen," states a young, White woman in an introduction to psychology course. Many college professors fail to engage their students with privilege topics due to fear of negative student responses (Boatright-Horowitz & Soeung, 2009; Henze, Lucas, & Scott, 1998). Many professors express concern about arousing feelings of defensiveness, anger, and other negative emotions, which are common student reactions (Davis, 1992). Additionally, a general lack of institutional and departmental support for teaching privilege topics contributes to the fears (Ahmed, 2008; Henze et al., 1998). However, professors working with privileged undergraduates can take some steps to manage these challenges.

Many students feel fear and guilt when presented with privilege concepts for the first time (McIntosh, 1988; Todd, Spanierman, & Aber, 2010; Wise &

Case, this volume). Students who possess multiple privileges may also feel threatened if they feel blamed for the oppression of others, especially given they perceive themselves as good people (Wise & Case, this volume). Modern-day aversive racism and prejudice lead many people to hold internalized negative societal messages and sometimes act on these beliefs, yet outwardly deny their own prejudicial attitudes (Gaertner & Dovidio, 1986). Recognition that one's privilege occurs at the expense of others may be quite painful to students (Swim & Miller, 1999; Tatum, 1992). The negative emotions indicate a realization of privilege as an insidious, harmful phenomenon (Sue et al., 2010). Students may employ a number of defense mechanisms such as denial, minimizing the true impact of privilege, or externalizing anger at the instructor to alleviate the discomfort (Case & Cole, this volume; Davis, 1992; Kernahan & Davis, 2007; Wise & Case, this volume).

Understanding and managing these common student reactions present perhaps the most challenging aspect of teaching about privilege topics, especially when the class is comprised of mainly privileged students. To this end, many of the classroom activities detailed in previous sections contribute to the learning goals of making the material personal, relevant, and non-threatening, which can reduce these negative emotions. One practical strategy involves having students work in small groups for more personalized discussion. This method offers students the opportunity to express feelings and thoughts in a safer venue. In a smaller discussion group format, students usually engage more as a result of feeling more comfortable. In addition, non-evaluative assignments, such as journal entries, where students privately dialogue about their reactions to the material, serve as a medium for conversation between instructor and student about difficult topics and emotional reactions. Other strategies for managing negative emotions involve starting simple with less threatening material. For example, it may be advisable to start with types of privilege that are slightly less controversial, such as able-bodied privilege, and work up to more emotionally laden privileges, such as white privilege (Wise & Case, this volume). While all forms of privilege cause harm and contribute to oppression, students tend to react more negatively to some types of content as compared to others. Some topics bring more or less emotional and political controversy to the conversation. For example, for issues related to race relations, often considered sensitive or taboo in our society, students may come in with strong opinions or personally difficult experiences with the topic (Tatum, 1992). By starting "easy," the instructor raises student consciousness about privilege without as many negative emotional responses (Wise & Case, this volume). As the curriculum moves into more "controversial" privilege topics, the instructor continues to model a calm and confident emotional demeanor, while explicitly validating the uncomfortable feelings that might arise in response to the material. This overt communication reinforces the message that privilege topics will push students in new and valuable ways.

Activity: Action Plans for Change

This classroom activity gives students an opportunity to develop creative ideas for incorporating proactive movement toward social justice and reducing the impact of privilege in their future endeavors. Students receive or choose a privilege topic, such as male or heterosexual privilege, and work with a partner or group to develop three different action steps they might take in the future to combat the assigned form of privilege. Students also receive action step examples, from "small steps" (i.e., confronting a friend who makes a sexist comment) to "large steps" (i.e., forming a campus awareness activity). Once students develop their action plans, they present the details of their plans to the larger classroom.

If time and course content allows, students complete this activity early in the semester and then attempt to implement their action plans over the duration of the course. Students then write or present the final outcome of their action plans by discussing the rewards and challenges of attempting to implement changes in their daily lives. For example, in a psychology of gender course, several students created an action plan to become more involved in a campus advocacy group for women. The students joined a campus club designed to raise awareness about sexual violence against women. As part of the club, they participated in helping develop the first Take Back the Night event (a women-centered rape awareness event) held on campus. At the end of the semester, the students documented their experiences being involved in the campus group and their analysis of the wider campus community's response to the event. One of the female students wrote, "I never really considered the true harm of male privilege until I fully considered how unsafe I feel walking alone at night." Another student observed:

> It seemed like only women participated in the march and campus events we put on. It made me wonder why the men on campus did not feel a need to be involved. I realize now this is an example of male privilege because they do not have to worry as much about sexual violence.
>
> (White female psychology major)

Another student wrote about her personal action step to stop using the word "gay" in a derogatory manner and felt the action plan activity increased her awareness of her own heterosexual privilege. She stated, "No one ever says, 'Oh that's so straight!' as an insult. I realized that I have the privilege of my sexual orientation not being seen as bad."

As many privileged students feel guilt when recognizing they benefit from privilege, this activity can channel those emotions into positive action for the future. There is considerable research demonstrating the positive impact of community engagement and service-learning activities for students (Jones & Hill, 2001; Mobley, 2011; Peterson, 2009). For example, as part of his action plan, one student participated in a service-learning activity at a local non-profit organization specializing in assisting African refugees. He wrote:

> After learning about the advantages I have in my life, I really wanted to fix things somehow. These concrete steps such as helping to offer support groups for the new refugees helped me not feel so guilty and hopeless and taught me a lot about my own privileges.
>
> (White male communication major)

For this student, concrete action through service learning provided a positive pathway to promote change in his community. Additionally, many students enjoyed being given the opportunity to feel productive toward social change in reducing privilege.

Educators may want to prepare for potential pitfalls associated with students' following through on their action plans. First, students are encouraged to start small, with less risky steps. These small steps could be as simple as refraining from using derogatory slang terms or calling their female friends "women" instead of "girls." By starting small, students more easily reach their goals, promote change, and reduce the likelihood of negative responses from their peers. As students move into taking larger steps, an educator can prepare students for responding to negative feedback from friends or the wider campus community. As developing allies, I encourage students to look for reasonable opportunities that have the greatest chances of success. Educators can remind students that, regardless of the overall scope of their action steps, they still contribute to implementing important changes for the future.

The Action Plans for Change activity addresses the three pedagogical learning goals of (a) increasing awareness, (b) increasing empathy, and (c) initiating future change. When students participate in experiential, action-oriented activities to promote change, they engage in a meaningful encounter with their own privileges and the oppression of others (Lawrence, 1998). By creating an action plan for change, they increase their basic knowledge and awareness of privilege by seeing the harm of privilege and oppression first hand. In taking action steps, they go from simply learning about privilege to interacting with those cultural and structural systems with the goal of initiating future changes.

Instructor Emotional Responses

Along with understanding the negative emotions of students, managing your own emotions as the educator in response to students requires preparation. Most educators with passion for social justice have significant emotional investment in student responses to this type of material (Case & Cole, this volume; Enns & Sinacore, 2005). In teaching students about difficult, sensitive topics like privilege, educators often pay a high price in terms of personal emotional energy (Nast, 1999). Teaching privileged students about these topics may feel like swimming against a tide of deeply rooted individual and systemic biases. This effort often leaves educators feeling defeated in the face of such overwhelming resistance (Enns & Sinacore, 2005).

Educators must strive to manage expectations of teaching about privilege topics and work with students at their current level, likely at the very beginning of the process. Multicultural identity development such as white identity development does not occur overnight (Helms, 1990; Tatum, 1992). Young undergraduate students from privileged backgrounds with limited real life experience with these topics and are only beginning to form their adult identities. It is also important to remember that valuable learning can come from uncomfortable, yet productive, emotions (Wise & Case, this volume). For many students, sitting with the uncomfortable feelings may help accomplish the learning goals more effectively than simple lecture or book learning (Ancis & Szymanski, 2001).

However difficult, modeling a calm, non-reactive stance even in the presence of racist or sexist student comments that demonstrate a lack of education about these topics will minimize resistance and promote open dialogue. An educator must articulate a composed, well thought out response to many common, negative student responses (Bell et al., 1997) while being patient with student development. Maintaining a calm demeanor as an instructor helps prevent students from becoming more entrenched in old views due to feeling misunderstood or attacked. An instructor must engage in non-reactive ways with students who hold values very different from his or her own in regard to privilege topics.

Instructors may also feel professional risk associated with teaching privilege topics. This risk may lead to lowered course evaluations (Boatright-Horowitz & Soeung, 2009), backlash from hostile colleagues or administrators (Nast, 1999), and losing overall credibility. These risks feel particularly salient for academic professionals without tenure or those who already face a lack of privilege and power such as faculty of color, women, LGBT faculty, etc. (Bell et al., 1997; Case, Kanenberg, Erich, & Tittsworth, 2012). While no simple solutions to eliminating this professional risk exist, instructors can take some steps to reduce these risks and improve their overall chance at success.

First, an instructor can be selective in when and where to introduce learning about privilege. For example, a faculty member may choose to only briefly discuss privilege topics for one or two days of a course initially and gradually build up to a more integrated framework in later course offerings (Case, McMullen, & Hentges, this volume). Additionally, appropriate framing of activities or course content about privilege may be of assistance. For example, prior to assigning a reading an instructor can explicitly state, "This reading is more controversial than some we have done thus far. Try to keep an open mind, and we will discuss it in class." In my psychology courses, I often state, "Diversity considerations are essential to understanding and working with people. Privilege can have a major impact on an individual's life experiences, so it is important we understand these topics." Framing the relevance of the material and its importance to course content gives it more creditability.

Seeking out other allies within the institution may reduce the negative professional impact of teaching about privilege topics. While such individuals may not be immediately obvious or overt, subtle communications or signs may be present if one is astute. There can be power in numbers even if an ally is not housed directly within one's department. Bell et al. (1997) also suggest team teaching with a tenured professor to reduce professional vulnerability.

Although difficult to accept, reaching every single student with maximized learning about privilege sets instructors up for unreachable goals. Not all students possess the willingness to engage in this type of material. Instead of perceiving these cases as pedagogical failures, instructors might consider that with more exposure, developmental maturity, and personal experience, even highly resistant students may be more willing to listen in the future, well after the course ends (Adams et al., 1997). As an educator, channeling energy toward the positive growth of students and appreciating the progress made in the classroom may help reduce negative emotions associated with feeling ineffective. Engaged students also model open-mindedness to resistant peers and serve as allies in the classroom (Young, 2003). Additionally, even if only a few students experience growth through learning about privilege, instructors must acknowledge these successes. The societal change that even one student could produce may not be something immediately tangible or visible but could still have a lasting impact (Enns & Sinacore, 2005).

Conclusion

Through teaching about privilege, educators promote a systemic, cultural shift in the awareness and actions of those who hold privilege and validate the experiences of those who do not. Education holds the key to this long-term goal (Wildman, 1996). The practical means of providing education involves making the material personal and relevant to highly privileged students, while also managing the negative emotions of both students and the self as an educator. Also, educators can be creative in allowing students opportunities to create change. The activities presented may be implemented in multiple types of courses such as social science, business, or education courses. Implementing clear learning goals also helps clarify what aspect of learning about privilege the instructor hopes to attain. Privileged undergraduate students can be advocates for future change and benefit from learning about the role of privilege in their lives. Highly privileged undergraduates benefit from the activities and strategies outlined above. Educators must start reaching those with the most power for change in our society (Wise, 2005).

References

Adams, M. (1997). Pedagogical frameworks for social justice education. In M. Adams, L. A. Bell, & P. Griffin (Eds.), *Teaching for diversity and social justice: A sourcebook* (pp. 30–43). New York, NY: Routledge.

Adams, M., Jones, J., & Tatum, B. D. (1997). Knowing our students. In M. Adams, L. A. Bell, & P. Griffin (Eds.), *Teaching for diversity and social justice: A sourcebook* (pp. 311–325). New York, NY: Routledge.

Ahmed, B. (2008). Teaching critical psychology of race issues: Problems in promoting anti-racist practice. *Journal of Community & Applied Social Psychology, 18*(1), 54–67. doi:10.1002/casp.912

Ancis, J. R., & Szymanski, D. M. (2001). Awareness of white privilege among White counseling trainees. *The Counseling Psychologist, 29*(4), 548–569. doi:10.1177/0011000001294005

Anderson, S. H., & Middleton, V. A. (Eds.) (2011). *Explorations in diversity: Examining privilege and oppression in a multicultural society* (2nd ed.). Belmont, CA: Brooks/Cole.

Armstrong, M. J., & Wildman, S. M. (this volume). "Colorblindness is the new racism": Raising awareness about privilege using color insight. In K. A. Case (Ed.), *Deconstructing privilege: Teaching and learning as allies in the classroom* (pp. 63–79). New York, NY: Routledge.

Bell, L. A., Washington, S., Weinstein, G., & Love, B. (1997). Knowing ourselves as instructors. In M. Adams, L. A. Bell, & P. Griffin (Eds.), *Teaching for diversity and social justice: A sourcebook* (pp. 299–310). New York, NY: Routledge.

Boatright-Horowitz, S. L., & Soeung, S. (2009). Teaching white privilege to White students can mean saying good-bye to positive student evaluations. *American Psychologist, 64*(6), 574–575. doi:10.1037/a0016593

Bohmer, S., & Briggs, J. L. (1991). Teaching privileged students about gender, race, and class oppression. *Teaching Sociology, 19*(2), 154–163. doi:10.2307/1317846

Bucher, R. D. (2004). *Diversity consciousness: Opening our minds to people, cultures, and opportunities.* Upper Saddle River, NJ: Pearson.

Case, K. A. (2012). Discovering the privilege of whiteness: White women's reflections on anti-racist identity and ally behavior. *Journal of Social Issues, 68*(1), 78–96. doi:10.1111/j.1540-4560.2011.01737.x

Case, K. A., & Cole, E. R. (this volume). Deconstructing privilege when students resist: The journey back into the community of engaged learners. In K. A. Case (Ed.), *Deconstructing privilege: Teaching and learning as allies in the classroom* (pp. 34–48). New York, NY: Routledge.

Case, K. A., Kanenberg, H., Erich, S., & Tittsworth, J. (2012). Transgender inclusion in university nondiscrimination statements: Challenging gender-conforming privilege through student activism. *Journal of Social Issues, 68*(1), 145–161. doi:10.1111/j.1540-4560.2011.01741.x

Case, K. A., McMullen, M., & Hentges, B. (this volume). Teaching the taboo: Walking the tightrope of Christian privilege. In K. A. Case (Ed.), *Deconstructing privilege: Teaching and learning as allies in the classroom* (pp. 188–206). New York, NY: Routledge.

Cole, E. R., Case, K. A., Rios, D., & Curtin, N. (2011). Understanding what students bring to the classroom: Moderators of the effects of diversity courses on student attitudes. *Cultural Diversity and Ethnic Minority Psychology, 17*(4), 397–405. doi:10.1037/a0025433

Davis, N. (1992). Teaching about inequality: Student resistance, paralysis, and rage. *Teaching Sociology, 20*(3), 232–238. doi:10.2307/1319065

Dill, B. T., & Zambrana, R. E. (2009). *Emerging intersections: Race, class, and gender in theory, policy, and practice.* Piscataway, NJ: Rutgers University Press.

Enns, C. Z., & Sinacore, A. L. (2005). *Teaching and social justice: Integrating multicultural and feminist theories in the classroom.* Washington, D.C.: American Psychological Association.

Gaertner, S. L., & Dovidio, J. F. (1986). The aversive form of racism. In J. F. Dovidio & S. L. Gaertner (Eds.), *Prejudice, discrimination and racism: Theory and research* (pp. 61–89). Orlando, FL: Academic Press.

Griffin, P. (1997). Introductory module for single issue courses. In M. Adams, L. A. Bell, & P. Griffin (Eds.), *Teaching for diversity and social justice: A sourcebook* (pp. 61–81). New York, NY: Routledge.

Henze, R., Lucas, T., & Scott, B. (1998). Dancing with the monster: Teachers discuss racism, power, and white privilege in education. *Urban Review, 30*(3), 187–210. doi:10.1023/A:1023280117904

Helms, J. E. (Ed.) (1990). *Black and White racial identity: Theory, research and practice*. New York, NY: Greenwood Press.

Howard, T. C. (2003). Culturally relevant pedagogy: Ingredients for critical teacher reflection. *Theory into Practice, 42*(3), 195–202. doi:10.1207/s15430421tip4203_5

Jones, S. R., & Hill, K. (2001). Crossing High Street: Understanding diversity through community service-learning. *Journal of College Student Development, 42*(3), 204–216.

Kernahan, C., & Davis, T. (2007). Changing perspective: How learning about racism influences student awareness and emotion. *Teaching of Psychology, 34*(1), 49–52. doi:10.1207/s15328023top3401_12

Kivel, B. D., Johnson, C. W., & Scraton, S. (2009). (Re)Theorizing race, experience, and leisure: Using critical ethnography and collective memory work. *Journal of Leisure Research, 41*(4), 471–492.

Lawrence, S. M. (1998). Unveiling positions of privilege: A hands-on approach to understanding racism. *Teaching of Psychology, 25*(3), 198–200. doi:10.1207/s15328023top2503_8

McIntosh, P. (1988). *White privilege and male privilege: A personal account of coming to see correspondences through work in women's studies* (Working Paper No. 189). Wellesley, MA: Wellesley Centers for Women.

Mobley, C. (2011). Diversity and service-learning: Finding common ground through social justice and mindfulness. In T. Stewart & N. Webster (Eds.), *Exploring cultural dynamics and tensions within service-learning* (pp. 83–103). Charlotte, NC: Information Age Publishing.

Nast, H. J. (1999). "Sex," "race," and multiculturalism: Critical consumption and the politics of course evaluations. *Journal of Geography in Higher Education, 23*(1), 102–115. doi:10.1080/03098269985650

Niehuis, S. (2005). Helping White students explore white privilege outside the classroom. *North American Journal of Psychology, 7*(3), 481–492.

Pence, D. J., & Fields, J. A. (1999). Teaching about race and ethnicity: Trying to uncover white privilege for a White audience. *Teaching Sociology, 27*(2), 150–158. doi:10.2307/1318701

Pendry, L. F., Driscoll, D. M., & Field, S. C. T. (2007). Diversity training: Putting theory into practice. *Journal of Occupational and Organizational Psychology, 80*(1), 27–50. doi:10.1348/096317906X118397

Peterson, T. H. (2009). Engaged scholarship: Reflections and research on the pedagogy of social change. *Teaching in Higher Education, 14*(5), 541–552. doi:10.1080/13562510903186741

Pryor, J. H., DeAngelo, L., Blake, L. P., Hurtado, S., & Tran, S. (2011). *The American freshman: National norms fall 2011*. Los Angeles, CA: Higher Education Research Institute, UCLA.

Pratto, F., & Stewart, A. L. (2012). Group dominance and the half-blindness of privilege. *Journal of Social Issues, 68*(1), 28–45. doi:10.1111/j.1540-4560.2011.01734.x

Snyder-Roche, S. (2011). Take a walk in my shoes. In M. Pope, J. S. Pangelinan, & A. D. Coker (Eds.), *Experiential activities for teaching multicultural competence in counseling* (pp. 185–188). Alexandria, VA: American Counseling Association.

Soble, J. R., Spanierman, L. B., & Liao, H. (2011). Effects of a brief video intervention on White university students' racial attitudes. *Journal of Counseling Psychology, 58*(1), 151–157. doi:10.1037/a0021158

Sue, D. W. (2010). *Microaggressions in everyday life.* Hoboken, NJ: Wiley & Sons Inc.

Sue, D. W., Rivera, D. P., Capodilupo, C. M., Lin, A. I., & Torino, G. C. (2010). Racial dialogues and White trainees fears: Implications for education and training. *Cultural Diversity and Ethnic Minority Psychology, 16*(2), 206–214. doi:10.1037/a0016112

Swim, J. K., & Miller, D. L. (1999). White guilt: Its antecedents and consequences for attitudes toward affirmative action. *Personality and Social Psychology Bulletin, 25*(4), 500–515. doi:10.1177/0146167299025004008

Tatum, B. D. (1992). Talking about race, learning about racism: The application of racial identity development theory in the classroom. *Harvard Educational Review, 62*(1), 1–24.

Todd, N. R., Spanierman, L. B., & Aber, M. S. (2010). White students reflecting on whiteness: Understanding emotional responses. *Journal of Diversity in Higher Education 3*(2), 97–110. doi:10.1037/a0019299

Wildman, S. M. (1996). Teaching and learning towards transformation: The role of the classroom in noticing privilege. In S. M. Wildman (Ed.), *Privilege revealed: How invisible preference undermines America* (pp. 161–176). New York, NY: New York University Press.

Wildman, S. M., & Davis, A. D. (1997). Making systems of privilege visible. In R. Delgado & J. Stefancic (Eds.), *Critical white studies: Looking behind the mirror* (pp. 314–319). Philadelphia, PA: Temple University Press.

Wise, T. J. (2005). *White like me.* Brooklyn, NY: Soft Skull Press.

Wise, T., & Case, K. A. (this volume). Pedagogy for the privileged: Addressing inequality and injustice without shame or blame. In K. A. Case (Ed.), *Deconstructing privilege: Teaching and learning as allies in the classroom* (pp. 17–33). New York, NY: Routledge.

Young, G. (2003). Dealing with difficult classroom dialogue. In P. Bronstein & K. Quina (Eds.), *Teaching gender and multicultural awareness: Resources for the psychology classroom* (pp. 347–360). Washington, D.C.: American Psychological Association.

LIST OF CONTRIBUTORS

Margalynne J. Armstrong, B.A., J.D., is an Associate Professor of Law and the Associate Academic Director of the Center for Social Justice and Public Service at Santa Clara University School of Law, California. Professor Armstrong teaches race and law, constitutional law, and property. Her scholarship in these areas has appeared in books, journals, newspapers, and online. Prior to teaching at Santa Clara University, she practiced in public employment law, was a staff attorney with the Legal Aid Society of Alameda County, California, and directed the Academic Support Program at the University of California at Berkeley Law School.

Cerri A. Banks, Ph.D., is the Vice President for Student Affairs and Dean of the College at Mount Holyoke College in South Hadley, Massachusetts. She received her Ph.D. in cultural foundations of education from Syracuse University, New York. Banks specializes in sociology of education, cultural studies, multicultural education, and qualitative research and draws from critical pedagogy, educational theory, feminist theory, and critical race theory in her scholarship and teaching.

Sriya Bhattacharyya, B.S., is a doctoral student in the Counseling Psychology Program at Boston College (BC), Massachusetts. She is a Diversity Fellow at BC, serves as a Young Ambassador through the U.S. Department of State, is a Student Affiliate of the American Psychological Association, and has been nominated a Changemaker by the Ashoka Foundation for her work in India. She served as an Orbis Fellow in Bhubaneswar, India, where she began her research in inter-caste ally development and taught a United Nations Millennium Development Goals Curriculum. She co-founded a micro-credit loan program in

Gisenyi, Rwanda, called Rwanda Sustainable Families. She currently is a research assistant at BC and is interested in social justice advocacy, multiculturalism, empathy development in international curricula, and wellbeing in international development.

Markie Louise Christianson (L. C.) Blumer, Ph.D., is an Assistant Professor at University of Nevada, Las Vegas. She is a licensed family therapist, and mental health counselor, clinical member, and approved supervisor of the American Association for Marriage and Family Therapy, and serves as an Editorial Board Member for the *Journal of Feminist Family Therapy: An International Forum.* Dr. Blumer's research primarily focuses on social justice practices and clinical considerations for persons identifying as sexual and gender orientation minorities, and she has published, presented, and received grant funding in this area. Other areas of interest include feminist family therapy, mentoring, clinical supervision, couple and family technology, and family and ecological sustainability.

Jenna M. Calton, B.S., is a doctoral student in the clinical psychology doctoral program at George Mason University, Virginia. She received her Bachelor of Science degree in psychology and her Bachelor of Arts degree in women's studies from the University of Florida. She is interested in social justice, and her current research examines intimate partner violence victims' perceptions of procedural and distributive justice while seeking support from the justice system.

Kim A. Case, Ph.D., is Associate Professor of Psychology and Women's Studies at the University of Houston-Clear Lake, Texas, and Director of the Applied Social Issues sub-plan in the Psychology Master's Program. Her research on prejudice confrontation and ally behavior focuses on dominant group responses to bias in various social contexts. She also studies strategies for raising awareness of heterosexual, gender-conforming, male, and white privilege in educational and community settings. She teaches courses addressing intersectionality, privilege and oppression (via gender, race, and sexuality), social issues methods, and career development. As an active member of the Society for the Psychological Study of Social Issues (American Psychological Association, Division 9), she has served as elected Council and Executive Council member, Early Career Scholars chair, Teaching and Mentoring Committee chair, and *Journal of Social Issues* editorial board member.

Elizabeth R. Cole, Ph.D., is Professor of Women's Studies and Psychology at the University of Michigan. Her research interests include intersectionality; class, race, and gender as social identities; the relationship between political attitudes and behaviors, particularly among African Americans and all women; and qualitative methods.

Adrienne B. Dessel, Ph.D., LMSW, an Associate Director of the Program on Intergroup Relations at the University of Michigan, teaches courses on intergroup dialogue, intergroup relations, global conflict and coexistence, and conducts research on prejudice reduction and intergroup dialogue processes and outcomes.

Abby L. Ferber, Ph.D., is Director of the Matrix Center for the Advancement of Social Equity and Inclusion, Professor of Sociology and Women's and Ethnic Studies at the University of Colorado, Colorado Springs. Her research explores issues of privilege, and the intersections of race, gender and sexuality. She has authored/edited seven books, including *Privilege: A Reader*, with Michael Kimmel (Westview, 3rd ed. forthcoming in 2013), *Sex, Gender, and Sexuality: The New Basics*, with Kimberly Holcomb and Tre Wentling (Oxford, 2nd ed., 2012), and *Home Grown Hate* (Routledge, 2004), and is a founding editor of *Understanding and Dismantling Privilege*, an online journal. She is on the national planning team of the annual White Privilege Conference, and Co-founder and Director of The Knapsack Institute: Transforming Teaching and Learning.

Mary Sue Green, Ph.D., is an Assistant Professor at Texas Woman's University. She is a licensed couple and family therapy therapist, clinical member and approved supervisor of the American Association for Marriage and Family Therapy, and member of the American Family Therapy Academy. She has researched, published, and presented on the topics of sexual minority issues in therapy. Her current research projects focus on lesbian and gay male therapist development, communication and decision making in same-sex couples, and the influence of religious beliefs on therapist and clergy comfort working with lesbian and gay male clients.

Parris M. Green, B.S., is a graduate student in the family therapy program at Texas Woman's University (TWU). He received his Bachelor of Science degree in education. He is a student member of the American Association for Marriage and Family Therapy and the National Council on Family Relations. He serves as Treasurer for TWU's Student Association for Marriage and Family Therapy and is on the executive board of the Student Government's House of Representatives. He has presented at the state and national level on sexual minority issues. He currently works as a research assistant and is interested in decision-making processes in blended families.

Martin Heesacker, Ph.D., is a Professor of Psychology at the University of Florida, where he has served as director of counseling psychology doctoral training and as department chair. A fellow of both the Association for Psychological Science and the American Psychological Association (Counseling Psychology and Men and Masculinity divisions), he conducts research at the interface of social psychology and counseling/clinical psychology, with a current focus on understudied processes in stereotyping and prejudice.

Beth Hentges, Ph.D., is an Associate Professor of Psychology at the University of Houston–Clear Lake. Her research interests focus on media representations of gender and race and their effect on children and adults. She teaches courses in child psychology, media and psychology, and critical thinking in psychology.

Andrea O'Reilly Herrera, Ph.D., is a Professor of Literature and Director of the Women's and Ethnic Studies Program at the University of Colorado, Colorado Springs. She is also a poet and essayist. Her publications include a collection of "testimonial expressions" drawn from the Cuban exile community and their children residing in the United States (*ReMembering Cuba: Legacy of a Diaspora*, University of Texas Press, 2001), a novel (*The Pearl of the Antilles*, Bilingual/Review Press, 2001), an edited collection of essays (*Cuba: IDEA of a Nation Displaced*, State University of New York Press, 2007); and a recent work monograph, *Cuban Artists across the Diaspora: Setting the Tent Against the House* (University of Texas Press, 2011).

Morgan B. Hopkins, M.A., is the Coordinator of Leadership Programs in the Centennial Center for Leadership at Hobart and William Smith Colleges in Geneva, New York. She received her bachelor's from William Smith College with honors in psychology and a minor in women's studies and her master's in psychology from the University of Houston-Clear Lake with concentrations in women's studies and applied social issues. Her areas of specialty include feminist theory, social psychological theory, and community organizing.

Rebecca R. Hubbard, M.S., is a doctoral candidate in the counseling psychology program at Virginia Commonwealth University in Richmond, Virginia. She is a member of the American Psychological Association for Graduate Students, the Society for the Psychological Study of Lesbian, Gay, Bisexual, and Transgender Issues (American Psychological Association, Division 44), and a student member of the Association of Black Psychologists. Rebecca's research interests include Black–White biracial identity development, social justice issues focusing on racism and heterosexism, and multicultural counseling.

Jill Lee-Barber, Ph.D., is Director of Psychological and Health Services at Georgia State University. She serves as co-chair of the Taking Action Against Racism in Media project within the Society of Counseling Psychology (American Psychological Association, Division 17) and has presented and published in the areas of integrating multicultural and feminist theories in psychotherapy. Dr. Lee-Barber is a licensed psychologist who received her Ph.D. in counseling psychology from the University of Houston, Texas. Her areas of specialty include both individual and systemic intervention in diverse university populations.

Johanna C. Massé is pursuing a joint Ph.D. in higher education and sociology at the University of Michigan. Her primary research interests include qualitative research methodologies, educational transitions from a life course perspective, and undergraduate social justice education.

Mike McMullen, Ph.D., is an Associate Professor of Sociology and Cross-Cultural Studies at the University of Houston-Clear Lake. His areas of interest include the sociology of religion, conflict resolution and mediation, organizational development and change, and religious mediation. He does academic research into various religious groups, as well as conflict resolution programs in the corporate and non-profit sectors and the public schools. He also worked for five years at the Martin Luther King, Jr. Center for Nonviolent Social Change in Atlanta, Georgia, as a researcher and workshop facilitator, training youth in conflict resolution techniques as well as civil rights history.

Kala J. Melchiori, M.A., received her bachelor's degree with honors from Marshall University, West Virginia, in 2008, where she won the Outstanding Student in Psychology award from both the honors and psychology departments. While an undergraduate, she took several courses with Dr. Williams that included experiential components, which she now strives to use in her own teaching. In 2011, Kala was awarded a master's degree in applied social psychology at Loyola University Chicago and is currently working towards her Ph.D. Her research interests include gender, prejudice, and discrimination, including how women respond to sexual harassment and what factors influence their choice to confront harassers.

Ruperto M. Perez, Ph.D., is a licensed psychologist with his Ph.D. in counseling psychology from the University of Missouri–Columbia. Previously, Dr. Perez served as Assistant Director for Clinical Services at the Counseling Center at the University of Florida and as Counseling Services Coordinator and Training Director at the Counseling & Testing Center at the University of Georgia. His areas of professional interest include counseling issues related to diversity and multiculturalism, gender issues, lesbian, gay, bisexual, and transgender (LGBT) concerns, outreach/consultation, and supervision/mentoring. In addition, Dr. Perez is the co-editor of the *Handbook of Counseling and Psychotherapy with Lesbian, Gay, and Bisexual Clients* published by the American Psychological Association.

Paul B. Perrin, Ph.D., is an Assistant Professor in the Department of Psychology at Virginia Commonwealth University, and he received his Ph.D. in counseling psychology from the University of Florida. He researches multicultural health psychology, and his primary career goal is to use psychology as a vehicle to work toward social justice against different forms of oppression, such as racism, heterosexism, and sexism, as they manifest themselves in various social systems, especially within the health care system. He teaches undergraduate and graduate courses on multicultural and community psychology, health psychology, psychopathology, and research methods.

Lisa F. Platt, Ph.D., is an Assistant Professor of Psychology at the College of Saint Benedict/Saint John's University in Collegeville, Minnesota. She received a M.Ed. in couples and family therapy from the University of Oregon and a Ph.D. in counseling psychology from Penn State University, Pennsylvania. She is also a licensed psychologist in the state of Minnesota. Her research and teaching interests involve exploring the psychological and social impact of privilege and oppression, particularly in regard to gender and sexual orientation.

Susan M. Pliner, Ed.D., is the Associate Dean for Teaching, Learning and Assessment and Assistant Professor of Education at Hobart and William Smith Colleges in Geneva, New York. She has a certificate of advanced graduate studies in social justice education and an Ed.D. in human development. Her areas of specialty include universal instructional design for teaching and learning, multicultural and social justice education, college student learning and development, and social identity development theory and practice in higher education.

Desdamona Rios, Ph.D., is an Assistant Professor of Psychology at the University of Houston-Clear Lake. Her research examines diversity in educational contexts and the impact of socialization processes on underrepresented groups in different roles in the academy. She uses mixed research methods to examine the role of curricular content on identity and attitudes about the self and others, the psychology of invisibility, and factors in the academic environment that facilitate a sense of fit for underrepresented groups.

Daniel J. Snipes, B.A., is a doctoral student studying health psychology at Virginia Commonwealth University in Richmond, Virginia. He received his bachelor's degree in psychology from California State University, Long Beach, and graduated *magna cum laude*. He is studying topics relevant to LGBT health, with specific interests in HIV risk behaviors and discrimination among LGBT populations.

Abigail J. Stewart, Ph.D., is Sandra Schwartz Tangri Distinguished University Professor of Psychology and Women's Studies at the University of Michigan, where she is Director of the ADVANCE Program. Her current research examines educated women's lives and personalities; women's movement activism, both in the United States and globally; gender, science, and technology among graduate students, postdoctoral fellows, and faculty; and institutional change in the academy.

Nicole L. Thomte, B.A., is a graduate student in the University of Nevada, Las Vegas (UNLV) Marriage and Family Therapy Program. She attained Bachelor of Arts degrees in Spanish and Theater, as well as a Secondary Education Teaching Certificate from the University of Texas at Austin. She holds a Bachelor of Arts in Psychology from the University of Nevada, Las Vegas, and is currently a student member of the American Association for Marriage and Family Therapy and the National Council on Family Relations. She has an interest in serving the lesbian, gay, bisexual, transgender, queer, and intersex community as a family therapist.

Lauren T. Walker, M.S.W., is an alumna of the University of Michigan School of Social Work. Her academic interests include diversity, access, and community engagement in higher education.

Stephanie M. Wildman, A.B., J.D., is the John A. and Elizabeth H. Sutro Professor of Law and Director of the Center for Social Justice and Public Service at the Santa Clara University School of Law, California. In 2007, she received the Great Teacher Award from the Society of American Law Teachers, the largest national organization of law school faculty. She was the founding Director of the Center for Social Justice at the University of California at Berkeley School of Law. Her publications include *Privilege Revealed: How Invisible Preference Undermines America* (1996) and the co-edited books *Women and the Law: Stories* (2011), *Race and Races: Cases and Resources for a Diverse America* (2nd ed., 2007), and *Social Justice: Professionals Communities and Law* (2003). She teaches law and social justice and gender and law. Her scholarship emphasizes systems of privilege, gender, race, and classroom dynamics.

Wendy R. Williams, Ph.D., received her doctorate in social psychology from the University of California, Santa Cruz, in 2005. She is currently an Associate Professor of Psychology and Women's Studies at Berea College, Kentucky, where she teaches courses on social psychology, research methods, and women's studies. She is the former Director of Women's Studies at Marshall University, and, in 2008, she was awarded the Pickens–Queen Excellence in Teaching Award for junior faculty. Her research focuses on documenting the lived experiences of low-income and working-class Americans, as well as examining the personal and political consequences of how low-income people are perceived.

Tim Wise is among the nation's most prominent anti-racist writers and educators. He is the author of six books on race and racism, and has spoken to over a million people in all 50 U.S. states, on over 700 college campuses, as well as to international audiences in Canada and Bermuda about the subject of white privilege and racial inequity.

INDEX